On Effective Leadership

Jepson Studies in Leadership

Series Editors: George R. Goethals, Terry L. Price, and J. Thomas Wren

Managing Editor: Tammy Tripp

Jepson Studies in Leadership is dedicated to the interdisciplinary pursuit of important questions related to leadership. In its approach, the series reflects the broad-based commitment to the liberal arts of the University of Richmond's Jepson School of Leadership Studies. The series thus aims to publish the best work on leadership not only from management and organizational studies but also from such fields as economics, English, history, philosophy, political science, psychology, and religion. In addition to monographs and edited collections on leadership, included in the series are volumes from the Jepson Colloquium that bring together influential scholars from multiple disciplines to think collectively about distinctive leadership themes in politics, science, civil society, and corporate life. The books in the series should be of interest to humanists and social scientists, as well as to organizational theorists and instructors teaching in business, leadership, and professional programs.

Books Appearing in This Series:

On Effective Leadership

Across Domains, Cultures, and Eras

G. Donald Chandler, III
and
John W. Chandler

palgrave
macmillan

ON EFFECTIVE LEADERSHIP

Copyright © G. Donald Chandler, III and John W. Chandler, 2013.

All rights reserved.

First published in 2013 by
PALGRAVE MACMILLAN®
in the United States—a division of St. Martin's Press LLC,
175 Fifth Avenue, New York, NY 10010.

Where this book is distributed in the UK, Europe and the rest of the world,
this is by Palgrave Macmillan, a division of Macmillan Publishers Limited,
registered in England, company number 785998, of Houndmills,
Basingstoke, Hampshire RG21 6XS.

Palgrave Macmillan is the global academic imprint of the above companies
and has companies and representatives throughout the world.

Palgrave® and Macmillan® are registered trademarks in the United States,
the United Kingdom, Europe and other countries.

ISBN: 978–1–137–30069–0 (PBK)
ISBN: 978–1–137–30070–6 (HC)

Library of Congress Cataloging-in-Publication Data

Chandler, G. Donald, 1950–
    On effective leadership : across domains, cultures, and eras / G. Donald
Chandler, III & John W. Chandler.
        p. cm.
    Includes bibliographical references.
    ISBN 978–1–137–30069–0 (alk. paper)—
    ISBN 978–1–137–30070–6 (alk. paper)
        1. Leadership. 2. Leadership—Case studies. I. Chandler, John W., 1923–
    II. Title.

BF637.L4C43 2013
158′.4—dc23   2012029560

A catalogue record of the book is available from the British Library.

Design by Newgen Imaging Systems (P) Ltd., Chennai, India.

First edition: February 2013

10 9 8 7 6 5 4 3 2 1

Transferred to Digital Printing in 2013

To Michele Moeller Chandler,
my inspiration and partner in life

In memory of Florence Gordon Chandler
with love and gratitude

The presidency is not merely an administrative office...it is pre-eminently a place of moral leadership. All our great presidents were leaders of thought at times when certain historic ideas in the life of the nation had to be clarified.

—*Franklin D. Roosevelt, governor of New York*

To lead the people, walk behind them.

—*Lao Tzu*

If the blind lead the blind, both shall fall into the ditch.

—*Matthew 15:14*

Anyone can steer the ship when the sea is calm.

—*Publius Syrus*

CONTENTS

Part IV   Transforming Visions   **159**

FOREWORD

This book grew out of a course we taught in the Leadership Studies Program at Williams College that focused on theories of leadership. In it, our students read selections from a number of contemporary scholars, together with a series of case studies of leaders. We then challenged them to assess whether any author had developed a comprehensive framework that convincingly explained how very different people became effective leaders in a wide variety of fields and cultural contexts. Every student concluded that although each theory was useful in describing or explaining some aspect of successful leadership, none met the test of comprehensiveness. We agreed.

Yet during the semester we became increasingly convinced that such a comprehensive framework was feasible as we tested the theories against the case studies and our personal experience. Prior to teaching leadership studies, each of us had a longtime interest in leadership and had read widely in history and biography. Our interest was further stimulated by careers in which we had been exposed to many executives and administrators, some of them highly effective leaders and others not. One of us was an academic whose career embraced roles as teacher, scholar, college president, college and university trustee, and adviser to approximately 40 colleges and universities in their search for new chief executives. The other was a management consultant who worked with for-profit and nonprofit institutions in several different fields over his career. From our respective experiences, we both were drawn to the question of what distinguished the effective leaders from the less effective ones we had observed. The combination of our reading and our practical professional experience served as a starting point for our assessment of contemporary leadership theory.

By the end of the course, we concluded that the answers to our question lay in a small number of factors, some of which had been identified by scholars and others that had not been fully explored or understood. Nor had all of the factors been integrated into one comprehensive framework. Accordingly, we wrote a paper that contained the core of the framework outlined in this volume. With the encouragement of Professors Susan Dunn, Al Goethals, and James McAllister, all of whom were at Williams College at that time, as well as Williams Professor Emeritus James MacGregor Burns, we continued our project by analyzing a number of additional case studies, conducting more research in the relevant literature, and further refining our framework. More recently, Professor Goethals pushed our thinking by challenging us to address in more depth the role of a leader's psychological profile. We benefited, too, from the critiques and suggestions of Professors Edward Burger and Bill DeWitt and Professor Emeritus Kai Lee of Williams College, and of Neil Janin and David Meen, directors emeriti of the international management consulting firm McKinsey & Company, Inc. In addition, we are indebted to several classes of fellows at the Oakley Center for the Humanities and Social Sciences at Williams for critically reviewing our manuscript at various stages in its development. We wish to thank as well several other colleagues and external experts who graciously reviewed specific case studies within their respective fields of expertise. These individuals include David Elpern, MD, Georgetown University professor and former US permanent representative to the United Nations Donald McHenry, Professor Ngoni Munemo and Professor Emeritus Fred Rudolph of Williams, and Wayne Wilkins, MD, as well as James McAllister and Kai Lee once again. The constructive criticism of all those named here significantly strengthened our project.

We wish to underscore several additional acknowledgments. We especially wish to recognize the groundbreaking work of leadership scholars who contributed significantly to the theoretical foundation on which we have attempted to build our framework. In particular, we have drawn insight and inspiration from the works of James MacGregor Burns, Howard Gardner, and Ronald Heifetz. John Kotter, too, has been a noteworthy influence on our thinking. We note with gratitude the dedicated and careful work of our four student research assistants, Caroline Bennett of Colorado College, Will Fogel of the University of Michigan, and Sarah Steege and Lily Wong of Williams College. Each made valuable contributions to our case studies. We are also deeply grateful to our editor, Milton Djuric, whose many thoughtful suggestions and questions have contributed notably to the crispness and clarity of the final product. We thank, too, the crack production team that guided our book into print—Leila Campoli and Erin Ivy at Palgrave Macmillan, Deepa John of Newgen Knowledge Works, and Lisa Rivero, our indexer.

Finally, we want to express our appreciation to Williams College and the Leadership Studies Program for their financial support of our project and to George Kennedy and his Williams classmates from the class of 1948 for their generosity and steadfast support of the Leadership Studies Program.

A word of explanation concerning our research methodology is in order. Our case studies were not intended to be comprehensive in presenting the facts of our subjects' lives or unearthing new information about them. Our intention was to test our framework by referring to the generally accepted and pertinent facts about our subjects' lives and careers. Would this framework provide a persuasive explanation for the essence of each leader's effectiveness or ineffectiveness? Consequently, we typically relied on a few authoritative sources for each case, although we also consulted a wider range of sources to ensure that the principal ones were presenting the commonly accepted facts and views about each leader.

Finally, we wish to make the customary disclaimer that while we have been helped greatly by the many people listed here, we take responsibility for any factual errors and for all the conclusions in our study. We also want to thank our spouses, our families, and our friends, who patiently put up with the inevitable demands on our time and attention in the writing of this book.

INTRODUCTION

The topic of leadership has engaged people in all eras, cultures, and walks of life. This is not surprising, since there are few experiences more fundamental to the human condition. We are social animals, and the group is central to our survival and development as a species. With every group, large or small, comes both the need and the opportunity for leadership. Thus, we have all felt the impact of leadership from early in childhood and on throughout adulthood. Occasionally, it has been as leaders ourselves and more often as followers, whether in our schools, in our working lives, or as citizens of a nation and an increasingly interconnected planet. Sometimes that impact has been bad, sometimes good, and occasionally even inspiring.

From Plato and Lao Tzu to Machiavelli and Max Weber, many of humanity's greatest thinkers have tried to explain this fundamental and elemental force, whether to instruct, to warn, or to prophesy. So, too, have countless other less-celebrated individuals, from coaches to politicians, psychologists, and management gurus, all of whom believe that they have distinctive insights based on their own experience or study. Like politics, leadership is a topic on which everyone has an opinion.

Over the past century, the attempt to understand leadership has become more formal, pioneered by the research of social psychologists in the 1920s and 1930s, first on the traits of leaders and then on their behavior. In the past few decades, scores of colleges and universities in the United States have introduced leadership studies programs. In addition, leadership training and education has become a small industry in the business world, fueled by the insatiable demand for more effective corporate leaders.

This intensified study of leadership has resulted in an improved understanding of many of its aspects—for instance, its psychological underpinnings, the interdependency between leaders and followers, and the roles of power and conflict. These efforts have not, however, resulted in the development of a robust, comprehensive framework that helps us understand leadership of all kinds, in every domain of human endeavor, across cultures, and over time. Why are some leaders effective, many ineffective, and only a few exceptional?

The quest for such a comprehensive framework may appear daunting. The range of leadership situations is almost boundless: from small groups to nation states, from hierarchical organizations to unstructured grassroots movements, from specialized domains populated by experts to broad constituencies composed of a mix of humanity. Moreover, these situations arise in different cultures with varying values and behavioral norms, and they have existed over time, including eras when the values and concerns of leaders and followers were widely different from those of a modern democracy.

Yet the development of a compelling comprehensive framework could bring many practical benefits. The ability of any group of followers (or any governing board) to choose leaders, and to replace them when necessary, might be enhanced. The effectiveness of leaders themselves perhaps could be improved by enabling them to analyze better the potential challenges they face and the broad array of strategies, tactics, and styles available to them. Finally, leadership training and education potentially could be made far more targeted and effective than the hodgepodge of offerings that now flood the marketplace.

Thus, this book will outline our hypothesis for a comprehensive framework that focuses on what Harvard psychologist Howard Gardner defines as the *direct leadership* of a group of followers, whether formal or informal, not the *indirect leadership* provided by artists and intellectuals, who influence others by way of the ideas they develop and disseminate through their work.[1] Most scholarly treatments of leadership approach the subject from the perspective of a particular academic discipline. Although one of us is a former management consultant and the other a philosopher/theologian with wide experience as an executive and consultant in higher education, we consider ourselves as generalists in our approach to leadership. We do not regard any particular discipline as primary or privileged in what it brings to the understanding of the complex phenomenon of leadership. Instead, we will attempt to integrate those elements we find most insightful from the full range of disciplines and leadership theories into one comprehensive but simple framework that, we believe, best describes the basis of effective leadership across domains, cultures, and eras.

PART I

Effective Leadership: A New Framework

CHAPTER ONE

The Leadership Conundrum

Before discussing what makes leaders effective or ineffective, it is important to define what leadership is and is not, since the term is often used loosely to describe a wide array of relationships between the formal or informal head of a group and its members. Because virtually all human beings experience leadership throughout their lives, most believe that they can recognize it when they see it, though few might define the term in precisely the same way. Thus, the definition of leadership on which any comprehensive theory is based must be broad enough to encompass the full range of relationships that most people would regard as leadership.

It may be best to begin with what leadership is *not* in order to bound its definition. First, in our view leadership is not the sheer exercise of power, which we define in this context as the use of physical, psychological, and other forms of coercion used to control followers' thoughts or behavior. Resorting to coercion alone, or even primarily, to induce the cooperation of one's followers, whether that power is exercised brutally through physical force or psychological terror, or subtly through rewards, sanctions, and propaganda, would be termed by most contemporary leadership scholars as despotism, tyranny, or simple thuggery, but not as leadership.[1] In such cases, the goals of the group cannot, by definition, be the same as those of the power-wielder, who is forcing submission to his will, not leading. Does this mean, however, that effective leaders never use power? No, in practice a perceptive and skilled leader will sometimes use a blend of persuasion and power in certain situations, especially if failure to do so would imperil the achievement of goals essential to the collective good.[2]

For example, during the Civil War Abraham Lincoln used his presidential power to suspend the civil right of habeas corpus and issue the Emancipation Proclamation, acts that were opposed by a substantial number of his constituents. His justification for these highly controversial actions was their importance to the ultimate goal he shared with his followers: the preservation of the Union. Only through the Union, he believed, would the Constitution, which guarantees all rights, be protected and slavery ultimately be abolished throughout the United States.

Thus, despite his distinctive powers of persuasion and his unquestioned moral core, even Lincoln felt obliged to use his positional power in the interests of what he saw as the collective good. Still, the use of power to supplement persuasion is a slippery slope upon which leaders must tread with care.

Second, if leaders must rely primarily on persuasion to mobilize their followers, does it follow that they can only gain their positions legitimately through democratic political means? Democracy as a widespread form of government is a relatively recent historical phenomenon. Intellectual historian Francis Oakley argues in his book *Kingship* (2006) that throughout most of history the legitimacy of the head of state in almost all cultures was based on his sacral role,[3] while the leaders of most civil, military, religious, and other institutions were drawn from a hereditary aristocracy. Though the Enlightenment led to the principle that legitimacy stems from the consent of the governed, even in the United States the rights of citizens to participate in the electoral process were limited for a long time, and the gradual expansion of suffrage has only been achieved through two centuries of struggle to eliminate economic, racial, and gender barriers to the ballot. Even today, in many domains ranging from business to education to sports, leaders gain their positions legitimately by inheriting them or through appointment by a governing board or other small elite body. In our view, the key criterion for legitimacy is whether a leader has gained her position through a widely accepted process wherein the followers willingly confer that power.

Third, does gaining an institutional position of authority through legitimate means automatically mean that the holder of the position is a leader? No, those who hold positions designed to ensure the efficient and effective operation of an institution are managers, not necessarily leaders.[4] In many cases, managers need neither to persuade nor to coerce subordinates to follow their directions so long as their goals are acceptable to, if not completely congruent with, those of their subordinates. Subordinates may comply in exchange for some form of gain from the institution, a job, for instance, or spiritual fulfillment, or an education. Indeed, in a stable environment good management may be all that a strong, well-organized institution needs. Usually it is only in an unstable situation or where management's objectives become unacceptable to subordinates that the calls for leadership tend to arise. This may occur, for example, when a corporation faces a new competitive threat and the possibility of layoffs, or when a church or school is perceived as violating the values it espouses. It is then that we learn whether these managers can also become leaders who convert their subordinates into followers.

Thus from the first three dimensions of what leadership is not, an inclusive definition of what leadership *is* begins to emerge. It is the use of persuasion as the primary means to achieve a goal mutually shared by a leader and a group of followers, whether that goal is relatively narrow and mundane or more fundamental and visionary. Such leadership can be exercised from a position of authority or without any formal authority at all, but it is always more than just capable management. In practice, it often is composed of a mix of persuasion and some judicious use of the power conferred by the leader's position, a position willingly bestowed by the group, whether the process for doing so is democratic or not. Moreover, the leader and his followers share the end goals, including when, as James MacGregor Burns suggests, the leader is making "conscious what lies unconscious among followers."[5]

The final dimension along which to define what leadership is *not* is the element of morality. Some contemporary commentators believe that morality is an essential element of leadership. Most notable is Burns, the author of *Leadership* (1978), who is viewed by many as the dean of modern leadership studies. Burns argues that leaders and followers must share mutual needs, aspirations, and values. These values include both ends, or collective goals, and means, or modes of conduct in achieving those ends. According to Burns, the act of leadership is the ability to persuade a group of followers, who are aware of the competing alternatives, to make an informed choice to pursue the goals advocated by the leader. When they do so in exchange for something they value—jobs in exchange for their votes, for example—Burns calls it *transactional leadership*.[6] When a leader's effort raises the aspirations of followers to an even higher level of morality and motivation such as the search for liberty, equality, and the pursuit of happiness, Burns terms it *transforming leadership*. When neither condition exists, it isn't leadership at all; it is power-wielding.[7]

We wish we could agree. Regrettably, however, there are many examples throughout history of leaders who persuade their followers—not force them—to pursue unethical goals and to use unpalatable means to achieve them, as judged by the commonly held moral standards of their times. From demagogues and street gang leaders to corrupt politicians and businessmen, the list is long. Indeed, even some leaders who qualify as "transforming" under Burns's definition used questionable means, such as Franklin Roosevelt's obfuscations while preparing the United States to enter World War II and Lincoln's aforementioned use of executive power to save the Union. Another complication of incorporating morality into the definition of leadership is that moral values can be very different across cultures, as with the treatment of women in traditional Islamic societies. Which culture's values should provide the ethical norms in judging whether an individual is acting as a leader? Even within a given society, different groups can have sharply conflicting definitions of moral goals, as the ongoing dispute between prolife and prochoice activists illustrates in contemporary America.

Consequently, we agree with those who contend that, while moral leadership is highly desirable, there is no compelling argument that morality must be a component of leadership.[8] Instead, for us the important distinction is between what we define as effective leadership and exceptional leadership. *Effective leadership* (and ineffective leadership as well) can be moral, immoral, or morally neutral. It is simply leadership that success-fully achieves the mutual purpose shared by the leader and his followers, followers who were won and motivated primarily through the leader's exercise of persuasion.

Exceptional leadership, however, cannot be immoral in either means or ends. What makes it exceptional is the combination of the leader's effective-ness and the worthiness of the goal achieved. This will often, though not always, mean the achievement of morally based ends. It will always, how-ever, meet Ronald Heifetz's broader definition of a "socially useful," even if morally neutral, goal such as the founding of a job-creating new company or an excellent new charter school.[9] It excludes, by definition, the achievement of an immoral goal, as judged by the larger, contemporary society and the verdict of history. At the highest level of achievement, as Franklin Roosevelt said of the great presidents, exceptional leaders are "leaders of thought at times when certain historic ideas...had to be clarified." The worthier the goal, the more difficult its achievement, and the more widespread its bene-fits, the more transforming and exceptional we regard the leader. It is on this basis that we revere leaders such as Roosevelt himself, as well as Washington, Lincoln, and Martin Luther King, Jr.

★   ★   ★

Our definition of leadership suggests some qualities a leader should possess—for instance, the skill of persuasion and the ability to set compelling goals. But can we give a comprehensive answer to the question of what makes some leaders effective, many ineffective, and only a very few exceptional? We argue that any comprehensive theory or framework must meet three criteria to be judged as robust and useful. First, a robust framework should be able to identify the key principles underlying effective, and ineffective, leadership in any domain or leadership situation. Second, the framework should be applicable across cultures and over time. Third and finally, in addition to *explanatory* power, the framework should have some *prescriptive* power, even if it is limited. More specifically, it should help in identifying those with the highest potential to become effective leaders and in deter-mining the best means for developing that potential. Ideally it would also help active leaders to analyze the leadership challenges of a given situation and formulate broad strategies to meet those challenges.

These criteria reveal the limitations of most traditional theories of lead-ership. The oldest and most durable is the *traits* or *Great Man theory*, which postulates that only those people with exceptional, even heroic, character, talents, and physical traits can be great leaders. This idea of leadership has held center stage for 25 centuries, from Confucius's notion of the supe-rior man to Plutarch's biographies of eminent Greeks and Romans, from Thomas Carlyle's focus on heroes to Max Weber's theory of charismatic authority. Most people still instinctively believe that great leaders must be, indeed can only be, great men or women, probably because such leaders often have important physical, emotional, and/or intellectual attributes that distinguish them in the eyes of followers.

Yet when twentieth-century social psychologists and management scientists tested the traits theory in an empirical, ostensibly scientific manner, they soon found that they could not identify a common set of traits that explained leadership success in all circumstances. When researchers shifted their attention from traits to *behaviors*, they encountered the same problem. Even when they added the elements of situation and contingency to the mix, the results indicated that successful leadership was marked by a bewilderingly large number of combinations of behaviors, situations, and contingencies, rather than a neat, predictable pattern, even among the limited number of situations studied.[10]

One painstaking attempt by psychologists Steven Rubenzer and Thomas Faschingbauer to find a correlation between the success of American presidents and their personalities illustrates the difficulty.[11] In their study, they enlisted more than 120 experts; at least 3 with detailed knowledge of a given president rated that president on a 592-item personality questionnaire. These data and more were reduced to an index of nine personality characteristics that the authors claim is predictive of successful presidents.[12] Yet on the resulting scale of suitability for the presidency, Richard Nixon and Millard Fillmore were equals with Washington, Jefferson, Jackson, and Truman. All were predicted to have only "average" prospects for presidential success. On the same scale, Jimmy Carter tied Woodrow Wilson as the fourth most "well-suited" for the presidency. James Polk, meanwhile, was predicted to be "poorly suited," despite his high rating by historians as a brilliant political operator who worked all the levers of government, party, and public opinion to fulfill his vision of America's "manifest destiny" by adding Texas, the Oregon territory, California, and the southwest to the Union.[13] Like another tough-minded politician Lyndon B. Johnson, Polk was a master of exploiting the political process to get his way.

Such findings do not provide much confidence that personality characteristics alone can either explain retrospectively the degree of a leader's effectiveness or predict prospectively who will be a successful leader. The best that decades of statistical research has been able to demonstrate is that five broad personality characteristics (known in psychology literature as the "Big Five") are most often correlated with effective leaders: extraversion/assertiveness, intellect/openness to experience, conscientiousness, emotional stability, and agreeableness.[14] Broad as these characteristics are, the statistical correlations are far from perfect, and counterexamples among successful leaders are legion.

The extent to which a leader is able to leverage her personal strengths and overcome her weaknesses seems a better explanation than simply her traits or broad personality profile. While George Washington was not particularly intellectual, he was able to use his charismatic presence, strong will, impeccable values, and steely self-control to become the "indispensable man" in the founding of the United States. Although John Adams was irascible, combative, and impolitic, as well as far from charismatic, his intellectual brilliance and tenacity enabled him to play a vital role in the nation's founding.

In summary, the variability in the combination of traits and behaviors exhibited by successful leaders in different situations is simply too great to be useful in explaining what makes leaders effective or ineffective. Even if a particular personality characteristic could be identified as common to effective leaders, clearly something else is missing if a comprehensive framework is to be developed.

CHAPTER TWO

The Temple and the Genome

Over the past few decades, several new promising theories of leadership have emerged, all of which focus on the core activities of leadership, instead of the physical or personality attributes of leaders. The most notable are those proposed by James MacGregor Burns, Howard Gardner, and Ronald Heifetz. Each of them brings a fresh perspective to the study of leadership based on his professional background as a political scientist, psychologist, and physician/educator, respectively. Together their theories illuminate several critical elements of effective leadership, and our proposed framework builds on the foundation they have created.

To view leadership as primarily a set of activities does not mean that personal traits and behaviors are irrelevant to a leader's effectiveness. In a given leadership situation they may help a leader gain initial credibility with a group and enhance the probability of his or her leadership success. Yet even in similar situations, different leaders with varying combinations of traits and behaviors can succeed.

What then makes these different leaders effective? Viewing leadership as a common set of activities has led us to the conclusion that it requires four highly integrated variables. The first three are what we view as the core skills of leadership: (1) developing a compelling, well-conceived vision for the achievement of a set of goals that are shared, or have the potential to be shared, by a group of followers; (2) persuasively communicating that vision in a manner appropriate to the group; and (3) building and managing an organization that effectively supports the implementation of the vision, ensures ongoing alignment between leader and followers, and institutionalizes the vision even after the leader is gone. Although the third variable has received less attention from historians and other scholars, all three have been recognized as critical to effective leadership in one form or another from the time of Thucydides.

The fourth variable, however, is almost never conceptualized as a key attribute of effective leaders. The most effective leaders—and all exceptional ones—demonstrate the proclivity to act selflessly. We understand the apparent paradox in this statement, since those who rise to significant leadership positions are often more ambitious, egocentric, and self-absorbed than most

>men. And rarely, if ever, are even exceptional leaders purely
when leaders act selflessly, it inspires devotion among their fol-
.forces group dedication to achieving mutual goals, enhances
t of their followers becoming leaders in turn, and optimizes the
chances ror enduring success. Conversely, if leaders do not transcend their
personal interests when necessary to serve those of the group, they will lose
the trust of their followers and eventually their leadership position, or they
will become despotic as a means to forcibly retain their position.

Why hasn't selflessness typically been identified as an element of effective leadership? Perhaps for some it is implicit. Those of the Great Man
school, for example, might argue that the interests of leaders and followers are identical. Indeed, they may presume that a great leader acts in
the interest of the common good, whether his followers know it or not.
For others, selflessness may be irrelevant or at least unnecessary. Effective
leadership in their eyes may be successful achievement of the leader's
vision, whose interests rightly predominate. In our view, both of these
perspectives underestimate the critical role of followers, who over the
long run almost always have a good understanding of their best interests
and whether a leader is acting on their behalf. When he isn't, they will
withdraw their support.

Consequently, a leader's success will be compromised profoundly if
there is a shortfall on any one of the four variables mentioned earlier,
especially the element of selflessness. To illustrate the importance of their
interdependence, our framework can be visualized as a Greek temple,
with selflessness forming the foundation while the other three elements
constitute the columns that support effective leadership (see figure). If

Effective Leadership

| Compelling, well-conceived vision | Persuasive communication | Capable supporting organization |

Selflessness

any one of these columns is weak, the resulting edifice is far more fragile, especially if it is under any stress. And if a column is missing or if the foundation is flawed, the entire structure may collapse.

For example, a compelling vision and superbly persuasive communication of it may not result in successful implementation if the leader's organization is inadequate. William Jennings Bryan was one of the leading orators of his day and had an attractive populist vision, yet he was never able to win the presidency, in part because he lacked a united, effective party organization backing him. Conversely, excellent communication and organizational skills unaccompanied by a wise and compelling vision do not result in effective leadership either. In his days as secretary of defense under Presidents Ford and George W. Bush, Donald Rumsfeld demonstrated superb organizational abilities and a combative and persuasive communication style. Through this managerial approach he accomplished many changes during his second tour as secretary of defense, deemphasizing nuclear weapons, enhancing Special Ops capability, and helping expand NATO eastward.[1] However, during the Iraq War, he proved that management alone was not enough; he lacked the wise vision based on a deep understanding of the situation needed to win the peace after the war was won.

Similarly, a potentially compelling vision that is not matched with an ability to communicate it persuasively is just as ineffective as a superb communicator who has nothing substantive to say. Vice President Al Gore arguably had the more compelling vision in the 2000 presidential election, but his inability to communicate it effectively contributed to his close electoral loss. Conversely, in the 2008 election, Senator Barack Obama was a far more gifted, inspiring, and persuasive speaker than his Republican opponent, Senator John McCain. That oratorical skill, combined with his compelling vision of change amid the collapse of the economy during the campaign, enabled Obama to win the presidency convincingly.

Finally, even if the vision is compelling, the communication superbly persuasive, and the supporting organization effective, all will founder if followers believe that the leader is selfish and would put his interests before theirs if a conflict existed between the two. Sometimes a leader is focused almost solely on his own self-interest, such as crooked business executives and politicians who have sought leadership positions primarily to gain personal wealth and power. In many other cases, selfish impulses coexist uneasily with a genuine intention to meet the shared goals of the leader's followers. President Clinton, for example, struggled throughout his career to control his libido amid the opportunities his personal charisma and public position offered to sate his sexual appetite and need to be loved. He managed to dampen the potential conflict between his impulses and the public interest until his dalliance with a White House intern and his dissembling about their relationship led many of his followers to feel betrayed, handicapping both his leadership effectiveness in his second term and the Democratic Party in the 2000 election.

In summary, the image of a Greek temple is intended to illustrate that the four key elements required for effective leadership are both constant and interdependent. Without a well-conceived vision and persuasive communication of it, there can be no effective leadership at all. At the same time, the enduring impact of that vision will be limited without a capable supporting organization that can institutionalize it. And critically, selfish behavior will dramatically diminish, or even eliminate, the leader's effectiveness no matter how strong she may be on the other three elements. Without the trust of her followers, the entire edifice will come crashing down.

At the same time, leadership as actually practiced by individual men and women is not as static or singular as the image of the Greek temple may suggest. While all effective leaders may possess the four elements the temple portrays, the particular pattern of strengths and weaknesses among the four, and their dynamic impacts on each other, are unique to each individual leader—much like each human being's distinctive genomic inheritance from her parents. Moreover, the natural abilities possessed by each individual on the four attributes represent only a potential for effective leadership—much as an individual's genetic pattern represents a potential, not a fixed, actuality. And just as that potential actuality can be modified within certain limits, so too can a potential leader learn how to enhance her natural strengths and shore up her weaknesses to varying degrees. Finally, the most effective leaders recognize that each situation they face is distinctive and modify their leadership actions and behavior accordingly—just as different genes are activated or suppressed in response to the environment.

Thus to fully capture the richness and complexity of effective leadership, the static image of the Greek temple needs to be supplemented with the dynamic analogy to the genome. Effective leadership requires all four elements pictured in the temple, but they can present themselves in an infinite number of distinctive combinations and be exercised in a variety of ways. They also do not have to be completely natural gifts because to some degree they can be developed. And finally, they must be adapted to the circumstances in each new leadership challenge in order to be employed successfully. In the balance of this chapter, we discuss each of the four elements in greater depth.

A Compelling Vision, Persuasively Communicated

The first two columns of the temple represent a synthesis of several key elements of the theories developed by Gardner, Burns, and Heifetz. Specifically, like Gardner, we believe that successful leaders in any field or culture must be able to persuade a group of followers to pursue a given goal by relating a "story," whether through words, other symbol systems, or personal example. Drawing on his background in cognitive psychology, Gardner argues in his 1995 book, *Leading Minds*, that to be credible and convincing, the leader must tell his story in a manner tailored to the sensibilities of his followers. For example, communicating persuasively to highly educated experts in a particular field is very different from reaching the "unschooled minds" of a group of nonexperts. In Gardner's view, the successful leader must also be able to react flexibly to competing counterstories and he must "embody" his own story.[2]

We follow the lead of James MacGregor Burns, however, in that our proposed framework places much more emphasis than Gardner does on the dynamic relationship, interdependency, and even interchangeability of roles between leader and followers. Like Burns, we believe that a successful leader must embrace the same goals as his followers, in terms of their needs or aspirations. Sometimes, as Burns states, a leader may help his followers articulate their unconscious goals, but without shared goals, he cannot lead effectively. Indeed, lasting achievement of these goals is the ultimate measure of successful leadership, and that will often mean that some of the followers become effective leaders in their own right.[3]

The classic model of a leader who combines the elements described by Gardner and Burns is Pericles, who for more than 30 years was the elected leader of ancient Athens. Thucydides memorably describes him in his *History of the Peloponnesian War* as the embodiment of Athenian values, a wise man who possessed a clear vision for defeating the Spartans and their allies, and a superb speaker who was able to present his views persuasively in the din of counterstories always circulating in democratic Athens. Indeed, Thucydides quotes Pericles as saying, "A man who has the knowledge but lacks the power to express it is no better off than if he never had any ideas at all."[4] He could stir his fellow citizens to higher levels of aspiration and embolden them to become leaders themselves. Perhaps most famously, in his oration at a public funeral for the war dead, he reinvigorated his audience's patriotism by enumerating the characteristics of Athens that made it a city and society worth dying for, thus turning a mournful occasion into an inspiring one.

Thucydides contrasts Pericles with Cleon, Alcibiades, and the other demagogues who succeeded him after his death from plague early in the Peloponnesian War. While gifted orators, they pandered to the emotions and prejudices of their followers to gain and retain power, and, as Thucydides recounts events, their imperial overreach, factionalism, and incompetence led to the defeat of Athens and the loss of its empire. But it is not only demagogues who may be gifted communicators and ineffective leaders. Countless well-intentioned politicians, corporate CEOs, and other leaders have persuaded their followers to pursue what turns out to be the wrong path because of flawed or empty visions.

Sometimes, of course, even a dedicated and able leader may lack the solution to a particularly difficult problem. Thus, our proposed framework also incorporates Ronald Heifetz's concept of leadership as at times mobilizing people (followers) by facilitating and mediating a process to solve hard and ill-defined problems. Both leader and followers are thereby deeply engaging in developing a solution. In contrast to technical problems where an expert with authority can provide the answer, the primary challenge of leadership in unclear, "adaptive" situations, Heifetz believes, is in getting people to face tough realities and develop creative solutions, artfully structuring the process and managing the attendant stress. Characteristically, the need for leadership becomes most apparent in times of crisis or instability when there is no obvious solution, as in the cases of climate change or the introduction of a potentially disruptive new technology. Sometimes there is no clear definition of the problem, as with the threat of global terrorism. In such cases, the leader must make a persuasive case for the urgency of the challenge and then facilitate the effort to devise a solution.[5]

For example, when President Kennedy faced the Cuban missile crisis in October 1962, he appeared to have no good options. Pursuing a diplomatic solution would take too long and likely leave the Soviets with a first strike nuclear capability only 90 miles off the US coast. An airstrike on Cuba, possibly followed by a ground invasion, was recommended by most of Kennedy's military and civilian advisors, yet it risked a nuclear holocaust. Fortunately, Kennedy rejected both options and instead led a small group of his advisors and other experts through a problem-solving process that eventually generated an alternative course of action, a blockade. That strategy succeeded, and the world survived one of its closest brushes with nuclear war through his superb adaptive leadership.

A Capable Supporting Organization

The third column in our metaphorical temple is a dimension frequently missing from theories of leadership: the need for an effective organization that supports the communication and implementation of the leader's vision and helps ensure alignment between her and her followers.[6] Sometimes an organization already exists, and the challenge is simply to manage it effectively. At other times, an organization must be created or rebuilt. Whatever the case, effective leaders will recognize the importance of having a capable supporting organization. If they lack the time or ability to manage it themselves, they will bring in others who can.

Management theorists and practitioners have long understood the importance of an effective organization in accomplishing a group's goals. What causes organizations to be effective (or not) are the complex and dynamic interrelationships between a number of elements that go far beyond the lines and boxes on an organization chart and that in turn must be integrated with the first two elements in our framework. For example, even if the vision of the leader is compelling and the leader's communication of that vision has been persuasive, success is unlikely if the institutional skills do not exist to implement the vision, or if the people chosen to play key roles in implementation are incompetent. Similarly, poor decisions are likely to result if vital information is unavailable on a timely basis, the incentives of key players are misaligned, or the structure of the organization is unwieldy. Research and experience demonstrate that if any one of these organizational variables is poorly designed, weak, or mutually inconsistent with the others, that organization will be much less effective than it could be.[7]

To illustrate the point, had Martin Luther King, Jr., and the other leaders of the Montgomery bus boycott in 1955 not developed an effective organization, their chances of sustaining the protest and ultimately achieving success would have been minimal, despite the justice of their cause. While King's moral vision, personal example, and soaring oratory inspired his followers, it was the Montgomery Improvement Association's car pool system and grassroots fundraising that enabled those followers to get to work and survive the economic hardships created by the boycott and the white community's hostile reaction. Although King himself was not a skilled manager, he recruited another local preacher to turn around the faltering car pool system when its inefficiency in getting people to their jobs threatened the boycott. In short, a successful leader needs to be able to manage an organization, as well as lead one, or he needs to be able to choose individuals for key positions who are capable of supplying the essential management.

The management theorist who has most clearly recognized the importance of both leadership and management to the success of individual leaders and organizations is John Kotter, a professor at the Harvard Business School. In his book *A Force For Change: How Leadership Differs from Management* (1990), he argues that leadership and management are different, although each is critical to success. Management is needed to generate "consistency and order," and thus is essential to the effective functioning of an organization, especially large, complex organizations. Management includes developing detailed plans and budgets, structuring and staffing the organization to achieve those plans, monitoring progress, and solving any problems that arise. Leadership, in contrast, creates "movement" and change by establishing a long-term direction and goals for the organization, gaining the commitment of the people involved, and inspiring them to pursue those goals despite inevitable obstacles.[8] Both are needed for enduring success. Overmanaged and underled organizations, Kotter notes, can become rigid, noninnovative bureaucracies,[9] subject to all of the dangers of "professional" management described by another management scholar, Henry Mintzberg of McGill University. Mintzberg worries, in particular, about the focus of professional managers on the short term, risk avoidance, specialization, compliance with bureaucratic rules, and control and predictability. These, he argues, tend to drive out creativity, judgment, and the value of deep expertise and experience.[10] On the other hand, as Kotter warns, overled and undermanaged organizations can result in chaos in which even the best strategies cannot succeed.[11]

We diverge, however, from Kotter's conclusion that leadership and management are separate though complementary functions. In our view, capable management is a necessary component of effective leadership. Still, the leader need not be the personal source of that capable management so long as she has the skills to choose and the will to delegate to others who are capable.

In summary, all leaders need an effective supporting organization to achieve enduring success and to institutionalize their impact once they are gone. When the leader is operating within an existing institution (as head of a government, business, or school), she often will need to enhance its effectiveness. If a leader initially is operating without any formal position (as with many grassroots activists), an effective organization will eventually need to be created in order for the prospective leader to disseminate her vision and support its implementation. In both cases, the effectiveness of the supporting organization will depend in turn on an appropriate balance of leadership and management.

Selflessness

The foremost determinant of a leader's enduring impact is the degree of his selflessness, a term we use instead of the more prosaic "unselfishness" to underline the point. Why is the proclivity to act selflessly so characteristic of the most effective leaders? The answer is very simple. As followers, most of us are inspired by leaders who demonstrate commitment to our mutual goals and pursue the steps necessary to achieve them, without thought of their personal gain, prestige, or other self-interested considerations. At the extreme, these steps might include dramatic acts of sacrifice, such as accepting imprisonment, damaging one's health, foregoing personal pleasures and fulfillment, or moving aside for younger or more capable leaders. More typically, a leader's selflessness is manifested through less dramatic, but still highly meaningful acts such as delegating, listening to other voices, sharing credit, admitting mistakes, mentoring other leaders, demonstrating care for others, and grooming capable successors. Such selflessness is more than enlightened self-interest, which expects an eventual reward for a near-term sacrifice. The result is that leaders who consistently act selflessly inspire greater trust, build greater group dedication to the mutual goal, are more likely to attract followers who will become leaders themselves, and thereby have a greater chance of achieving enduring success.

Many argue, however, that human beings are incapable of real selflessness. From Darwin's description of evolution as a brutal, relentless struggle, which only the fittest survived, to Sigmund Freud's claim that human behavior is driven fundamentally by such basic drives as hunger, thirst, and sexual appetite, much of both biological and psychological theory has rested on assumptions that human beings always and inevitably act on the basis of self-interested motives, whether conscious or unconscious.[12] Yet those assumptions overlook Darwin's own evidence for the survival advantages derived from cooperative and unselfish behavior. In *The Descent of Man* (1874), he wrote: "Selfish and contentious people will not cohere, and without coherence nothing can be effected." A tribe rich in the social and moral qualities of sympathy, fidelity, and courage, Darwin went on, "would spread and be victorious over other tribes; but in the course of time it would, judging by all past history, be in its turn overcome by some other tribe still more highly endowed. Thus the social and moral qualities would slowly tend to advance and be diffused throughout the world."[13] In the last 30 years, scholars have turned to this neglected aspect of Darwin's thinking and questioned the dominance of the selfish gene, noting the widespread human quest for activity and stimulation, competence and power, security and social approval. Social psychologists Michael and Lise Wallach suggested that caring for others may "be a quite direct consequence of our biological heritage."[14]

In support of such claims are recent experiments in which neuroscientists scanned the brains of human volunteers who were presented with a scenario in which they could ponder whether to keep a large sum of money or donate it to charity. The contemplation of donating the money to help others activated the same part of the brain that usually lights up in response to food or sex. Thoughts of keeping the money brought no such pleasurable response. The experiment suggests that altruism is prewired in the brain and is very likely the product of evolutionary processes that began ages ago.[15]

Where Darwin spoke of "coherence," contemporary evolutionary biologists speak of "synergy" and "symbiosis." They go so far as to note that the human organism, like other complex bodies, is an agglomeration of organisms that are parasitically interdependent. Each of us is host to billions of germs and viruses, most of them beneficial and even essential to our survival and well-being. The Nobel Prize–winning cell biologist Christian de Duve has added his voice to the argument that selfless behavior is rooted in our biological natures and contributes to the survival of our species.[16]

Yet such views remain highly controversial in the scientific community. In 2012, famed sociobiologist Edward O. Wilson ignited a firestorm among evolutionary biologists with his new book, *The Social Conquest of Earth*. In it he retracted his earlier view that the individual organism is the single foundational locus of evolution and contended instead that the group also is central to the spread of beneficial genes.[17] Thus, evolution is a multilevel process that facilitates the survival of both the fittest individuals of the species and the fittest groups.

In explaining what we ourselves mean by selflessness, we note that the social organization and behavior of human beings include a pivotal causal factor that is not present in the "eusocial" insect societies (ants, bees, wasps, and the like) that have been the principal subjects of Wilson's scholarship. Eusocial insects, in assuming particular roles and sacrificing their individual well-being for the good of the nest or the hive, act on biological instincts. Humans, on the other hand, have cognitive abilities that enable them to change, adapt, and invent. In the case of leaders acting on behalf of the group, they use these cognitive abilities to calculate the benefits, risks, and probable costs of various possible responses to the challenges and crises that they constantly face. It is in this context of a group of followers who depend on the leader that the virtue of selflessness we see as central to the leader's long-term success is exercised. We are thinking of a selflessness that is rooted in the knowledge that humans are tribal in nature, not selflessness in the universalistic terms that distinguish the views of some of the great religious leaders.

Indeed, we recognize that few leaders have been or ever will be purely selfless. As noted earlier, men and women often must be ambitious and egocentric in order to gain a position of leadership. Moreover, like most human beings, a leader's instinctive impulses toward selfishness and his higher motivations to be selfless constantly battle, with his character reflecting the balance that he individually achieves over a lifetime. For some leaders, that balance is relatively stable, whether it is predominantly selfish or selfless, and for others, it is uneasy. Selflessness may reflect a fundamental element in the leader's character and be central to his impact, as with the great religious leaders. In other cases, a selfless action by a particular leader might be out of character, much as a cowardly soldier who unexpectedly leaps on a grenade to save his companions. The spectrum is wide, and under stress, even a strong character can crack, while a weak one can show surprising strength. Nonetheless, in the most effective leaders whose impact is enduring, the balance is usually stable and tilts toward selflessness, which results in leaders consistently placing their followers' interests before their own when a conflict arises—and in followers trusting that their leaders will do so. Few are willing to bet that a selfish leader will overcome his characteristic impulses and jump on that proverbial grenade.

In advocating selflessness as the foundational element in our framework, we are mindful of Robert Greenleaf's widely influential theory of "servant leadership." Although he does not use the term "selflessness" in his original essay, "The Servant as Leader," one could argue it is implied in his description of a caring servant. However, Greenleaf's theory is centered on a type of leadership style and on a set of leadership goals that differ from selflessness as we define it. As he put it, the "servant-leader *is* servant first... [and] the best test... is this: Do those served grow as persons? Do they, *while being served*, become healthier, wiser, freer, more autonomous, more likely themselves to become servants?"[18] While we admire what Greenleaf advocates, we see no evidence that all effective leaders have been or need be "servants" to their followers, in the emotional and spiritual sense in which Greenleaf defines the term. Again Pericles comes to mind as a good example of a leader who could act selflessly, but who led from the front, not from behind as Leo, Greenleaf's inspiration for the concept of servant leadership, did in Hermann Hesse's *Journey to the East*. Indeed, Thucydides recounts that Pericles

> could respect the liberty of the people and at the same time hold them in check. It was he who led them, rather than they who led him, and, since he never sought power from any wrong motive, he was under no necessity of flattering them: in fact he was so highly respected that he was able to speak angrily to them and to contradict them...[19]

An American counterpart to Pericles as a selfless leader is George Washington. He was, of course, the indispensable man: commander-in-chief of the Continental Army, a key presence at the Constitutional Convention, and the unanimous choice as the first president. While he was undoubtedly self-confident and ambitious, he was nonetheless motivated by what he felt was honorable and right for his people and his country, not by the achievement of personal power or wealth. Indeed, when King George III was told that Washington planned to retire to his plantation after the Revolutionary War, he purportedly said: "If he does that, he will be the greatest man in the world." Washington did retire, until, urged by his countrymen, he reluctantly left Mt. Vernon to preside over the Constitutional Convention and then assume the presidency.

While acting selflessly was arguably a core attribute of the disciplined Washington and of most highly effective leaders, as noted earlier it is possible for a leader to be effective in whom selfish and selfless impulses are inextricably entangled if he or she is able to resist the powerful selfish impulses and act selflessly at critical moments. Lyndon Johnson provides a good example of such a psychologically complex leader. In the aforementioned study of presidential personalities, he was rated lowest among all his peers on the factors of character, altruism, and modesty.[20] He bullied his staff and when he could, his colleagues, while behaving obsequiously with those in a position to advance his career. He sometimes acted unscrupulously in pursuit of his own ends. Yet when he had the chance as president in the wake of Kennedy's assassination to pass landmark civil rights legislation, he did so knowing that it would cost him southern white votes and quite possibly a second term. Perhaps Johnson had his eye on cementing his place in history. Perhaps, too, his early experiences struggling through college and teaching poor Mexican children genuinely catalyzed an enduring sense of social justice on his part and a corresponding belief that government's role should be to help all of its citizens and protect their rights. Whatever his actual motivations may have been, his moral courage in pressing for civil rights was exemplary, although not reflective of his entire character. As *New York Times* columnist Russell Baker summarized Johnson, he was "a human puzzle so complicated nobody could ever understand it...a storm of warring human instincts: sinner and saint, buffoon and statesman, cynic and sentimentalist, a man torn between hungers for immortality and self-destruction."[21] Yet some-how he overcame his more self-centered impulses and exhibited the will-power to act selflessly on behalf of the weakest, most oppressed group of Americans.

Like selflessness, selfishness can display itself in a variety of forms. At its most egregious, it manifests itself through a lust for power or wealth that has characterized many despots, even if they gained their initial leader-ship positions legitimately. Less dramatic, but equally selfish, is the leader who cares far more about his own image, rewards, and success than he does about the good of his followers. David Halberstam, in his book on the Korean War, *The Coldest Winter* (2007), cites a number of examples from General Douglas MacArthur down to junior field officers, where those serving under them quickly sensed that these men were far more concerned with achieving glory and advancing their own careers than pre-serving the lives of their troops.[22]

Perhaps the most subtle and insidious form of selfishness is the egocen-tric leader who not only holds strong beliefs, but cannot or will not listen to competing views, and thus is temperamentally unable to discern when the course of action in the group's best interests is in conflict with his own views. At the extreme, such leaders can be virtually messianic in their beliefs and rigid in their mindsets. They may be brilliant, but arrogant or narcissistic to the point of hubris. Or they may be driven by deep-seated personal insecurities. Whatever the cause, the resulting inflexibility in their thinking limits their ultimate effectiveness, even if their goals are morally admirable, thus hobbling their prospects of ever becoming truly exceptional leaders. For example, Woodrow Wilson's unwillingness to compromise or share credit resulted in his failure to gain Senate ratifica-tion of the Treaty of Versailles and the League of Nations. The lack of American participation in the League crippled that promising body and shattered Wilson's ambition to be a truly transforming leader. In contrast, a high degree of selflessness was a crucial ingredient in the exceptional leadership of Generals Eisenhower and Marshall during World War II, as exemplified by Marshall's gracefulness in yielding field command for the Normandy invasion to Eisenhower, and Eisenhower's intention to assume personal blame should the invasion have failed.

★   ★   ★

In summary, we believe that the critical components of a simple, but robust, comprehensive framework are in place when the ability of a leader to persuasively communicate a compelling vision to her followers is combined with her ability to ensure the development of an effective, supporting organization and transcend her personal interests in order to serve those of the group. These elements help explain leadership success and failure in a range of domains; they are agnostic about the myriad combinations of personal traits and behaviors other than selflessness

that can lead to success in any given leadership situation; and they provide broad guidance to the challenges facing a leader in any particular
situation.

To test our hypothesis, we analyzed eight sets of case studies, drawn
from a range of domains, cultures, and time periods. While they may not
qualify as a scientifically valid sample, we believe these cases represent a
good initial illustration of our framework's explanatory power. Each set
examines first a less effective and then a more effective leader in a given
domain. Each set also illustrates how one of the three columns in the
temple—vision, communication, or organization—particularly impacted
a given leader's effectiveness. Each shows as well how a leader's relative
selflessness or selfishness amplified his or her effectiveness or ineffectiveness. Finally, in addition to demonstrating how the four elements of our
metaphorical temple are critical to each leader's effectiveness or ineffectiveness, our case studies show the distinctive, genomic pattern formed by
each leader's strengths and weaknesses on these four variables, the degree
to which this pattern changed over time, and the leader's ability to adapt
to different situations and challenges.

The eight sets of case studies are discussed in the next three parts of the
book: "Organizing Change," "Powers of Persuasion," and "Transforming
Visions."

"Organizing Change" first examines three women who played foundational roles in the feminist social movements of the nineteenth and early
twentieth centuries: Margaret Sanger, who is best known for her leadership
of the birth control movement, and Susan B. Anthony and Elizabeth Cady
Stanton, who worked so closely together in the women's rights movement that we have chosen to treat them as a powerful example of team
leadership. We then assess the leadership of two US cabinet secretaries,
Robert McNamara, the secretary of defense under Presidents Kennedy
and Johnson, and John Gardner, the secretary of health, education, and
welfare under President Johnson. While they headed huge government
bureaucracies, they were also in the position of middle managers in any
organization who report to superiors. Last, we analyze the leadership of
two legendary business entrepreneurs in the twentieth-century automobile industry who operated in very different cultural settings, Henry Ford
in the United States and Soichiro Honda in Japan.

"Powers of Persuasion" begins with a set of cases drawn from the realm
of higher education, G. Stanley Hall, the flawed first president of Clark
University, and his contemporary, William Rainey Harper, the founding president of the University of Chicago, whose leadership catapulted
that institution into the ranks of great research universities. We then analyze two leaders in the domain of science, Edward Teller, a controversial
nuclear physicist who greatly influenced US defense policy in the latter
half of the twentieth century, and Sir William Osler, a leading physician
at Johns Hopkins University at the turn of the twentieth century, who
played a critical role in advancing the scientific practice of medicine. We

end with a pair of familiar military and political leaders who founded empires separated by 18 centuries, Napoleon and Caesar Augustus.

"Transforming Visions" first assesses two leaders of religious movements, John Humphrey Noyes, the founder of the controversial Oneida Community in nineteenth-century America, and George Fox, founder in seventeenth-century England of the influential Quaker movement that continues even today. We then conclude our case studies with a comparison of the leadership of Robert Mugabe in Zimbabwe and Nelson Mandela in South Africa, two political leaders who epitomize the foundational impact of selfishness and selflessness, respectively, on their legacies.

Finally, the epilogue discusses the implications of our comprehensive framework for choosing leaders, for developing leaders, and for guiding active leaders.

PART II

Organizing Change

While all three pillars of the metaphorical Greek temple are essential to leadership effectiveness, typically one of them is the key to understanding an individual leader's success or failure. Sometimes it may be a particular strength that, given the dynamic interplay among all three pillars, buttresses the other two relatively weaker ones. Alternatively it may be a critical weakness that places undue stress on the other supporting pillars and can even topple the entire edifice. In every case, a leader's selflessness or selfishness will amplify the impact of each strength or weakness on the stability of the structure as a whole. And on occasion selflessness can even counterbalance an apparent weakness, while selfishness can undermine a strength. It is this unique combination of strengths and weaknesses in all four elements—and the interactions among them—that creates the distinctive pattern for each individual leader, which may be likened to the unique genomic code that defines each individual member of a species.

The next three chapters focus on case studies where the ability to build and manage a capable supporting organization provides the best starting point for understanding each leader's relative effectiveness. We begin with social activists Margaret Sanger, Susan B. Anthony, and Elizabeth Cady Stanton. We then examine cabinet secretaries Robert McNamara and John Gardner. We conclude with legendary businessmen Henry Ford and Soichiro Honda.

CHAPTER THREE

Margaret Sanger and Susan B. Anthony/ Elizabeth Cady Stanton: Social Reformers

Despite their exclusion from college-level educational opportunity and the right to vote, American women provided an inordinate share of the energy and initiative that organized and drove the principal social reform movements of the nineteenth and early twentieth centuries. Noteworthy were movements to abolish slavery, curb alcohol abuse, and establish equality for women. The focus of our attention in this chapter will be on three primary exemplars of that energy and initiative, three women who became national leaders and exerted international influence.

Two of the women, Elizabeth Cady Stanton and Susan B. Anthony, worked so closely and in such a complementary fashion throughout the second half of the nineteenth century that we treat them as a leadership team. While many successful leaders depend on the support of others, few are equal partnerships where the strengths of one are a near-perfect match for the weaknesses of the other. In still fewer instances is this division of labor paired with a fully shared set of visions and goals. In the case of Stanton and Anthony, the vision was equality for women, and the immediate goal was women's suffrage. With Stanton as the visionary author and radical firebrand and Anthony providing the organizational and political genius, their partnership was critical to enhancing women's rights during their lifetimes and to the eventual passage of the Nineteenth Amendment, which gave women the right to vote, years after their deaths. Their story is one of epochal and exceptional leadership.

Margaret Sanger was born more than a half century after Stanton and Anthony, and her pioneering campaign for birth control, both in the United States and internationally, extended the range of their work in emancipating and empowering women. While Sanger's leadership of the birth control movement is justly celebrated, limitations and flaws become apparent when we juxtapose it with that of Anthony and Stanton. These flaws were manifested, in particular, in her repeated failures to build and manage capable organizations to implement her vision, as Anthony and Stanton had done. In our attempt to understand what explains effective leadership, we shall look at Anthony and Stanton as more perfect illustrations and Margaret Sanger as a less perfect example of effective leadership.

Margaret Sanger

The Revolution came, but not as it has been pictured nor as history relates that revolutions have come. It came in my own life. It came in my very being...I would strike out—I would scream from the rooftops. I would tell the world what was going on in the lives of these poor women. I would be heard. No matter what it should cost. I would be heard.[1]

—Margaret Sanger

Margaret Sanger wrote this dramatic statement some time after the death of a poor woman named Sadie Sachs in 1912, who died trying to abort an unwanted pregnancy. Sanger was then working as a nurse in New York City and had been present months earlier when a physician warned Mrs. Sachs that another pregnancy might kill her. The only contraceptive advice he could or would give her, however, was that Mr. Sachs sleep on the roof. Sanger was appalled and used this story as a powerful symbol of the conditions that led her to devote her life to women's reproductive freedom, especially poor women whose large families became a trap that prevented economic and educational advancement. At the same time, Sanger used Sadie Sachs for her own origins story, her claim that she was the first to identify a problem and its solution. This claim to primacy in the birth control movement would contribute to an almost messianic imperiousness that ultimately diminished the effectiveness of her leadership, especially her ability to build capable supporting organizations.

★　★　★

On September 14, 1879, Margaret Higgins was born in Corning, New York, to Irish Catholic parents, the sixth of 11 children. Her mother died at 48 of tuberculosis, an early death that Margaret blamed on excessive childbearing, the same factor she held responsible for her family's low economic status. Margaret was well acquainted with the even poorer residents of the nearby flatlands. From an early age, she perceived large families as the root of conditions there: "poverty, unemployment, drunkenness, cruelty, quarreling, fighting, debts, [and] jails."[2] She envied the rich of Corning with their smaller families and greater leisure.

The experience of caring for her dying mother stimulated in Margaret an interest in medicine, and though her family lacked the money for college or medical school, nursing was open to her. Thus in 1899, with the help of a friend's mother, she entered the nursing program at the White Plains Hospital in Westchester County near New York City.

More than becoming a nurse, though, what Sanger wanted was to join the growing affluent class that she had envied so much in Corning. Eagerly she yielded to the courtship of William Sanger, a successful architect, and in August of 1902, they were married, shortly before the completion of her nursing program. After they settled in Hastings-on-Hudson, a suburb of New York City, the first of three children arrived in 1903. Sanger, though, found herself disappointed and bored with suburban life. Her husband, who was a longtime member of the Socialist party, felt similarly, and in early 1912, the Sangers moved to the city, where they became deeply involved in the bohemian scene. Through her husband's connections, Sanger met leading radicals of the day, including Eugene Debs and Emma Goldman. She too joined the Socialist party as a women's organizer. Gradually her amorphous resentment of the affluent classes was reshaped into a more radical estrangement from the American social order, and she became a committed activist for wide-ranging reforms through education and direct action.

In her early efforts, Sanger used her nursing skills to address the problems of poor immigrant women on the Lower East Side whose ignorance about sexuality and their own bodies resulted in a high incidence of venereal diseases. To educate them, she began writing articles on feminine hygiene for a radical political daily, *The Call*. Late in 1912, however, just after Sadie Sachs's tragic death had deepened her sense of mission, the Post Office Department, acting under the authority of the Comstock Law, banned *The Call* from the mails because of Sanger's "obscene" articles on venereal disease.

Her newfound political voice muted, Sanger welcomed the opportunity to travel with her family to Paris in the fall of 1913, her first trip abroad and the beginning of a pattern of frequent and extensive international travel that distanced her even more from mainstream American values and assumptions. In France, England, Holland, Japan, India, and elsewhere, she would learn specific methods of birth control and practical political techniques for the education of both poor women and the general public. She later maintained that on this first trip she discovered basic knowledge about contraception suppressed in the United States, suggesting that she personally imported birth control to benighted Americans. While this knowledge actually was available in the United States, it was not easily accessible, and it is not clear how much Sanger knew before her trip. In any event, it certainly is true that she swiftly became birth control's American evangelist and popularizer, helping her stake yet another large claim to primacy in the movement. At the same time, she had become discontented with her marriage and left her husband behind when she returned with her children to New York in December 1913.

Sanger plunged back into the city's cauldron of radical politics and the cause of reproductive freedom. Beginning in March 1914, she began to publish the *Woman Rebel*, a newspaper with the banner slogan "No Gods, No Masters" and a focus on contraception. Its June issue introduced the

term "birth control" for the first time.[3] Even though she never wrote
about contraceptive practices in detail, Sanger was indicted in August
under the Comstock Law for distributing obscene materials through the
mail. Later that autumn she fled the country, setting sail for England, but
not before she arranged for the illegal distribution of 100,000 copies of a
pamphlet she authored titled *Family Limitation*, which outlined all of the
contraceptive techniques she had brought home from France.

In England, the fugitive was greeted as a hero in radical circles, gaining
her instant access to influential reformers from whom she learned how to
create concrete programs for change in contrast to the relatively abstract
and ineffectual ideas of American radicalism. That new appreciation led
her to Holland, where the infant mortality rate was the world's lowest,
to investigate a system of clinics that taught mothers about contraception.
In the clinic of Dr. Johannes Rutgers, a physician who trained nurses and
midwives in contraception, she learned how to examine women, advise
them on contraceptive methods, and fit them with what later came to be
known as the diaphragm. On this trip, as biographer Elyse Topalian notes,
Sanger "realized for the first time the importance of the medical community's involvement in the birth control movement and the necessity of
keeping records, doing follow-up studies, and compiling data."[4] She also
realized that she had to temper her radical posture and appeal to a much
greater cross-section of the American public if she was going to make any
real headway.

In the fall of 1915, Sanger returned from Europe to a storm of publicity
in New York provoked by the arrest and trial of her husband, William,
for giving a copy of Sanger's *Family Limitation* to an undercover Comstock
agent. It proved to be a pivotal year for Sanger and therefore for the birth
control movement. First, on her return she found that, inspired by her own
efforts and William's martyrdom, a number of organizations had formed to
advocate birth control. Disconcertingly to Sanger, while she was a widely
recognized and powerful figure in the birth control movement, others
were jockeying with her for recognition as its leader. She deeply resented
this rivalry and became determined to establish and preserve her unique
status as the movement's pioneer and principal leader.

Her return home also meant that she faced prosecution and prison
for her violations of the Comstock Law, though the government, faced
with her newfound celebrity, decided at the last minute to drop the case.
Finally, within a month of her return, her oldest daughter, Peggy, died
of pneumonia, leading to a nervous breakdown for Sanger and a vow to
sacrifice all for the movement as a means of vindicating her daughter's
death. Sanger's future path was set. From this time forward, she would be
focused exclusively on leading the new birth control movement—and she
would tolerate no rivals.

There is no question that Sanger provided effective leadership to the
birth control movement over the next five decades. Not only was her
vision of gaining reproductive freedom for women a noble one, her

strategy of proceeding on two fronts was sound. First, she concentrated on repealing the Comstock Law, which dated from 1873 and placed not only written materials about birth control but also contraceptive devices under the category of obscenity. Anthony Comstock, a US senator from Connecticut, had also been a Congregational minister, and powerful religious forces continued to provide strong support to his law. The battle to overturn Comstock was won not in legislatures, but in the courts, where a case Sanger incited led to a crucial victory in a 1936 federal appeals court ruling that enabled physicians to provide information about contraception and supply birth control devices to patients.[5]

The second front involved programs to educate the public and to assist women in their use of birth control methods. In 1916, Sanger launched this campaign with a speaking tour and the introduction of the *Birth Control Review*. Displaying her **persuasive skills**, she mixed "a captivating potion of charm, logic, statistics, often maudlin sentiment, and high idealism" that transfixed audiences and created a devoted group of followers.[6] She was careful, though, to present the appearance of a demure and earnest wife and mother in order to appeal to the educated and affluent liberal middle class that was critical to the ultimate success of the movement.[7]

Sanger used every possible rationale—social, economic, political, and moral—in support of birth control. She became expert in tailoring her message to key constituencies with differing agendas. In the 1920s, she appealed to influential white Anglo-Saxon Protestants, who worried about their future powers of social control as generations of poor immigrants with large families filled American cities. During the Great Depression, she argued that birth control would help reduce the demands on New Deal welfare programs and improve the standard of living for many families. Following World War II, Sanger pointed out the value of birth control in controlling population growth, given the uncertain prospects for the postwar economy and the long-term dangers of overpopulation. Other birth control arguments she used at various times included relieving the suffering of the poor, boosting the health and welfare of children, eliminating birth defects (through incentive-based sterilization), and enhancing the quality of sexual relationships. Birth control, it appeared, was the solution to almost any problem, and she had the persuasive powers to convince many of that.[8]

The results of Sanger's efforts to promote birth control over the 50 years following her daughter's death were nothing short of revolutionary, culminating with the introduction of "the Pill" in 1960, the first contraceptive that gave women control over fertility and whose development Sanger sponsored and helped to fund. In 1965, the Supreme Court, in *Griswold v. Connecticut*, struck down the last remnant of Comstock by lifting all restrictions on the use of contraceptives by married couples, while expanding individuals' right to privacy. Sanger's vision held out the prospect of economic betterment, educational attainment, enhanced opportunity, improved health, and greater family happiness. Especially after she had moderated her resentment toward the powerful individuals and interests who dominated the American scene, she became an exceptionally effective fundraiser and networker. Her charisma and intelligence gained her access to the inner circles of wealthy and influential people who were sympathetic or curious enough to want to meet her. More often than not, she left with their friendship and financial support. Moreover, she had celebrity-level mass appeal and recognition as the world's foremost figure in the birth control movement. Already in 1925, at an international conference on birth control Sanger organized, the delegates tried to elect her as the president, but she demurred in favor of having a scientist head the movement. In 1959, when she was still active in her beloved cause at the age of 80, delegates at the International Planned Parenthood Federation convention voted her president emeritus for life. Such plaudits indicate that Sanger had a vision and a narrative that were compelling. As a result, she generated a committed following throughout the world of those who shared her faith that reproductive freedom was key to a life of dignity and opportunity for mothers and their families.

Yet the adulation and admiration showered upon Sanger came primarily from people who viewed her at a distance. Those who shared responsibility for the various organizations that she led saw her in a much less favorable light. What they experienced was a poor administrator, who preferred direct action and disliked organizations, even though she understood their necessity.[9] Her need for complete autonomy and control inevitably strained her relationships with these subordinates over time. As a result, she was always more successful in founding organizations than in running them, especially the kind of large, centralized organization needed to plan and direct complex campaigns.

Sanger's failings as a leader were best illustrated by her difficulties with her principal organization, the American Birth Control League (ABCL), which she founded in 1921. It grew rapidly and spread widely, achieving a membership of 27,500 within the first three years. But a few years later, Sanger had lost control of the ABCL. Many of the junior staff revered her, but she had alienated the senior staff. As biographer Deborah Bachrach points out, they came "to resent her dictatorial methods, her failure to acknowledge their contributions, [and] her insistence on making all [policy] decisions."[10] Because her second husband, J. Noah H. Slee, a wealthy patron of birth control whom she married in 1920 after formally divorcing William Sanger, was a major contributor to the ABCL, she also insisted upon complete control of its spending. This caused additional friction. "Essentially," Bachrach notes, "many people had grown to oppose what they considered to be a one-woman movement."[11] Consequently, after an 18-month absence from the United States, Sanger returned to New York in March 1928 to find her presidential authority diminished by the board of directors. She angrily resigned the presidency in June and later in the year quit the organization entirely. Critically, she did not leave over differences in policies or goals, but because of her inability to compromise over who exercised power. She seemed incapable of subordinating her personal desires and needs for the good of the movement. In short, she failed the tests of both *organization building* and *selflessness.*

Following her exit from the ABCL, Sanger began to focus upon the development of birth control clinics under the auspices of the Clinical Research Bureau, which she had founded in 1923. Once again, she demonstrated her effectiveness in leading an organization in its early phases. She was very successful at raising money, publicizing the clinics, and recruiting outstanding physicians and nurses to lead them and conduct related research. As a result, by 1930 there were 55 clinics in 12 states. But here again, Sanger's compulsion to control got in the way of her leadership. Because of her unwillingness to let the clinics be managed by licensed medical groups, she exacerbated the separation between mainstream medicine and birth control. With no uniform guidance from the medical profession, many women still did not know which birth control providers were legitimate and which were "quacks" or worse. Indeed, another Sanger biographer, David Kennedy, speculates that had she been willing to entrust more authority to professional medical personnel, the clinical dimension of the birth control movement might have developed far more rapidly and extensively.[12]

By 1938, it had become clear that the work of the ABCL and Clinical Research Bureau needed to be coordinated. Despite the vigorous opposition of Sanger, who feared she would be overshadowed, the two organizations merged, becoming the Birth Control Federation of America under the leadership of a male doctor. Four years later, with Sanger again objecting, its name was changed to the Planned Parenthood Federation of America.

Yet by then, perhaps weary from battling, or perhaps wiser with experience, Sanger had, as she put it, "spiritually left the front and joined the ranks."[13] By the end of World War II she was little more than a figurehead.[14] Even though the plaudits would continue, biographer Ellen Chesler observes that Sanger "would essentially live on borrowed time, age and illness magnifying her eccentricities and compromising her effectiveness."[15] Her combative, militant style was viewed as a liability in the movement that was largely her creation. The qualities that had brought energy, credibility, and recognition to the cause were no longer the qualities most needed. Even though in some ways she had adapted to new leadership demands through the years, she failed to display the selflessness needed to keep her priorities straight, to retain the respect and loyalty of many who had looked to her for leadership, and thus to lead a strong, supporting organization. Indeed, concludes Bachrach, "she became selfish, claiming full credit for victories won along the way with the help of numerous faithful followers."[16] While the movement and organizations she founded did indeed evolve in new directions and ultimately achieved her goals, this was accomplished largely through the initiatives of others and despite her opposition.

Susan B. Anthony and Elizabeth Cady Stanton

I am the better writer, [and] she the better critic. She supplied the facts and statistics, I the philosophy and rhetoric, and together we have made arguments that have stood unshaken by the storms of...long years; arguments that no man has answered. Our speeches may be considered the united product of our two brains. So entirely one are we that...not one feeling of envy or jealousy has ever shadowed our lives.[17]

—Elizabeth Cady Stanton on her relationship
with Susan B. Anthony

Elizabeth Cady was born in Johnstown, New York, on November 12, 1815, the eighth child of Judge Daniel Cady and Margaret Livingston Cady. The Livingstons were an old aristocratic family with deep roots in the Hudson River Valley, and throughout her life Elizabeth proudly referred to herself as a "Daughter of the Revolution."[18] Although her father lacked so distinguished a pedigree, he was a prominent lawyer. Elizabeth was drawn more to him than her mother, seeking his approval and spending much time in his law office. As a young child she was with him there when a woman named Flora Campbell came to ask for legal assistance. Flora's father had left her a farm, but her husband had mortgaged it. Now the husband's creditors were preparing to take it over. Young Elizabeth never forgot Judge Cady's devastating response to Flora Campbell: there was nothing he could do. Flora's inheritance belonged to her husband. As Stanton would often testify, this incident inspired her lifelong work to remedy such injustices. Another formative episode concerned the death of her brother Eleazar soon after his college graduation. As she tried to comfort her grieving father, who had already lost three other sons in infancy, he said, "Oh, my daughter, I wish you were a boy!" At the age of 11 Elizabeth resolved to fill the void, "to be all my brother was."[19]

It would be a mistake to ascribe too much of Stanton's motivation to a desire to accomplish things that would make her father proud of her. Even before Eleazar died, she believed that she was the equal of the local boys and had been eager to compete with them in reciting Greek. Moreover, despite her fond recollections, there is little evidence Judge Cady encouraged his daughter's attempts to better herself. Indeed, when Elizabeth tried to enter all-male Union College at the age of 15 and was predictably denied admission, Cady did not intervene on behalf of his bright and ambitious daughter. He did, though, allow himself to be persuaded by a son-in-law, Edward Bayard, to let Elizabeth attend the Troy Female Seminary, run by the well-known educator Emma Willard. Nonetheless, Cady remained ambivalent at best about Elizabeth's ambitions and eventual public role. He and his wife were pillars of the established order. They did not want to be embarrassed by children who publicly questioned the status quo.

Instead, Elizabeth won support and sympathy from other members of her extended family. In addition to Bayard, she found the home of her mother's cousin, Gerritt Smith, a place where she could participate in energetic conversations about abolition, temperance, and other reform movements, and where she could try out her own opinions with friendly audiences.

But what Elizabeth most needed was independence from her parents, and in 1839, at the age of 23, she met and eventually accepted the marriage proposal of Henry Brewster Stanton. Ten years older than Elizabeth, Stanton was a well-known orator in abolitionist circles, but Judge Cady and Edward Bayard regarded him as something of a dilettante and persuaded Elizabeth to break off the engagement. A few months later, though, when Henry Stanton announced that he was going to London for eight months to attend the first World Anti-Slavery Conference, Elizabeth was emboldened by the prospect of joining him. The wedding plans were revived, and they were married in Johnstown on May 1, 1840, after both agreed not to use the word "obey" in the ceremony and that she would henceforth use her full name, Elizabeth Cady Stanton, not the conventional Mrs. Henry Stanton.[20] She was determined to maintain her equality and independence.

In London, Elizabeth began to find her voice as well. While women attended the conference, they were not allowed to participate, separated from the men by a screen. Angered by the exclusion, Stanton met and came under the influence of another woman delegate, Lucretia Mott, a prominent American Quaker preacher, abolitionist, and advocate for women's rights. Stanton adopted Mott's motto of "truth for authority, not authority for truth." Over the next two years, as she was exposed to the ideas of free thinkers, Quakers, Unitarians, and Transcendentalists, she grew estranged from the conservative Presbyterian worldview with which she had been raised.[21]

Back in the United States, though, living first in Boston and then in Seneca Falls, New York, Elizabeth's life was conventional as she gave birth to three sons between March 1842 and September 1845. Eventually she would have seven children. Feeling increasingly tied down in her roles as wife and mother, a catalyzing event occurred in 1847 that eventually propelled her into a public role and made equality for women her battle cry. In Seneca Falls, she joined others in trying to bring relief to impoverished Irish refugees from the potato famine in a shantytown near her home. Stanton was appalled by what she saw. The burden of meeting the needs of the refugees fell primarily on their women. Uneducated and penniless, they were oppressed, often abused by heavy-drinking husbands, and handicapped by impossible odds. Stanton, with her privileged background, saw in the plight of the Irish women a parable of what was wrong with women's lives in general.[22]

Soon after this experience, in July of 1848, Stanton was having tea with Quaker friends including James and Lucretia Mott. As she later recounted: "I poured out the...torrent of my long-accumulating discontent, with such vehemence and indignation that I stirred myself as well as the rest of the party to do and dare anything."[23] The discussion resulted in the convening of the first Women's Rights Convention in Seneca Falls on July 19 and 20, 1848. It was held only days after Stanton's outburst at a tea party that would have ramifications for American life almost as great as the more famous one in Boston less than a century before.

The Seneca Falls Convention was the birthplace of the American women's rights movement. Some 300 people, including 48 men, attended. James Mott presided, and Elizabeth Cady Stanton was principally responsible for drafting the documents for the convention. Using the Declaration of Independence as her model, she and her colleagues drew up a Declaration of Sentiments that defined the purpose of the meeting. Declaring that "all men and women are created equal," it proceeded with fiery passion and eloquence to list the "injuries and usurpations" of men toward women that have as their object "the establishment of an absolute tyranny over her." As one imagines Stanton's reading of the Declaration, its indictments must have landed like hammer blows, one after another, on the ears of her audience:

> He has never permitted her to exercise her inalienable right to the elective franchise. He has compelled her to submit to laws, in the formation of which she had no voice. He has withheld from her rights which are given to the most ignorant and degraded men—both natives and foreigners...He has made her, if married, in the eye of the law, civilly dead. He has taken from her all right in property, even to the wages she earns...He has denied her the facilities for obtaining a thorough education, all colleges being closed against her...He has endeavored, in every way that he could, to destroy her confidence in her own powers, to lessen her self-respect, and to make her willing to lead a dependent and abject life.[24]

Stanton also came armed with 11 resolutions containing specific demands that would empower women to pursue their own "true and substantial happiness."[25] The assembly moved smoothly through the agenda until the ninth resolution came to the floor. It was the boldest, most shocking proposal on the list, a declaration that women must secure for themselves the right to vote. Even Lucretia Mott feared that such a demand would "make the convention ridiculous."[26] But Stanton firmly insisted that without suffrage, no other rights could be secure. Then Frederick Douglass, the former slave who had become a powerful voice for abolition, weighed in eloquently and persuaded the majority to support the resolution calling for women's suffrage.

Stanton's Declaration of Sentiments became a galvanizing document, and among its signatories were Susan B. Anthony's parents and sister. While Susan was not at the convention, women's suffrage was to become the center of her life's work. Born in 1820 in Adams, Massachusetts,

Anthony was the daughter of a prosperous Quaker mill owner. Beginning at age 15, she taught school, initially for her own improvement, but after the nationwide economic depression of 1837 ruined her father's business, to help support her family. She was paid, though, just one-quarter of a man's salary, an inequity she never forgot. Over the next few years, she rose in the teaching profession and learned to enjoy a career woman's independence. In 1846 she became headmistress of the Female Department of the Canajoharie Academy. As for marriage, she told a female interviewer later in her life that "I never felt I could give up my life of freedom to become a man's housekeeper. When I was young if a girl married poor she became a housekeeper and a drudge. If she married wealthy, she became a pet and a doll. Just think, had I married at twenty, I would have been a drudge or a doll for 55 years. Think of it!"[27]

In 1848, seeking a new challenge, Anthony helped start a local chapter of the Daughters of Temperance, and as the "Presiding Sister" she gave her first public speech early in 1849. Very soon, she realized that her passion was for reform, not teaching. As Stanton later wrote of her, "In ancient Greece she would have been a stoic; in the era of the Reformation, a Calvinist; in King Charles's time, a Puritan; but in the Nineteenth Century, by the very law of her being, she is a reformer."[28] By the autumn of 1849, Anthony had quit teaching, returned to the Rochester farm where her family had moved in 1845, and joined a local temperance chapter. Unlike Stanton, Anthony enjoyed the wholehearted support of her parents, with their belief that men and women were equal before God and their devotion to the temperance and abolition movements. By 1850, Anthony, too, was involved in abolition, as the family farm became both a stop on the Underground Railroad and a meeting place for like-minded reformers, including Douglass, John Brown, and William Lloyd Garrison.

In May 1851, Stanton and Anthony finally met, introduced by their mutual friend, Amelia Bloomer, inventor of the women's pantaloon of the same name. Their partnership seemed predestined. As one of their biographers, Geoffrey Ward, points out: "Stanton, brimming over with indignation but pinned down by domestic responsibilities, needed to have someone to carry her message into the field. Anthony, unfettered and possessed of almost manic energy, was eager for action," but she "needed someone to put her own indignation into words."[29] Within a year, they had teamed up in the temperance movement. When Anthony attended a statewide convention in Albany of the Sons of Temperance in January 1852, the chairman ruled that "the sisters were not invited...to speak but to listen and learn."[30] That remark prompted her to start the Woman's State Temperance Society, and she invited Stanton to be its first president and to write a speech for Anthony to deliver at the inaugural meeting. Stanton agreed with the sole condition that she be permitted to write the uncensored truth as she saw it, thus setting the pattern that the two would follow for the next four decades. Stanton's inaugural address in April 1852 far more stridently advocated a broad women's rights agenda than the attending temperance crusaders had expected, and the next year, at the second annual convention, conservative women deposed Stanton as president, prompting her and Anthony to resign from the group they had founded.

Now the two focused their own efforts on women's rights and on women's suffrage in particular, without which, they believed, any gains in rights could easily be withdrawn at the pleasure of the male ruling class. In 1854, Stanton became the first woman invited to speak to the New York state legislature on the inequality of women before the law and Anthony's organizational skills made sure that the speech's impact was magnified many times over. She circulated 50,000 copies to the press and other reform groups nationwide and arranged for Stanton to deliver the same speech to the New York Woman's Rights Convention that year. The results of this public relations campaign included speaking invitations from all over the state and an offer to Stanton from Horace Greeley, the reform-minded editor, of a regular column in his *New York Tribune*.[31]

For the balance of the 1850s, Stanton remained tied down by her family responsibilities. She worked largely behind the scenes, writing articles, letters, and speeches for Anthony, who became a powerhouse, a very popular lecturer as well as the executive manager of the women's rights movement. The two women recognized the value of their partnership. Anthony understood that Elizabeth was more skilled at conceptualizing an overall strategy and articulating their vision. Stanton saw that her more radical ideas would be better received when presented by the temperate and empathetic Anthony. Stanton, more ebullient and emotionally tough, was glad to serve as a lightning rod in sheltering Anthony. As Stanton later wrote: "So closely interwoven have been our lives, our purposes and experiences, that separated, we have a feeling of incompleteness—united, such strength of self-assertion that no ordinary obstacles, difficulties, or danger ever appear to us insurmountable."[32] Theodore Tilton, who worked with the two in the late 1860s and early 1870s when they were producing the radical weekly newspaper *The Revolution*, concluded that "neither has any selfish ambition for celebrity; but each vies with the other in a noble enthusiasm for the cause to which they are devoting their lives."[33]

In March of 1860, all of their efforts resulted in a major triumph for the women's rights movement when an important expansion of New York's Married Woman's Property Act of 1848 was passed by the state legislature, after a multiyear campaign that included Stanton's address to the Judiciary Committee. The law gave women the right to own property, keep their earnings, engage in business on their own, sue and be sued in court, and share custody of their children. Eventually other states passed similar bills. With the onset of the Civil War, however, the energy behind further reform lessened as the focus of many in the movement shifted toward abolition and supporting the Union, in hopes that their work would be rewarded with suffrage after the war.

Stanton and Anthony would need all of their optimism and persistence over the coming decades as one disappointment followed another.

In 1862, for example, the New York legislature repealed the shared custody provision of the 1860 Act. Following the war, women's rights activists were repeatedly rebuffed in their attempts to have women's suffrage included in the Fourteenth and, especially, the Fifteenth Amendments, which guaranteed the voting rights of former male slaves. Women who for decades had labored on behalf of abolition felt betrayed. Stanton lashed out, opposing passage of the Fifteenth Amendment and acidly noting that while the freedmen were largely illiterate, the women who sought the vote were generally prepared to bring an informed perspective to the political issues of the day. Splitting from their erstwhile abolitionist allies, Stanton and Anthony formed the National Woman Suffrage Association (NWSA) in 1869 to pursue women's suffrage through a constitutional amendment of their own and through the courts. Meanwhile, those former colleagues who favored the Fifteenth Amendment started the rival American Woman Suffrage Association (AWSA), which focused on achieving suffrage at the state level. Not until 1890 would the two combine forces, with Stanton and Anthony assuming the leadership of the resulting National American Woman Suffrage Association (NAWSA).

Despite repeated disappointments over the coming decades, Stanton and Anthony slowly made progress in shifting the mindsets not only of women, but also of politicians and the average male voter. This shift, while excruciatingly slow, set the stage for the eventual triumph of the suffrage movement. Thus, for example, every year after the Civil War the petition drives of the suffragettes led more and more state legislatures to debate and vote on women's suffrage, including by 1869 the states of Ohio, Michigan, Missouri, Kansas, Wisconsin, Minnesota, and Wyoming. By the election of 1880, the presidential candidates felt the need to explain both publicly and in private to the movement's leaders why they would not endorse women's suffrage. Stanton and Anthony succeeded in generating powerful conviction among women and broad sympathy among men for their cause. And the many local, state, and national initiatives they and others sparked eventually engulfed American society and spread to many other parts of the world.[34] Nonetheless, by the time of Stanton's death in 1902 and Anthony's in 1906, women had been granted the right to vote in only four states (Wyoming, Utah, Colorado, and Idaho) and a handful of municipal and school board elections elsewhere. The continuing opposition of certain special interests (such as the liquor industry, which rightly worried that women's suffrage would bring prohibition) and competing political priorities would delay the ultimate passage and ratification of the Nineteenth Amendment until 1920.

★   ★   ★

How did Stanton and Anthony succeed in establishing the justice of their *vision*, despite the deeply embedded economic and legal forces empowering men, forces that were sanctioned in turn by millennia of custom and religious teachings? They did so by compellingly communicating their case, leveraging their impact as individual leaders through superb organization of their followers (many of whom became effective leaders in their own right), and selflessly embodying their values and message.

The backbone of their *communications* was the visionary, and sometimes incendiary, writings of Stanton. She was not only a regular columnist for Greeley's *Tribune*; she contributed articles to any other newspaper or journal around the country that would print them. Stanton and Anthony published *The Revolution* as well, until it ran into financial trouble. They also were masters of garnering publicity for their cause. For example, for the nation's centennial in 1876, they wrote and distributed copies of a new *Declaration of Rights for Women* to the prominent politicians attending the July 4 celebration in Philadelphia. And over the following decade, they wrote a three-volume work titled *The History of Woman Suffrage*. In addition to publications, they communicated their message through the media used by any effective political campaign of the period. Traveling by rail, both women lectured tirelessly across the country. In one year alone, Anthony gave over 170 lectures and traveled 13,000 miles. They also presented petitions, addressed state legislatures, testified before Congressional committees, and lobbied politicians. Indeed, Anthony ensured that NWSA held its convention in Washington every year—and always made Congress feel its presence.

Stanton and Anthony's effectiveness in delivering their message was amplified dramatically by Anthony's *organizational* genius. It was she, for example, who organized petition drives that generated six thousand signatures in only six weeks in 1853 demanding the New York legislature expand the Married Woman's Property Act. She gathered ten thousand signatures in 1865 supporting the inclusion of woman suffrage in the Fourteenth Amendment. She worked tirelessly to place Stanton's articles in newspapers nationwide, ran *The Revolution*, and found the publisher for *The History* and arranged for its distribution to schools and libraries. Over 50 years, she traveled throughout the land renting halls for meetings, raising funds, running petition campaigns, speaking, and training in organizational techniques the thousands of women who flocked to her. She seeded the entire American landscape with local organizations, multiplying her impact many fold in the process. She also left a very strong organization and leadership team behind her in the form of NAWSA, which was led first by Carrie Chapman Catt and then by the Reverend Anna Howard Shaw.

As their colleague Theodore Tilton indicated, Stanton and Anthony worked together *selflessly* in pursuit of their cause. Indeed, Anthony remained single so that she would be unencumbered in the struggle for equality for women. They both were prodigious writers and lecturers who undoubtedly could have cashed in on their celebrity—and notoriety— and made a very good living indeed. Instead, they settled for economic self-sufficiency. Their eyes never strayed from the prize. Moreover, they did not cling to the levers of power. For example, Stanton resigned as president of NAWSA in 1892. Anthony, who succeeded her, in turn resigned in 1900, telling activists she preferred to "see you all at work while I am alive, so I can scold you if you do not do it well."[35]

A final evidence of their selflessness—and their effectiveness as a leadership team—is the way they consistently transcended the tensions inevitable in any partnership to present a seamless leadership profile to their followers. They worked side by side in facing the challenges and strains on the movement, even when Stanton's radical views and impetuousness created problems for the broad-based coalitions that Anthony was trying to build and lead. Their unity held after the Civil War, for example, when the alliance between the movements for abolition and for women's rights foundered on the decision to give priority to the rights of former male slaves over those of women.

Even when they had real divergences of opinion, they believed, as Stanton wrote, "To the world we always [must] seem to agree and uniformly reflect each other...Like husband and wife, each has the feeling that we must have no differences in public."[36] Their united front held despite Anthony's belief that it was wise to concentrate on the right to vote, while Stanton was more inclined to maintain a broad attack on the range of injustices women suffered. Stanton's views, moreover, became increasingly radical. She was drawn to socialism and openly questioned Christianity. Thus, when Anthony carefully cultivated the powerful Women's Christian Temperance Union, Stanton expressed concern to her about cozying up with an organization whose agenda was so openly religious.

Their relationship faced its greatest strain as the result of another controversy prompted by Stanton's brashness, the publication in 1895 of *The Woman's Bible*, her bold and brilliant attack on the Christian foundations of the oppressive sexism that ascribed a secondary and humiliating role to women. The public received this radical text with a mixture of shock and titillation. At NAWSA's annual convention in 1895, a resolution dissociating the organization from Stanton and her ideas was approved. Anthony defended her friend vigorously, warning of "a revival of the Spanish inquisition."[37] But when Stanton insisted that she resign the presidency in protest, Anthony agonized for three weeks, before telling her that it was her duty to stay, to provide guidance, and work to have the resolution withdrawn at the next convention. Indeed, by this point, Anthony had become the better-known and gentler face of the movement to the young feminists whom she called "her nieces," and Stanton occasionally envied the adulation they heaped upon "Aunt Susan."

Still, these instances of tension and jealousy within their lengthy relationship always remained small and private undercurrents that never interfered with their steady focus and combined public efforts. They were both paragons of selfless devotion to the cause of justice and equality for women. Both appreciated the symbiotic character of their distinctive partnership. Stanton's bold and colorful pronouncements created controversy, but they also brought valuable attention to the movement's goals. Meanwhile, Anthony's single-minded focus on the issue of suffrage and her coalition-building skills created the broad support critical to the eventual passage of the Nineteenth Amendment. Together, they provided exceptional leadership to the movement for women's suffrage in particular and women's rights more broadly.

★ ★ ★

In summary, while Stanton, Anthony, and Sanger were all legendary figures in the movement for women's rights, they were strikingly different in the style and effectiveness of their leadership. They were similar in their passion for the cause and in their ability to persuasively communicate a compelling vision to both their followers and the public at large. They differed, however, in the ability to build effective, long-lasting organizations and to develop worthy successors to carry on their work. While Stanton may have resembled Sanger in wishing to dominate any organization of which she was a part and in being more radical than many mainstream members could comfortably tolerate, she had Anthony to balance these tendencies. Moreover, Stanton was selfless enough to allow Anthony to lead in applying the organizational skills and unifying power that eventually enabled the creation of the National American Woman Suffrage Association, the building of coalitions with a series of allies, and the development of a number of worthy successors, who finally succeeded in passing the Nineteenth Amendment. Sanger, in contrast, was a poor manager whose ego would tolerate no rivals. As a result, the creation of what eventually was called the Planned Parenthood Federation and the development of a number of other important leaders in the birth control movement happened despite, rather than because of, Sanger's leadership. In short, all three women made enormous contributions to the women's rights movement, but only the team of Stanton and Anthony demonstrated exceptional leadership.

CHAPTER FOUR

Robert S. McNamara and John W. Gardner: Lyndon Johnson's Cabinet Warriors

Lyndon Baines Johnson took the oath of office as the 36th president of the United States on November 22, 1963, aboard Air Force One as it readied to carry the body of his slain predecessor from Dallas back to the capital of a stunned and grieving nation. Johnson inherited a military commitment in Vietnam that Presidents Eisenhower and Kennedy had undertaken, a commitment he was convinced was necessary to contain communist aggression not only in Southeast Asia but throughout the world. Johnson was also strongly committed to the civil rights legislation that his predecessor had advocated, and he harbored aspirations for a larger agenda of reforms to address the problems of economic inequality. In effect, Johnson's grand vision for his presidency was a two-front war, one against international communism and the other a domestic war on poverty. The domestic war he would eventually put under the command of John W. Gardner, whom he appointed to head the Department of Health, Education, and Welfare (HEW) in 1965. The military commitment in Vietnam was already under the oversight of Robert S. McNamara, who had served President Kennedy as secretary of defense since 1961.

McNamara and Gardner became Johnson's two most powerful cabinet secretaries based in significant measure on their organizational talents. Because of the size and complexity of the military forces, one expects the secretary of defense to be powerful, but McNamara, by building on his exceptional skills as a manager, became an unexpectedly influential advisor to Johnson. HEW, in contrast, was not historically a platform for power or influence. Gardner's standing reflected his success in coordinating a vast bureaucracy of 105,000 civil servants and in melding a plethora of mandates and agencies into a coherent, effective instrument of the policies that represented the domestic priorities and commitments of President Johnson and his administration. Yet despite the power each man accumulated, he served at the pleasure of the president, was expected to support his policies, and needed the cooperation of other departments to accomplish many of his goals. In short, McNamara and Gardner were in the position of many middle managers, whether high or low in an organization. How well did each rise to the challenge and lead?

Robert S. McNamara

Running the Department of Defense is not different from running Ford Motor Company, or the Catholic Church, for that matter. Once you get to a certain scale, it's all the same.[1]

—Robert McNamara, 1962

On November 29, 1967, President Johnson announced that McNamara was leaving the Defense Department to become head of the World Bank. McNamara later said that he did not know whether he had resigned or was fired, but given the collapse of his relationship with the president, it was most likely the latter. When he left, he was among the most controversial cabinet secretaries in US history, and more than 40 years later the debate about his role in America's Vietnam debacle is still very much alive. Why did McNamara continue to push for the escalation of the war for several years both in public and within the Johnson administration, even as his private doubts and the body counts grew? When he finally concluded that the war was unwinnable, why did he still appear to think that his primary responsibility was to the president's failed policies of escalation and bombing rather than to the hundreds of thousands of soldiers he was sending to fight that war or to the American people? In short, given the uniquely influential position he held among President Johnson's advisers, why was he not a more effective leader? The answers are complex, as befits the complexity of McNamara's personality, but at the core, we conclude, McNamara was much more of a manager than a leader.

★ ★ ★

Robert McNamara was born in 1916 and grew up in Oakland, California. He was an excellent student at the University of California at Berkeley where he experienced "defining moments" that shaped his approach to every job he ever held. Ethics courses, he would write in his memoirs, "forced me to begin to shape my values; studying logic exposed me to rigor and precision in thinking." And his mathematics professors taught him "to see math as a process of thought—a language in which to express much, but certainly not all of human activity. It was a revelation. To this day, I see quantification as a language to add precision to reasoning about the world."[2] He went on to excel at the Harvard Business School, where he received an MBA in 1939 and became especially adept at statistical analysis. These skills led to employment by Price Waterhouse, the large accounting firm, but within a year after his graduation, Harvard Business

School attracted him back to teach accounting as its youngest and highest paid assistant professor.

Soon after he began his second year of teaching, the United States entered World War II. McNamara's participation in the military effort began at Harvard where he taught young Army Air Corps officers to use statistical methods in developing military logistical systems. Excelling at this, in early 1943 he was assigned to the Air Corps Office of Statistical Control with the rank of captain. His most significant work during the war was the design, through statistical analysis, of plans for the most effective and efficient use of the new long-range B-29 bombers. McNamara's task was to help maximize the impact of bombing missions while minimizing plane losses. His study contributed to the decision by General Curtis LeMay, who, according to McNamara, "focused on only one thing: target destruction," to firebomb Tokyo—a largely wooden city—and to shower incendiary bombs on almost 70 other Japanese cities. These attacks resulted in the deaths of upward of a million people, the vast majority of them civilian noncombatants.[3]

Half a century later McNamara was still haunted by his role in that awesome demonstration of the human capacity and willingness to inflict destruction upon fellow human beings. In the award-winning documentary film by Errol Morris, *The Fog of War* (2003), McNamara stated, "LeMay said if we'd lost the war, we'd all have been prosecuted as war criminals, and I think he's right. He, and I'd say I, were behaving as war criminals." Yet elsewhere in the film, McNamara insisted that he served as merely "part of a mechanism," a cog in the machine.[4] This apparent dichotomy between self-awareness and self-delusion, between unbending principle and situational ethics recurred throughout McNamara's career, especially during the Vietnam conflict.

By the time he left the Army Air Corps in early 1946, McNamara had achieved the rank of lieutenant colonel and been awarded the Legion of Merit. He still thought of himself as an academic, but because of family medical expenses he needed more money than he would earn as a professor. He joined the Ford Motor Company as one of the ten "Whiz Kids" who had served together in Statistical Control. Ford Motor, once a wonder of industrial capitalism, had become a deeply troubled company after decades of mismanagement by its founder, Henry Ford. Ford Motor was paying a dear price for the absence of financial controls and planning mechanisms and the founder's stubborn refusal to hire accountants or even permit audits of the company's books. His grandson and the new president, young Henry Ford II, was desperate for help in turning around the fortunes of a company that trailed far behind General Motors, the world's leading automobile manufacturer, and was hemorrhaging losses at the rate of $10 million a month. Over the next 15 years, the Whiz Kids he hired reshaped Ford Motor and restored its prosperity and reputation.

At Ford, McNamara honed the management approach that would become his modus operandi at the Defense Department. As he expressed it in his memoirs, it was to define a clear objective, "develop a plan to achieve that objective, and systematically monitor progress against the plan. Then, if progress was deficient, one could either adjust the plan or introduce corrective action to accelerate progress."[5] At Ford, his objectives included identifying target market segments and improving the safety features of Ford cars. Demonstrating McNamara's strong personal values, one of his proudest accomplishments at Ford was the introduction of seatbelts, padded instrument panels, and collapsible steering wheels in 1957,[6] years before Ralph Nader began promoting auto safety. In every case, gathering relevant statistics and undertaking fact-based analyses were the keys to developing and monitoring the plans to achieve his goals. McNamara's approach was, in short, a paradigm of modern, professional management, and in the relatively stable environment of the postwar automotive industry and amid rising national prosperity, it worked.

While at Ford, however, McNamara also displayed some disturbing aspects of his personal style that prevented him from attracting many followers. While considerate to a few people he respected, he was a bully to most. According to biographer Deborah Shapley, "[H]is instinct of treating all but a chosen few as antagonists, of slighting people who were really his partners in a common effort, hurt cooperation, morale, and his claim to leadership."[7] Perhaps some of his behavior was calculated to shake up a sclerotic culture, but either way, without a critical mass of followers it is impossible to be a leader. He also had a practice of shading his views to demonstrate his loyalty to his bosses and preserve his power base. Shapley writes that if McNamara knew Henry Ford or another superior opposed something, "he would develop factual arguments against it. If he knew they favored a plan, McNamara tempered his objections—and sometimes fixed his statistics—to stay on the team."[8] Nonetheless, for Henry Ford II, the results that this Whiz Kid achieved were far more important than any doubts about his personal style. McNamara's reward was to be named the first president of Ford Motor from outside the founding family on November 9, 1960.

★ ★ ★

One day earlier, the United States had elected a new president, John F. Kennedy. McNamara was still settling into his new duties at Ford when in mid-December he was summoned to Washington to meet Kennedy, who was impressed by this Republican businessman with a relentlessly analytic mind. Kennedy offered him a choice of two cabinet posts— Treasury or Defense. McNamara quickly decided that Defense offered the greater and more interesting challenge, and in characteristic fashion, he immersed himself in understanding the data and issues of the Defense Department so that within a week he impressed the Kennedy people as being completely in control.[9] With an agenda of scores of urgent issues that he wanted to address—nicknamed the "Ninety-nine Trombones" within the department[10]—and a team of highly talented principal subordinates (five of whom later became cabinet members themselves[11]), he soon had groups studying each of the issues. McNamara was confident that the management approach that had served him so well at Ford would also be effective in his new role. "I had no patience with the myth that the Defense Department could not be managed," he said decades later. It was an immense organization with 4.5 million people and an annual budget larger than the national budget of any NATO ally in 1961. But McNamara had spent, he said, "fifteen years as a manager identifying problems and forcing organizations—often against their will—to think deeply and realistically about alternative courses of action and their consequences."[12]

Especially early in his tenure, McNamara's approach worked in achieving his and Kennedy's goal of "security for the nation at the lowest possible cost."[13] He and his team instituted systems analysis and the use of such tools as the Planning-Programming-Budgeting System (PPBS), cut duplication and waste in weapons development, closed a number of obsolescent military bases, and reduced interservice rivalries. Such changes, he claimed, contributed to cost savings of $14 billion in the five years beginning in 1961.[14]

Perhaps his most important contribution was his support of President Kennedy's policy of reorienting US defense strategy. Kennedy was deeply concerned about "the danger of irrational or unpremeditated general war" provoked by nuclear weapons, as he told Congress in March 1961. At the same time, in order "to prevent the steady erosion of the Free World through limited wars," he believed that the United States needed choices other than the "inglorious retreat or unlimited retaliation" of nuclear warfare.[15] In response, McNamara promoted the development of flexible forces that would improve the United States' ability to wage both conventional and limited wars. Sharing Kennedy's horror of the destructive power of atomic weapons, he worked hard to shake up conventional thinking about nuclear policy, both in the Pentagon and among the NATO allies. Perhaps the largest challenge was the negotiation of the 1963 Limited Test Ban Treaty, for which Kennedy and McNamara faced enormous opposition from the Joint Chiefs of Staff and from influential civilians such as the nuclear scientist Edward Teller, among others.[16] It was a tense and difficult time in government circles in the early 1960s with Cold War tensions high. According to close observers such as his bright young civilian aide, Daniel Ellsberg, McNamara played his part impressively.[17] But with the military brass, he prevailed not by his compelling vision or his persuasive skills, but by bulldog and bullying persistence. As David Halberstam describes it in *The Best and the Brightest*,

> On the test-ban treaty McNamara virtually locked them [the Joint Chiefs] in a room for a week to fight it out with them. He made them promise that once he had broken an argument they could not go

back to it...So, for a week, hour after hour, he went through every objection they had, breaking them down point by point, until finally he won. He read his victory as a conversion. His aides felt differently, however; they felt he had shown how important the treaty was to him, and as one said later, it was virtually a case of going along with him or resigning.[18]

The limitations of McNamara's managerial approach became most apparent when the environment in which he was operating became unstable, when the unpredictable variables involved in confrontation and conflict made impracticable his reliance on clear objectives, well-developed plans, and careful, quantitative measures of progress. Unlike in peacetime, objectives often are unclear in war or are subject to sudden change. Monitoring systems end up measuring the wrong factors, and timely and reliable data are often not available. It is much more imperative that one have a deep knowledge of the enemy and the enemy's motivations and context. Just as essential is an appreciation of what one does not know. With that mindset, one is much more likely to possess the insight to develop a creative strategic and operational vision for how to engage that enemy, and the ability to adjust quickly and flexibly to the unanticipated. It is also more likely that one will listen to others, especially those with more relevant expertise and experience, and involve them in the problem-solving process. In short, being an effective war secretary, not just a peacetime defense secretary, calls for more than just management; it calls for leadership.

In the fledgling administration's first great test—the Bay of Pigs fiasco in April 1961—McNamara acknowledged that he had allowed himself to become a "passive bystander" to the planning of the operation.[19] Like the president, McNamara was a novice in military affairs and covert action, and both men deferred to the CIA and accepted its invasion scheme almost uncritically. In the aftermath of humiliating failure, Kennedy, who took full responsibility for it, decided that its most important lesson was to be skeptical regarding recommendations from his military and intelligence advisers. He determined that in the future he would ask for all viewpoints to be expressed, encourage open debate and dissent, and thoroughly explore the full range of alternatives before coming to a decision. McNamara too embraced skepticism toward the judgment of his military subordinates and the intelligence community, but in characteristic fashion, his remedy was not to seek the counsel of a wide range of experts but to become the expert himself.

It was not long before Kennedy and McNamara had an opportunity to apply the lessons they had learned. Some six months later they were confronted with an urgent plea to dramatically escalate American intervention in Vietnam from the current commitment of 8,000 military advisors by sending in a small contingent of combat troops as the vanguard of a gradual build-up to as many as 205,000 troops. The recommendation was contained in a report prepared by General Maxwell Taylor, the new chairman of the Joint Chiefs, who in October 1961 had led a fact-finding team to Vietnam at the president's behest. Taylor's proposal was heavily conditioned—if not predetermined—by his belief in the "domino theory" that the fall of South Vietnam to the communists would be the prelude to the extension of communist control to the rest of mainland Southeast Asia and Indonesia.

McNamara embraced the domino theory and, initially, Taylor's recipe for escalation in Vietnam. But, cued perhaps to Kennedy's distaste for that course, McNamara quickly withdrew his recommendation and prepared another that envisaged only civilian aid to South Vietnam. In either case, McNamara, as he later acknowledged, knew little about the "history, language, culture, or values" of East Asia and Indochina.[20] Nor did he understand at the time what he did not know, or pursue a problem-solving process that would allow him to fill in the gaps through seeking the counsel of experts with opposing views and encouraging open debate. Instead, unable to realize that "we were confronting problems for which there were no ready, or good, answers,"[21] he proceeded with enormous confidence in the power of his own intellect and his management approach, eventually becoming his own principal desk officer on Vietnam.[22]

In contrast, President Kennedy pushed back vigorously against the argument of the Taylor report—and the advisers who supported its conclusions. He pointed to the risk of simultaneous military involvement in Europe and Asia. He doubted the effectiveness of conventional military means against guerilla forces and expressed apprehension about the amount of domestic and international support that such a response to Vietnam would draw. The discussions ended with a focus on immediate next steps regarding Vietnam, but with no agreement to adopt the recommendations of the Taylor report.

Over the next two years, McNamara became the dominant voice in the government's policy discussion on Vietnam.[23] He was widely perceived both within and outside the administration as brilliant, driven, principled, and completely in control of whatever problem he tackled. As the de facto principal desk officer for Vietnam, he took inspection trips and crunched the numbers that ostensibly measured the situation there, becoming the key arbiter between the optimistic military assessments and more skeptical State Department appraisals. However, unlike Kennedy after the Bay of Pigs, McNamara did not seek out dissenting views or sufficiently question the assumptions and statistics that the military was feeding him. He did not turn his talented civilian staff to developing independent sources of information with which to test the military's claims, as he had in such mundane areas as budgets and weapons development programs. The predictable result was that he consistently supported the military's optimistic evaluation of the situation.[24]

Despite McNamara's optimism about the chances for military victory, President Kennedy firmly held the line against the introduction of large numbers of American combat troops in Vietnam, although over a period of about two and a half years he gradually approved increases in the number of military advisers so that by the time of his assassination in November 1963 they numbered approximately 17,000. Nonetheless, while some of them fought in combat—and about 500 had been killed—they were primarily engaged in training Vietnamese forces and advising them on strategy and tactics.

Not long before his death, President Kennedy had begun to reexamine his conclusions about the American commitment to South Vietnam. In late September 1963, Kennedy once more dispatched McNamara and Taylor to South Vietnam to assess the situation. Their report encouragingly emphasized what was described as South Vietnamese military progress. But this time, as McNamara better understood Kennedy's concerns about the government in Saigon, the report also stressed the corruption, ineffectiveness, and unpopularity of the regime of President Ngo Dinh Diem, and expressed doubt that pressure from the United States would produce the reforms needed to continue "the present favorable military trends."[25] The report went on to recommend that the United States should work toward the goal of training Vietnamese to take over all military functions and aim for the withdrawal of American forces by the end of 1965. Meanwhile, it called for initial troop reductions of 1,000 by the end of 1963. Tape recordings of White House meetings at that time indicate that McNamara was firmly committed to getting out of Vietnam.[26] Kennedy wanted the troop reductions to occur through attrition and normal troop rotation, and without any public announcement. In a meeting on October 5, 1963, Kennedy told McNamara, "Let's just go ahead and do it, without making a public statement about it."[27]

Yet even after ordering this quiet initial withdrawal in late 1963, Kennedy continued to talk publicly about South Vietnam's strategic importance in resisting the spread of communism. Doubtless the president was concerned about the domestic fallout of withdrawal and its impact on his reelection chances in 1964. Moreover, an American retreat was premised on the ability of South Vietnam to defend itself against the communist North. But the corruption and incompetence of the Diem government was rapidly eroding the effectiveness of the South Vietnamese military effort. A succession of dramatic suicides by Buddhist monks who doused themselves with gasoline and burned to death heightened popular hostility to Diem. Kennedy and his advisers, alarmed by these deteriorating conditions, lent tacit support to South Vietnamese generals who were plotting against Diem and finally killed him and his brother in a coup three weeks before Kennedy's own assassination. It quickly became evident that the conspirators who brought about the coup were hardly more competent or less cruel than Diem and his coterie. The issue facing American policymakers was stark: if the United States withdrew, could South Vietnam survive?

Decades after his service as secretary of defense, McNamara expressed the belief that had John Kennedy lived he would have avoided the deep

US military involvement in Vietnam that Lyndon Johnson ordered. McNamara believed that Kennedy viewed the war as not winnable, and that this view was correct. Still, even though McNamara had backed JFK's proposed pullout of American troops, shortly after Kennedy's death he characteristically switched, supporting, with no less forceful logic and apparent conviction, Johnson's decision to Americanize the war by greatly expanding the US commitment and attacking North Vietnam.

As at Ford, McNamara tailored his advice according to what his boss wanted to hear. Halberstam describes his practice of keeping his recommendations in draft form while issues were under discussion and unresolved. Once the president (whether Kennedy or Johnson) had made his decision, McNamara's position paper would be revised to conform to that decision so that the official record would not reflect any differences between the secretary of defense and the president.[28] McNamara's understanding of duty and loyalty revolved around support for the president's position. As historian H. R. McMaster writes, "McNamara could sense the president's desires and determined to do all that he could to fulfill them. He would become Lyndon Johnson's 'oracle' for Vietnam."[29] Was McNamara intellectually dishonest, an ambitious and amoral courtier to his superiors? Or did his principled desire to serve the country and support two presidents he greatly admired, combined with his lack of experience and judgment, enable him to rationalize and even powerfully support the president's position? Our belief is that the latter interpretation is closer to the truth and better explains the complexity of McNamara's personality and record. While brilliant and principled, he lacked wisdom and the ability to learn the right lessons from experience. Consequently, his modus operandi was to defer to the president, even when the accumulating weight of evidence led to increasing personal doubts as the Vietnam War escalated.

The Johnson administration's expansion of the war was enabled by a murky series of events in early August 1964. The facts are that the USS *Maddox*, a destroyer on patrol in the Tonkin Gulf, reported attacks by North Vietnamese boats on two separate occasions. Long after the war was over, it was confirmed that the first attack on the *Maddox* was ordered by a local commander and so did not represent a decision by the government in Hanoi to widen the war, as American leaders claimed to justify attacks against North Vietnamese territory. Moreover, what was interpreted as a second attack two days later was almost certainly a misreading of radar data by edgy crew members on the *Maddox*. However, in September, members of Congress, relying on the administration's version of events, adopted the Tonkin Gulf Resolution, which was the functional equivalent of a declaration of war, the legal basis for the steady escalation of the American force level in Vietnam and expansion of the war through direct attacks on North Vietnam.

Supporting his boss as always, McNamara was one of the Johnson administration's most forceful public advocates for the Tonkin resolution and for all-out escalation. At the same time, however, his luster began to tarnish, and over the next three years, he became the administration's most controversial figure. Indeed, Senator J. William Fulbright, the outspoken chairman of the Senate Foreign Relations Committee, would charge in 1968 that McNamara had used his formidable reputation to deceive Congress on the Tonkin episode and justify escalation of the war.

The initial response to the alleged Tonkin attacks was a massive bombing campaign against North Vietnamese targets. Then, in July 1965, President Johnson authorized sending 175,000 combat troops to South Vietnam. Four months later, in November, the first major clash between American and North Vietnamese ground forces occurred in the Ia Drang Valley. Though the Americans won the battle, their casualties were higher than expected and, worse, the army realized that it was severely underestimating the infiltration of enemy fighters. "The buildup rate is predicted to be double" the previous estimate, McNamara now learned.[30] As a result, the American commander, General William Westmoreland, requested and received an additional 200,000 troops.

Even as McNamara was sending more and more Americans to fight in Vietnam, his pessimism about their chances intensified. As the war's statistician-in-chief who measured progress—or its absence—by body counts, troop ratios, force multipliers, and other such indices, he could not reconcile his expectations with realities on the ground. The figures, he would say, did not add up. While he rejected withdrawal as "a political humiliation," he feared that further escalation might mean nothing more than "stagnation at a higher level" of violence.[31] As he grew convinced that the war was "unwinnable militarily,"[32] he came to believe that the best Americans could hope for was a political settlement, a compromise that would fall short of the triumph the Johnson administration continued to promise Americans.

McNamara was among those making such promises. He justified his persistent public optimism on the war by his belief that military pressure on North Vietnam was necessary to win the United States better terms at the bargaining table. Yet even in memos to the president and in administration meetings he continued to give the appearance of agreement with LBJ's uncompromising policy. He defended the massive air campaign he himself had designed known as Rolling Thunder that brought death to tens of thousands of civilians and approved his military commanders' requests for additional troops. Indeed, the growing inconsistency between his private doubts and public positions contributed to charges that he was lying. For example, George Ball, the undersecretary of state, consistently argued against US military involvement in Vietnam.[33] Although in private discussions McNamara at times indicated agreement with Ball, in administration meetings that followed, with Johnson present, he would cold-bloodedly turn coat and strongly argue against Ball's position.[34] It was not until McNamara's testimony in August 1967 before the Senate Armed Services Committee that he publicly revealed any doubts about administration policy when he said that he no longer believed "any bombing campaign, short of one which had population as its target, would by itself force [the North Vietnamese] regime into submission."[35] He followed this with a confidential memo to Johnson in early November stating his belief "that continuation of our present course in Southeast Asia would be dangerous, costly in lives, and unsatisfactory to the American people."[36] The alternative, he suggested, was a unilateral bombing halt and increased reliance on the South Vietnamese army, a proposal that never got a response from Johnson. By this time the United States was inextricably involved, and 20,000 American soldiers had already been killed. It would be another six years, two administrations, and the deaths of an additional 38,000 Americans before the United States would reach a peace settlement with North Vietnam.

For his part, Johnson thought, according to a close aide, that McNamara "was letting his emotions get into it too much."[37] Later in November Johnson announced that McNamara was leaving the government to become president of the World Bank. He left disillusioned with the war while both Johnson and the American people were disillusioned with the secretary of defense. Even so, in February 1968, LBJ gave him a gracious send-off, honoring him with the Presidential Medal of Freedom and the Distinguished Service Medal. A month later, Johnson announced that he would not seek reelection.

★ ★ ★

Returning to our initial questions, how should we regard Robert S. McNamara as a leader in his role as secretary of defense and close advisor to two presidents? Given his influential and powerful position, he was a critical player in shaping the United States' role in the world and assessing the geopolitical implications of its actions. Moreover, in light of his analytical brilliance, forceful personality, experience with Kennedy, and his private doubts, he was well-positioned to help craft a more sensible US policy in Vietnam. Why was he not more successful? In our view, it was because McNamara exhibited the characteristics of the ultimate "organization man" in his years as secretary of defense. He put far too much faith in rational systems and his own analytical powers, and he lacked a wise and independent vision in those instances where it mattered most. In short, he was a manager, not a leader.

In an important sense, McNamara had no strategic *vision* of his own throughout most of his time as secretary. At the macro level, he accepted the conventional view held by the political leaders of both parties at the time and the great majority of Americans that the United States should lead the effort to contain the expansion of international communism. McNamara had neither the breadth of experience nor the judgment to develop (or to facilitate the development of) an independent, effective vision for handling the situations that confronted him, whether the Bay of Pigs, the Cuban missile crisis, or the Vietnam conflict. He took his cues from the conventional wisdom and from the president he served, whose vision he adopted rather than helped to shape. Unwilling to listen to those inside the administration and out who opposed escalation in Vietnam, it was only after he saw proof after proof of the conflict's intractability and experienced agonizing doubt that he finally concluded that the Vietnam War was unwinnable and not in America's interest, far too late for him to have any impact. Even where he was successful as secretary, for instance, in enhancing the Pentagon's efficiency and in reorienting the US nuclear and defense programs, it was in the execution of Kennedy's vision. His personal vision, in contrast, appeared to be largely managerial: please the president, save money, and avoid extremes. The picture that emerges is one of a loyal and on some dimensions gifted follower, whose achievements and failures depended on the quality of the man he served. As David Halberstam concludes, "The combination of Kennedy–McNamara seemed to work well. The president had a broader sense of history, a sense of skepticism, and it blended well with McNamara's sheer managerial ability...Kennedy understood the gaps in McNamara; even if he was brilliant, he was not wise."[38] The combination of Johnson and McNamara was clearly less optimal. Johnson had his own serious doubts about the war, but feared that if he "lost" Vietnam to communism, the political firestorm would destroy his Great Society initiatives. McNamara's vision was much more limited, and Johnson, in awe of McNamara's brilliance—"The ablest man I've ever met," Johnson called him[39]—was less perceptive about his shortcomings.

One of the things that both Kennedy and Johnson most appreciated about McNamara was his *ability to communicate*, whether in public forums or private meetings. He had an intimidating command of the facts, he was articulate, and he exuded public confidence. In short, he presented the image of a person in charge. If you wanted to win a debate, McNamara was a good person to have on your side. The problem was that his communication style was only to tell, not listen, to overwhelm (and at times to bully), not to persuade and inspire. Far from creating followers, he instead intimidated subordinates. Again, this is not a model of effective leadership. It is much more the communication style of a capable manager, who is on top of the facts and uses the power of his position to enforce his will.

Not surprisingly, McNamara's *organizational skills* were his strongest capability. In enhancing the Pentagon's efficiency, for example, McNamara pulled a wide range of managerial levers, including: the institution of systems analysis as well as the use of improved, computer-based information networks; the consolidation of intelligence and communications from all three service branches into a centralized Defense Intelligence Agency and a Defense Communications Agency; the establishment of the Defense Supply Agency to centralize procurement, distribution, and inventory management; the shift from a one-year to a five-year planning cycle; and a campaign to alter the culture of the Pentagon, including a change in the tenor and tone of senior meetings away from rote reporting and toward discussions of the policy issues underlying those reports.

To help with these organizational changes, McNamara brought with him to the Pentagon a team of deputies from elite universities and think tanks such as the Rand Corporation—in effect, his own group of Whiz Kids. They were self-assured, bright, and analytical. They were, in fact, very much like their boss—for the most part too much like him—and they were intensely loyal to him.[40] In choosing his team, McNamara again behaved much more like a manager than a leader. Although the circumstances were quite different, the contrast with Abraham Lincoln and the "team of rivals" that comprised his cabinet is illuminating. Lincoln wanted candor and disagreement in order to arrive at truth and positions that could withstand spirited debate. Moreover, through his personal style, he often turned rivals into admirers and devoted followers.[41] In contrast, McNamara dealt with subordinates in a manner suggesting a man determined to elicit agreement and suppress dissent. On Vietnam, according to the State Department's director of intelligence, Thomas Hughes, McNamara's effect on the bureaucracy was "regularly one of intimidation, hobbling if not silencing those in government who were prescient about the war."[42] The secretary usually arrived at meetings with decisions already made, armed with statistics that would stifle exchanges with all but those who agreed with him. The inwardly skeptical had every incentive to keep silent. Although a few like the independent-minded Ellsberg thought that he listened, most of McNamara's subordinates swiftly learned to shade things when talking to him, to say what would please him, just as he did with his bosses.[43] Even with subordinates who had an independent power base—the Joint Chiefs—McNamara was, according to his old boss, General Curtis LeMay, iron-handed and dismissive of views that challenged his own.

At Ford, an anonymous official said that McNamara ruled "the place through fear."[44] Within the Department of Defense, the pattern was similar. He was never able to build an effective culture within the organizations he headed, much less a critical mass of followers. Whatever he accomplished was through his centralized authority and the organizational machinery that he created. In summary, while McNamara's organizational capability was great, his poor interpersonal skills were his Achilles' heel, a handicap for a manager and a deadly liability for a leader.

Finally, a first glance at McNamara might suggest that when we apply the test of *selflessness* to the quality of his leadership he passes with flying colors. McNamara came across to many who worked closely with him as idealistic, highly principled, and above such matters as power battles and status. For years he suppressed his doubts and anguish as he loyally served President Johnson by expanding the American military commitment in Vietnam. Yet on a closer and more critical view, McNamara failed that paradoxical litmus test of effective leadership—selflessly subordinating his own interests to those of his followers when the two were in conflict.

An effective leader will, for example, be willing to assume personal responsibility for mistakes, as Kennedy did after the Bay of Pigs. McNamara would not take that responsibility in the case of the Vietnam War, even 30 years after it ended. In *The Fog of War*, documentary filmmaker Errol Morris asked McNamara: "When you talk about responsibility for something like the Vietnam War, whose responsibility is it?" Unhesitatingly, McNamara replied:

> It's the president's responsibility. I don't want to fail to recognize the tremendous contribution I think Johnson made to the country. I don't want to put the responsibility for Vietnam on his shoulders alone. But I do—I am inclined to believe that if Kennedy had lived, he would have made a difference. I don't think we would have had 500,000 men there.[45]

This statement bore no suggestion that McNamara recognized any personal responsibility for Vietnam, for his own failure to make a difference. In this film and the various writings where McNamara acknowledged—forcefully and sometimes tearfully—that Vietnam was a great tragedy brought about by wrong-headed policy assumptions and decisions, nowhere did he personally apologize or show contrition. War, he explained, is a fog, and warriors must cope with so many variables and unknowns that they can scarcely be held accountable for inevitable errors of perception and judgment.

Another part of the picture is McNamara's apparent lack of clarity about whom he ultimately served. Was his fundamental responsibility to the president, to the 4.5 million troops and civilians in the Defense Department, or to the American people? Surely, a man as bright and principled as McNamara would answer that, in some sense, he was responsible to all three parties. But at an operational level, he primarily served the president, first Kennedy and then Johnson, with a loyalty that took precedence over all other loyalties. Loyalty to Johnson kept him silent even while tens of thousands of Americans and hundreds of thousands of Vietnamese died in a cause he had come to believe was counterproductive to its professed aims. His decades-long silence after he left the Pentagon indicated the continuing grip of that loyalty. But, as historian George C. Herring asks in a review of McNamara's *In Retrospect*, "[W]hat about loyalty to the truth, and does not loyalty to the Constitution, the welfare of the nation, indeed to the president demand a willingness to confront him with the unpleasant truth, to try any means available to force him from his self-destructive course?"[46] In less dramatic and consequential settings, any middle manager in a large organization may encounter such questions.

The last part of the picture is what we would characterize as McNamara's hubris, an arrogance rooted in his past successes. Until the Vietnam War, McNamara had never failed at anything, a record that reinforced his confidence in his own highly managerial approach to problem-solving and running organizations. He also was absolutely convinced of the purity of his principles and motivations in seeking to serve the country.

In short, McNamara's selfishness was not the egregious form that seeks naked power or wealth. It was the far more subtle form of egoism or self-centeredness that does not even recognize itself as selfish. Instead, he saw himself as a loyal and dedicated public servant working in the country's interest through its president at the great personal cost of concealing and indeed denying his own growing doubts about the course being taken. We contend that the subtlety of his selfishness and the hubris that underlies it at least partially explain the dichotomies described earlier between McNamara's self-awareness and his self-delusion, between his public self and his private self, and between his strong principles and his situational ethics. In his view, he was doing the right things for the right reasons, and consequently, concealing his private doubts in public, before Congress, and in administration meetings was ethically justifiable. As he stated in *The Fog of War*, "One of the lessons I learned early on: Never say never. Never, never, never...And secondly, never answer the question that is asked of you. Answer the question that you wish had been asked of you. And quite frankly, I follow that rule. It's a very good rule."[47]

★ ★ ★

In summary, in his role as secretary of defense (as well as in his earlier activities at Ford Motor and during World War II), McNamara was the quintessential manager but a poor leader. His vision, especially as it related to the Vietnam conflict, was narrow and conventional; his communication style was intimidating and power-based rather than persuasive and inspiring; his organizational capability, though strong on many dimensions, was handicapped by his weak interpersonal skills; and in an important, albeit subtle way, he was very self-centered, which in turn amplified his weaknesses on the first two variables and handicapped his strength in organization. Consequently, he created relatively few real followers within the organizations he headed.

John W. Gardner

Confusion between leadership and official authority has a deadly effect on large organizations. Corporations and government agencies everywhere have executives who imagine that their place on the organization chart has given them a body of followers. And of course it has not. They have been given subordinates. Whether the subordinates become followers depends on whether the executives act like leaders.[48]

—John Gardner

John William Gardner, then president of a major philanthropic foundation, the Carnegie Corporation, came to the attention of President Kennedy in 1961 soon after the publication of his celebrated book, *Excellence: Can*

We Be Equal and Excellent Too? Kennedy so admired it that he nominated Gardner for the Presidential Medal of Freedom, the nation's highest civilian honor. President Johnson, who also thought highly of Gardner, conferred the award in 1964—and the next year asked him to head the Department of Health, Education, and Welfare (HEW), the principal agency for implementing Johnson's Great Society program. Johnson was passionate about the large and historic domestic agenda that he had undertaken and he entrusted Gardner with the massive effort of transforming sweeping legislation into practical programs. This represented an enormous risk on the president's part since Gardner would be moving from a small organization with a staff of 36 to a huge public department with 105,000 employees, a budget of $12.3 billion, and a hodgepodge of separate agencies that routinely was characterized as a mess. One of Gardner's predecessors, Abraham Ribicoff, was quoted as saying on his way out in 1962 that HEW was the "department of dirty water, dirty air and dirty looks. I feel sorry for the so-and-so who is going to take my place."[49] As it turned out, Johnson's trust was well placed as Gardner reshaped HEW into a far more effective organization and did an exemplary job of leading the implementation of Great Society legislation against great odds. Why was he so successful, and what in particular differentiated him from his cabinet colleague, Robert McNamara?

★   ★   ★

Like McNamara, Gardner was a Californian, born in Beverly Hills in 1912. He was also an excellent student. After marrying in his senior year, he graduated with honors from Stanford in 1935 and then went to the University of California at Berkeley to pursue a PhD in psychology. Although attracted by the idea of writing fiction, he realized that earning a graduate degree with the prospect of employment would mean a less risky life. His first job as a psychology teacher was at Connecticut College, followed by an appointment at Mount Holyoke College. During World War II, Gardner joined the Marine Corps and was assigned to the Office of Strategic Services, with its elite cadre of young intelligence officers who formed the vanguard for what eventually became the CIA. From his experience in the Marines and OSS assignments in Italy and Austria, Gardner learned to his surprise that he enjoyed managing and leading, and after the war, he sought a life and career that would enable him to combine reflection and practical action.[50]

In 1946, he was offered a job with the Carnegie Corporation, where he would work for 19 years and become its president in 1955. He was able there to pursue his interests in human development and societal change, sponsor promising programs with those aims, and then see which succeeded or failed.[51] His innovative educational programs, such as the White House Fellows, the Model UN, and the Russian Research Center at Harvard University, attracted wide attention. He became well known for both his capacity to envision alternative futures and his realism. His counsel was sought in government, education, and business, including President Eisenhower's invitation to chair a White House conference on education. Indeed, it was as chairman of another educational panel that he authored a report titled "The Pursuit of Excellence." It formed the basis of the book that so impressed President Kennedy.

Thus, as Lyndon Johnson capitalized on the wave of public sympathy following Kennedy's assassination to pass several of the late president's proposals for civil rights and other reforms, he too turned to Gardner for assistance as he crafted his own even more ambitious program—the "Great Society"—dedicated not only to a declared "War on Poverty" but to the promotion of equal rights and the improvement of education, medical care, housing, transportation, and the environment.

Johnson and Gardner shared a vision of that Great Society and even expressed it in similar language. The president's most comprehensive and publicly influential articulation of it came in a commencement address at the University of Michigan on May 22, 1964. His speechwriter Richard Goodwin is usually credited with having coined the "Great Society" label, but the way in which Johnson used the expression in his Ann Arbor speech sounds like an echo of what John Gardner had written three years earlier in *Excellence* when he asserted that Americans had long ago committed themselves, "as free men, to the arduous task of building a great society—not just a strong one, not just a rich one, but a great society."[52]

Speaking directly to the graduates before him at Ann Arbor, but indirectly to all Americans, Johnson said,

> Your imagination, your initiative and your indignation will determine whether we build a society where progress is the servant of our needs, or a society where old values and new visions are buried under unbridled growth. For in your time we have the opportunity to move not only toward the rich society and the powerful society, but upward to the Great Society.[53]

It was an inspiring and heartfelt address that caught the imagination of the nation and foreshadowed the programs Gardner would oversee. Regardless of who coined the term "Great Society," clearly Johnson and Gardner shared each other's visions.

President Johnson chose a propitious time to launch his Great Society initiative. The Democrats enjoyed large majorities in both houses of Congress, and the elections of 1964, when Johnson won a landslide victory over Senator Barry Goldwater, significantly augmented the ranks of congressional liberals. Johnson had been a highly effective Senate majority leader and thus knew how Congress worked and how to get things done. Even more important, perhaps, the American economy grew rapidly in the 1960s, and federal revenues correspondingly mounted. Still, amid unprecedented prosperity, large numbers of Americans—almost a quarter of the total population—were mired in poverty. Many of them were held back by racial discrimination, educational disadvantages, and poor health care. Teaching young Mexican Americans in Texas had given Johnson a firsthand view of the grinding poverty in which many of them lived. As a Southerner, he was acutely aware of the history of discrimination against African Americans. And as an aggressively ambitious man, he was anxious to make his mark on history. Thus, despite his complex personality and often selfish behavior, these factors added up to an opportunity to address the needs of those who had been left out of the American dream, and a president determined to make the most of it.

In the summer of 1964 Johnson named John Gardner the chair of a task force on education that consisted largely of private citizens. Because it was not an official government group, the task force was able to work quietly, and it obeyed Johnson's injunction to avoid press leaks that could ensnare it in partisan battles and attract lobbyists.

Gardner submitted the task force's report to the White House in mid-November 1964. Moving with astonishing speed, staff members in the office of US Education Commissioner Keppel began to transform the broad recommendations of the report into a legislative proposal. Within a couple of weeks Douglass Cater and Bill Moyers of the White House staff took over the effort of refining the legislation, and over the Christmas season President Johnson and his senior aides and various cabinet officers met at the president's ranch in Texas and put the proposal into final shape. On January 12, 1965, Johnson sent it to Congress. By overwhelming majorities, both houses of Congress passed the bill and President Johnson signed it on April 11. The rapidity with which Gardner's proposal became law was all the more impressive because the Elementary and Secondary Education Act (ESEA) represented a radical new approach to school financing by providing substantial federal funds to K-12 education for specific purposes, like the education of disadvantaged children. It became the cutting edge for a wider federal role—through regulations and court decisions as well as laws—in what had historically been a state and local responsibility. Since the new act targeted both urban and rural problems and directed money to 90 percent of the nation's school districts and 95 percent of the counties, it enjoyed widespread support.[54]

Soon after Gardner's proposal was transformed into far-reaching law, Johnson named him as secretary of HEW. Many of Gardner's friends were apprehensive that he would find it impossible to bring coherence, order, and an overarching vision to an organization with so many offices and programs that seemingly had little in common, an organization that was expanding mightily as President Johnson's Great Society program came into being. From 1965 to 1968 Congress passed an astonishingly large number of laws that fell under the purview of HEW. In 1965 alone, there were 25 major pieces of legislation affecting the department. As a result,

HEW's 150 programs would touch the lives of nearly all of 200 million Americans, from the very young (the new Head Start preschool initiative) to the very old (a new Administration on Aging). Its mandate included aid to the most vulnerable, including the 35 million Americans classified as poor (the expanded Welfare Administration), the 5.5 million physically and mentally disabled (Vocational Rehabilitation), and 3 million African American children in segregated public schools in the South[55] (new federal funding guidelines administered by HEW's Office of Education that required integration). The Food and Drug Administration served HEW's broad responsibilities for public health, as did the Office of the Surgeon General, the National Institutes of Health, and a conglomerate of field hospitals, clinics, and research centers across the nation. The department was also the spearhead for the federal government's fledgling efforts to control air and water pollution.

HEW administered Social Security as well, distributing $25 billion annually to 21.7 million Americans. On July 30, 1965, Congress enlarged the benefits system by creating Medicare and Medicaid to provide health care for the elderly and the poor. These were two of the greatest victories in the War on Poverty, but the implementation, especially of Medicare, was daunting, described by President Johnson as "the largest single management effort since the Normandy invasion."[56] Most crucial was Medicare's rapid partnering with health care providers across the country: by early 1967, the new program was working with a vast network of 6,750 hospitals, 2,500 nursing homes, 250,000 physicians, 133 Blue Cross and other insurers, as well as all 50 state health agencies.[57]

It was this extraordinarily vast, various, and complex set of responsibilities that Gardner faced as HEW's secretary, and by almost all accounts, he succeeded in melding the department into a remarkably effective and cohesive organization, a model for the Great Society. He immediately reorganized HEW, consolidating it from 14 agencies to 11. By 1967, that number was further reduced to 8. With respect to building his leadership team, Gardner was especially fortunate that when he arrived at the department, 15 of the top 23 positions were vacant. President Johnson instructed him to ignore political considerations as he went about choosing the people to occupy those positions. Unlike Robert McNamara, Gardner preferred to work with capable people willing to stand up to him, despite the risks that posed. He wrote: "I'd rather work with strong people and take the occasional heat of conflict than work with weak people and have to mop up after them."[58] He was no micromanager; he gave his people wide latitude. For example, instead of monopolizing communication with the White House, he allowed eight to ten different people to establish their own relationships with various members of Johnson's staff, feeling that the risk of not always conveying precisely the same message was far outweighed by the advantage of having multiple routes into the White House for delivering and receiving information and impressions.[59]

In a letter that he sent to all his employees in July 1967, Gardner called for an open culture, for HEW

> to live in an environment of ideas. I want discussion of where the Department is headed and why, and what that means for government policy and for the future of the Nation. I want argument about what the most important problems are, and whether we're turning our backs on them or solving them or making them worse. I want criticism of our basic assumptions.[60]

Unlike McNamara, Gardner did not view himself to be infallible, and he wanted a culture of constant questioning. Through such displays of self-confidence, as well as by his energy and stirring rhetoric, he inspired his subordinates and colleagues in HEW to believe that they were doing extraordinarily important work and that they could do it well. Eighteen months into Gardner's tenure, HEW's regional director for a five-state Southwest area testified that "I haven't always been as enthusiastic as I should have. But John Gardner is something else. He believes in working your way out of a bad situation, not just spending your way out. And he wants to run these programs from the community involved, not from Washington."[61]

Gardner faced not only the task of mastering the organization and delivering the services that had been promised; he also played a key role bringing into being the new laws and programs that added to HEW's mandates in ways that had a transforming effect on the cultural norms and personal lives of Americans. In doing so, he had to puzzle out the workings of Congress, whose members took an acute interest in the programs they created and funded. It was crucial, he said, to appreciate their needs and difficulties, "to respect the best people there, to respect the good parts of those who weren't the best, and to understand the system even if it was your intention to fight it."[62]

Gardner had to play policeman as well because HEW was an enforcement agency responsible for ensuring compliance with the rules and regulations that governed its grants and programs. He understood acutely that the deep cultural changes the new Great Society laws were intended to bring about would come with great difficulty, especially in the highly charged arena of civil rights. Enforcement depended upon the lure of money but also required coercive measures such as withholding funds and bringing suits against public officials. For example, Gardner cut off federal funds to Alabama for maintaining segregated schools and hospitals.[63] He also warned the Chicago school board that it was in danger of losing federal money because of slow progress in integrating its public schools. And he urged New York and New Jersey to impose more stringent controls over the pollutants that made their air so foul that if it were regulated by the FDA it could not be shipped to other states because it was unfit for human consumption.[64]

In fulfilling all of these roles, Gardner would often be the public face of Johnson's Great Society. He saw the communication of HEW's mission to its many constituencies, to Congress and the press, and to the American people at large as central to his leadership role. He later wrote,

> I had strong people whom I came to rely on for a lot of the managing, but they just couldn't do many of the leadership tasks. They weren't visible enough and they didn't have the attention of the media the way a cabinet member did. HEW had a terrible image because nobody told the story of the department. It became clear that my job as the leader was to tell the story. The story I told was: "Our goal is to proctor human fulfillment within a framework of values and laws. We deal with obstacles to human fulfillment, whether poverty, or ignorance, or sickness, or trouble with the police. We're the department of people."[65]

It was a story he told relentlessly, infusing it with his characteristic optimism. "What we have before us," he would say, "are breathtaking opportunities disguised as insoluble problems."[66]

In summary, Gardner became one of the strongest and most trusted members of Johnson's cabinet, along with, ironically, Robert McNamara. The president himself offered Gardner his highest praise. He was a "can-do man," who could, Johnson added, "hold any job in Government."[67] His cabinet colleague Dean Rusk waxed extravagant: "The 18th century produced a lot of men who had a truly universal approach—Benjamin Franklin and Thomas Jefferson, for instance, and that's what I see in John Gardner. The future is his business. His object is to anticipate the problems of tomorrow and help people to become prepared for it."[68]

Yet after only three years in office, Gardner resigned his post in early 1968 and departed from Johnson's cabinet at approximately the same time as McNamara and for kindred reasons. McNamara lost faith in the Vietnam War and could no longer serve the president to whom he had been so loyal. In late 1967, when the president told his cabinet officers that he was planning a series of dinners to get their thoughts on his reelection campaign, Gardner quietly reflected on the matter and concluded that Johnson could no longer unify the country, and thus he could not support the president's reelection effort. He wrote a thoughtful letter to that effect and personally delivered it to Johnson. He and the president had a cordial conversation. Johnson's announcement soon thereafter that he would not seek reelection undoubtedly was influenced by many considerations, but it would be reasonable to conclude that Gardner's action played a part. Johnson was agonizingly aware that the war in Vietnam had become a large obstacle politically to the achievement of his ambitious domestic agenda. He also knew that the nation could not pay for both the Great Society programs and the war indefinitely. Congress and the American public had not made that a major issue largely because of the exceptionally healthy economy, but also because of Johnson's skill at hiding the costs of the war.

When McNamara and Gardner left Johnson's cabinet in the late winter of 1968, none of the three of them could have foreseen the horrendous events that would shake the United States by the summer: the assassinations of Martin Luther King, Jr. and Senator Robert Kennedy, then a candidate for president; and riots in more than a hundred American cities, with downtown Newark and large areas of Washington and Detroit destroyed by fire. The grand political coalition that Johnson had put together to enact his reforms fractured, its power and influence rapidly eroding. The decline of the Democratic Party had begun, its bitter divisions over civil rights exploited by Republican conservatives who vowed to wage war on the Great Society. The mood of the country was no longer ripe for reform, and over time, there would be a rollback of many of the welfare features of the Great Society. But, after decades of political attacks and budget wars, the edifice that remains standing is impressive—Medicare, Medicaid, the Civil Rights Act of 1964, the Voting Rights Act of 1965, Head Start, the Public Broadcasting Corporation, the National Endowments for the Humanities and for the Arts, the Food Stamp Act, the Air Quality Act, the Water Quality Act, auto safety regulations. This edifice is a worthy monument to the work of the principal partners in the building of the Great Society—Lyndon Johnson and John Gardner.

★　★　★

It will come as no surprise that we conclude John Gardner was an exceptionally effective leader in an environment where good management is the usual hope and good leadership is typically only a dream. The question is what made him an exceptional leader? And how was he different from Robert McNamara?

First, Gardner had a clearly articulated, personal *vision* of the mission of HEW in building the Great Society, unlike McNamara in handling the Vietnam conflict. The alignment of his vision with President Johnson's was the foundation for their powerful partnership of intellectual and political skills. Moreover, Gardner was able to persuasively *communicate* this vision in an inspiring way to numerous constituencies, to the American public as well as to the 105,000 employees of HEW who were responsible for administering the many programs created to benefit that public.

Gardner based his approach to leadership and communication on several fundamental principles. One was that leadership is a process of persuasion, not intimidation.[69] A second was that real communication went far beyond the exchange of position papers: "We're more primitive than we think. The memo doesn't do it. We want to hear the tone of voice and see the body language."[70] Expressing an insight that apparently eluded

Secretary McNamara until it was too late to apply to the Vietnam tragedy, Gardner wrote,

> [I]n the tasks of leadership, the transactions between leaders and con-
> stituents go beyond the rational level to the nonrational and uncon-
> scious levels of human functioning. Young potential leaders who have
> been schooled to believe that all elements of a problem are rational
> and technical, reducible to words and numbers, are ill-equipped to
> move into an area where intuition and empathy are powerful aids to
> problem solving.[71]

A third principle, another one McNamara never learned, was that communication—whether with Congress, vested interests, citizen activists,
or the department's employees—needed to be based on mutual respect. A
fourth principle was to listen as well as talk. "What mattered was not just
what I thought or what I was ready to talk about, but my role as a representative, a human representative in a big, anonymous government."[72] A
fifth was always to search for a patch of common ground, no matter how
small. Gardner wrote that even in the bitterest conflicts "there are probably seven intermediate positions that you can repair to that take the heat
out of it. A word change, a phrasing change, and you can find a ground
for moving ahead."[73] Sixth and finally, Gardner grasped that there is an
element of theater to high public office. As he put it, "There is almost
a requirement that you be something of an actor, something of a ham,
something of an exhibitionist, which was very contrary to my nature. I'm
happy to say I acquired a fair amount of skill in this department."[74] The
contrast to McNamara on many of these principles is dramatic.

Of course, none of Gardner's inspiring rhetoric would have had
long-lasting impact inside or outside of HEW had results not been
achieved, had his *organizational and managerial capabilities* not proved
equal to his other leadership skills. Paradoxically, they proved to be stronger than those of the archetypal professional manager, McNamara. To
Gardner, for example, staffing was the critical element in an organization's effectiveness, and he wrote that he "dropped everything when a
high post had to be filled. I had to have the right person in that job."[75]
At HEW, he found very good people at every level even though its poor
reputation might have caused McNamara not even to look.

Gardner did not neglect the more mundane managerial tools at his dis-
posal to enhance the department's cohesion and effectiveness. He managed
HEW with three primary tools: by controlling top staff appointments; by
controlling legislative proposals, having learned from Johnson the importance of discipline and detail in legislative success; and by controlling
the budget. In addition, he made sure to preserve his access to "thick,"
front-line information, in Henry Mintzberg's terminology, that enabled
him to keep his pulse on what was really happening inside and outside
of HEW. Otherwise, he delegated to the strong people he appointed.

Interestingly, one of them was a former McNamara Whiz Kid from the Pentagon, William Gorham, who used systems-analysis techniques to determine which HEW programs were most cost-efficient.[76]

The result of the efforts of Gardner and his team was a far more effective HEW. For example, when the Medicare program was brought online, there were, not surprisingly, many glitches. Gardner and his colleagues quickly corrected those problems, however, and both Medicare and Medicaid became models of efficiency. More than 40 years later, they remain so, attesting to Gardner's capacity to create durable organizational structures that are the institutionalized embodiments of aspirations, an objective that Gardner believed was a core test of effective leadership.[77]

Last, was John Gardner a *selfless* leader, as we have postulated that exceptional leaders need to be? Our earlier account of the principles that guided him strongly underscores our belief that the answer is yes. When he was asked to go to the Carnegie Corporation he did not inquire about the salary, stating that if he liked the work, it would not matter, and if he didn't like it, it would not matter either.[78] He knew who he was, what his most effective contributions could be, and in what settings he could make those contributions. Though a Republican, he gladly served in Johnson's Democratic administration because he believed in the president's vision of the Great Society. Had he accepted Governor Nelson Rockefeller's offer of Robert Kennedy's Senate seat after he resigned from HEW he would have had the limelight and, very possibly, a secure seat with a long tenure. But he already knew that his great talent was in thinking and acting creatively to ensure the constant renewal of institutions, organizations, and people. While the US Senate would have given him leverage and opportunities in those areas, it would also have constrained him. Thus he quickly said no to that prospect, and he probably spent even less time pondering the chance to be Richard Nixon's running mate in 1968. He was selfless in that he was driven not by the lure of fortune or fame but by the dream of helping with the realization of the highest human potential by ensuring that our institutions and physical environment facilitated that realization.

Perhaps the most persuasive demonstration of Gardner's putting first the causes and people that he represented came when he decided to resign from the cabinet, having become convinced that Johnson could not lead the country, and to promote those same interests and causes through the voluntary organizations he helped to found and led—the National Urban Coalition, Common Cause, and Independent Sector—and through his writings, especially *No Easy Victories* (1968), *In Common Cause* (1972), and *On Leadership* (1990). With his record of success and innovation, it would have been easy for him to conclude that he had done his part for the advancement of the goals of the Great Society and settle into a well-remunerated job as chief executive of a foundation, university, or business corporation. Instead, for the rest of his life he continued to work for the betterment of the human condition through self-renewal and effective leadership, and in opposing conditions and interests that obstructed progress toward those goals. For example, after Nixon succeeded Johnson in the White House, Gardner became a vocal opponent of US participation in the Vietnam War. In addition, through Common Cause, he sued the Democratic and Republican parties for violations of campaign finance laws. By suing Nixon's reelection committee in 1972 for failing to report campaign contributions, Gardner earned the unique distinction of appearing on both Nixon's roster of potential running mates and his notorious "enemies list."

★ ★ ★

John Gardner was Lyndon Johnson's field commander in the War on Poverty and the battle for civil rights. He was successful in this task because, unlike McNamara, he was both an effective leader and an effective manager. He was optimistic, upbeat, and thoroughly absorbed and fulfilled in his work. He shared Johnson's vision of a Great Society, he could communicate that vision in an inspiring way to every constituency, and he could mobilize a vast bureaucracy to turn inspiring ideas into practical programs. Yet for all his success, Gardner never became arrogant or succumbed to the dangers of hubris. He encouraged an environment of debate and critical thinking, he listened carefully to all, and he never assumed himself infallible. He served President Johnson and his country well.

Robert McNamara, in contrast, was the quintessential manager during his years as secretary of defense, who brilliantly supported and promoted President Johnson's escalation of the Vietnam War. However, he lacked the depth and breadth to develop a wiser strategic vision for Vietnam, as well as the personal style and selflessness to learn from others and to use his influence more constructively with the president. Consequently, for almost two years after he concluded that the war was not winnable, he continued to defend the president's uncompromising policies in public while managing their implementation at the Pentagon. Thus he did President Johnson and his country a grave disservice. Only later in his life did he make some valuable "indirect" leadership contributions by drawing some insightful lessons from his studies of the Cuban missile crisis and the Vietnam War, but even then he would not admit any personal responsibility for the Vietnam tragedy. In sum, we view him as a brilliant and complex man, but as far more of a manager than a leader, as an executor not a visionary.

CHAPTER FIVE

Henry Ford and Soichiro Honda: Business Entrepreneurs

Soichiro Honda and Henry Ford, legendary business entrepreneurs, were similar in important ways. They were mechanical geniuses who founded two of the greatest automobile companies in the world. They had a passion for their work and overcame great adversity. And they had ferocious tempers when their standards were compromised.

However, their differences determined their long-term effectiveness as leaders, with Honda leaving his company in a healthy, growing condition, while Ford left a company on the verge of bankruptcy. These differences were rooted in all four elements of our comprehensive framework, but especially in the contrast between the self-centeredness and insecurities of Ford and the self-assurance and magnanimous spirit of Honda. Those differences translated into the effectiveness of Honda's organizational leadership compared with Ford's failure. Honda recognized his lack of administrative skill, and he was flexible and secure enough to delegate the management of the company to his talented partner, Takeo Fujisawa. In contrast, Ford refused or could not recognize his weaknesses, and he was threatened by having other strong-willed men around him. Consequently, he forced out his principal management partner, James Couzens, along with every other talented senior executive, thus creating a highly dysfunctional organization. Indeed, only the intervention of World War II and Ford's reluctant retirement under family pressure saved the company from extinction.

Henry Ford

> If only Mr. Ford was properly assembled! He has in him the makings
> of a great man but the parts are laying about him in disorder.[1]
> —Ford Motor Sociological Department head
> Samuel Marquis

Born in 1863 and raised on a farm in Dearborn, Michigan, young Henry
Ford exhibited a predilection for taking apart any mechanical device to
see how it worked. As one contemporary put it, "Every clock in the Ford
home shuddered when it saw him coming."[2] At times Ford's curiosity was
even dangerous, as when he plugged a teakettle to see what would happen
and it blew up, or when he built a steam turbine, which also exploded.[3]

Overall, however, Henry's remarkable mechanical talent was seen as
a great gift. So adept was he in dismantling and reassembling machines
that William, his father, made him responsible for maintaining the farm's
equipment at an early age. According to Henry's sister, Margaret, William
was "very understanding of Henry's demands for new tools for the shop
and ours was one of the best equipped in the neighborhood."[4]

Because farming had made this Irish immigrant prosperous and respectable, William was insistent that Henry become a farmer and not a mere
tinkerer. Father and son were on a collision course by the time Henry's
mother Mary died in 1876, when her ninth pregnancy ended in a stillbirth.
Following her death, Henry became withdrawn, explaining to a teenage
friend, "It is not necessary to expose your inner self to anyone."[5] Henry
had always been closer to Mary than William. Among other things, she
had taught him the simplistic moral lessons promulgated by the popular
McGuffey's Eclectic Readers that influenced generations of schoolchildren
in the nineteenth century. Following a moral code that was intolerant of
human frailty, Henry disapproved of his father's drinking and blamed him
for contributing to his mother's death. As one of his biographers, David
Bak, summarizes, "Taking his lead from McGuffey—and his mother—
Henry tended to reduce life's complexities into simple questions of black
and white, good versus evil."[6] This perspective, together with his lack of
openness and need for control, would eventually have significant implications for his leadership of Ford Motor.

Henry was only 12 when his mother died, much too young to strike out
on his own. Two experiences would prove pivotal in shaping his future
path. The first was his father's journey to the Centennial Exposition in
Philadelphia, a celebration not only of the nation's first century, but also
of its inventors, entrepreneurs, and scientists. When William returned
home with tales and brochures about the latest locomotives, hydraulic
rams, steam engines, machine tools, and other devices, Henry devoured
the literature and peppered him with questions.[7]

The second experience came as he was riding to Detroit with his father in
a horse-drawn wagon and encountered for the first time a steam-powered

vehicle lumbering along the road. Henry leapt off the wagon excitedly and began to interrogate the operator, who, he would recall almost a half century later, "was very glad to explain the whole affair." It was a transforming event for Henry Ford. "From the time I saw that road engine as a boy of twelve right forward to to-day, my great interest has been in making a machine that would travel the roads."[8] The experience made him all the more determined, as another Ford biographer Allan Nevins puts it, to "win a personal experience of the machine shops and factories of Detroit."[9]

Three years later, at 17, Ford took an apprenticeship in Detroit with a manufacturer of railway boxcars. After six days he solved a problem that had stymied experienced employees. This feat resulted not in recognition or celebration but his summary dismissal. The lesson, he would later say, was "not to tell all you knew."[10]

The next dozen years, in Detroit and then back in Dearborn, brought valuable knowledge and experience in a succession of jobs. He also acquired a wife, marrying Clara Jane Bryant in 1887 on her twenty-first birthday. She was attracted by his seriousness of purpose, as well as the charm he could display when he chose. Ford affectionately nicknamed her "The Believer" for her faith in his ingenuity and future success.[11]

Ford continued to dream of building horseless vehicles and spent his spare time experimenting with engines. While most of his machines were steam-operated, his voracious reading taught him that a German, Nikolaus Otto, had patented a gasoline-powered engine in 1876. Others, including Gottlieb Daimler in Paris in 1886 and the Duryea brothers in the United States in 1889, had introduced crude gas-powered automobiles. While repairing an Otto engine at a soda-bottling plant in 1891 Ford realized how he could harness the internal combustion of a gas engine to power a horseless carriage.[12]

Ford's knowledge that electricity sparked combustion in gasoline engines inspired him to move to Detroit in 1891 to take a job with the Edison Illuminating Company and learn about electricity. Working there would also provide the money to support Clara and pay for the equipment he needed to pursue his vision. Ford quickly achieved success at Edison and was appointed chief engineer in 1893, shortly after the birth of his and Clara's only child, Edsel. His handsome salary enabled him to experiment in a backyard workshop. Colleagues from Edison and elsewhere assisted in his efforts. They were attracted by an interest in the problems at hand and also by Ford's charisma. As one member of the group later reflected, "Henry had some sort of a magnet. He could draw people to him; that was a funny thing about him."[13] Paradoxically, despite the lack of openness and the suspicion that infected his personality after his mother's death, he also was known for his good humor, ambition, self-confidence, and general attractiveness. These attributes would shortly become major business assets as well.

Among the friends helping Ford was Charles Brady King, who in March 1896 built and drove a gasoline-powered automobile of his own design through the streets of Detroit. Three months later, it was Ford's turn. Next to King's 1,300-pound behemoth, which trundled along at six miles per hour, Ford's "Quadricycle," as he called it, was a marvel of lightness and speed, weighing only 500 pounds and racing at up to 20 miles per hour. With this success, Ford continued to refine his design, aiming to build a simple and practical car powered by an efficient engine. Commented one well-regarded engineer who had worked with Charles Duryea: "Simplicity, strength and common sense seem to be embodied in Mr. Ford's carriage."[14] Ford's efforts attracted enough attention that a group of investors put up $15,000 to found the Detroit Automobile Company with Henry as a partner and the chief engineer. Although he had to share ownership of his pending patents and did not have full authority to manage the business, Henry leapt at the opportunity and resigned from Edison in 1899.

Early reviews of the company's prototype vehicle, a delivery wagon, were positive. But 15 months after the company's founding Ford resigned in disgust with his partners' focus on short-term profits. In fact, the need to virtually custom-build each vehicle led to $86,000 in operating losses for the investors and after Ford left, the company went out of business. David Bak argues that Ford himself bore blame. Chafing and petulant about his lack of control over the company's operations, Ford would disappear for hours in a nearby woods. "If they ask for me," he once told an employee as he skipped out on a directors' meeting, "you tell them that I had to go out of town." Bak concludes that faced with new design and manufacturing challenges, "the eternal tinkerer had been in over his head."[15]

Ford's behavior in this first business venture foreshadowed aspects of his later leadership style: his need for control and secretiveness, his blaming others for failure, a black-and-white worldview, and spitefulness. His reaction to its failure, however, also showed his persistence, resourcefulness, and magnetism. He and his family moved in with his father to save money. He focused on building race cars in order to attract the attention of new investors. Within a year he parlayed the reputation he gained from winning a major race in Grosse Pointe into the founding, in November 1901, of the Henry Ford Company. Backed by five investors, Henry was given a one-sixth share of the company and named chief engineer. Almost immediately, though, he came in conflict with his board, which insisted that he focus on building mass-market passenger cars, not racers. From his experience with the Detroit Automobile Company, however, Henry had concluded that in racing he could make "$ where I cant [*sic*] make cents at Manufacturing."[16] In response, the investors brought in the respected engineer Henry Leland to run the business, provoking Ford's resignation, this time only four months after the company's founding. Ford said that he was "determined never again to put myself under orders."[17] The Henry Ford Company was reorganized and renamed Cadillac and under Leland's leadership began to establish its brand reputation for high quality.

Ford quickly went back to designing and building racers, including an 80-horsepower beast; "the roar of those cylinders alone," Ford bragged, "was enough to half kill a man."[18] But with two failures behind him, he was anxious about getting a third chance. He hedged his bets by revisiting his earlier ideas of building a simple and affordable passenger car. With rough plans for a prototype, Ford courted Alexander Malcomson, a well-established Detroit businessman with a streak of recklessness. By August 1902 they were partners in search of capital. Although Ford's business failures made finding new investors difficult, they finally succeeded. In June 1903, the Ford Motor Company was incorporated with $100,000 in capital. Ford and Malcomson controlled 51 percent of the 1,000 shares issued, and Ford was named vice president, while the largest single investor, Malcomson's uncle, became the titular president. Finally, Henry seemed to be on the road to having the control he felt that he needed and deserved.

The company got off to a good start with two critical hires. On the engineering side was C. H. Wills, who had helped Ford design both a racing car and the prototype for the new family car to be produced by the Ford Motor Company, the Model A. On the business side was James Couzens, a dour Canadian who was Malcomson's office manager and counselor. Couzens was a managerial genius whose close partnership with Ford and the meshing of their respective skills were vital to the company's success over the next dozen years.

The first sale of the Model A was in July 1903 for $850. Demand was strong and within six months the company declared a 10 percent dividend and began work on the Model C, which was to sell for $800. Already, however, conflict was brewing between Ford and Malcomson, as Henry wanted to produce an affordable and reliable family automobile that could compete with industry leader Olds, whose car sold for $650. Malcomson, though, thirsted for the larger margins of higher-priced cars. He also wanted Ford Motor to keep racing for publicity and marketing purposes. Reluctantly, Ford acquiesced. Working with Wills to revamp an old racer, the Arrow, Ford himself was the driver who set a world record of over 90 miles per hour in 1904 on a 1-mile course. This success had the impact that Malcomson sought, as demand for the company's more expensive models increased. Ford grudgingly designed the Model K, a six-cylinder car that could reach 60 miles per hour. It weighed a ton, though, and was costly to produce. Even priced at $2800, each of the few Model Ks Ford sold was a loss to the company.

Ford's frustration mounted over the next two years as he and Malcomson repeatedly clashed. Indeed, when Couzens sided with Ford, Malcomson tried to become business manager himself, only to be vetoed by the board. Demonstrating a ruthlessness that would become more pronounced later in his career, Ford finally joined with Couzens and other shareholders—but not Malcomson—to start a company that would become the sole provider of parts to Ford Motor and charge such high prices that it would shift the manufacturer's profitability to the new entity. A furious Malcomson retaliated by launching his own automobile company to produce a luxury vehicle, the Aerocar. That created a glaring conflict of interest and the board demanded Malcomson's resignation. He agreed to sell his 255 shares to Ford for $175,000 in 1906, shares that within a decade or so would be worth tens of millions of dollars. The Aerocar, by contrast, rapidly devoured Malcomson's wealth; in September 1907 his company filed for bankruptcy.

At last Ford was the majority shareholder and had full control to pursue his vision of a "universal" car for the multitudes.[19] The key to profitability, he had remarked in 1903, was "to make one automobile like another automobile, to make them all alike, to make them come through the factory just alike; just as one pin is like another pin when it comes from a pin factory."[20] This insight would eventually transform industrial economies worldwide.

Ford had been working secretly on the Model T even before Malcomson's exit. Now he gave it his undivided attention, collaborating closely with a talented team of associates that included Wills. To the men on the shop floor, Ford was a model of motivational leadership. As one front-office type observed, workers responded to his good-natured enthusiasm and passion. "God, he could get anything out of the men...He'd never say, 'I want this done!' He'd say, 'I wonder if we can do it. I wonder.' Well, the men would just break their necks to see if they could do it."[21]

The next decade would prove to be Ford's heyday as a business leader. The Model T was introduced in 1908 and transformed the automobile from a rich man's novelty into every man's necessity. It was an immediate success, and in 1910, a huge factory in Highland Park, Michigan, was opened to meet the growing demand for what became affectionately known as the "Tin Lizzie" or the "flivver." It was also where the mass manufacturing techniques of precision standardized parts, specialized repetitive labor, and the modern moving assembly line were perfected. The results were stunning. For example, from 1913 to 1915, the time required to assemble a Model T dropped from 12 hours and 28 minutes to 93 minutes.[22] This enormous increase in productivity was shared with both workers and consumers. By 1915, the price of a Model T was down to $440 from $850 in 1908,[23] and by 1914 Ford's market share was almost 50 percent, up from 10 percent in 1908.[24] At the same time, unit sales of cars were growing exponentially as the average American could now afford one. In 1916, 785,000 Model Ts were sold, up from 10,600 in 1908.[25] These trends would continue for the next decade or so with the price dropping to a low of $260, and by 1927, when the car's run ended, over 15 million Model Ts had been produced.[26]

Not only did these results produce enormous profits for Ford—$60 million in 1915—they earned him near-mythical status in the eyes of most Americans.[27] With his ingenuity, common sense, and modest background, he seemed to be one of them. His legend was further burnished when Couzens convinced him in early 1914 to announce a reduction in the workday for Ford employees from nine to eight hours and an increase in the minimum wage from $2.34 to $5 per day. The Five Dollar Day policy brought the company enhanced productivity, substantial savings due to lower turnover and absenteeism, and invaluable advertising publicity. It made Henry Ford the working man's hero. As one worker said, "I felt that Mr. Ford was doing something to help me and I wanted to show my appreciation by doing better than ever."[28]

So as 1915 began, Ford appeared to have everything he had dreamed of: complete control of his company, an enormously successful product, unimagined wealth, and the adulation of his employees and the public. Yet within a few short years, the company's fortunes would begin to decline. After reaching a peak of 67 percent in 1921, Ford's market share fell to 46 percent in 1926.[29] Although the suspension of the Model T and introduction of the Model A in 1927 temporarily revived the company's fortunes, General Motors, with its large investments in research and wide choice of models and brands, was establishing itself as the dominant automobile company. By 1933 Ford had fallen to number three in market share behind General Motors and Chrysler.[30] Ford's profits disappeared along with its sales. In 1931 the company was in the black for the last time until after Henry's 1945 retirement, when the company's fortunes began to revive under the leadership of his grandson, Henry Ford II.

Automobile technologies were changing rapidly during these years, stronger competitors were emerging, and the Great Depression was enormously disruptive. Still, these were not the primary reasons for Ford Motor's reversal of fortunes. The main cause was the highly ineffective leadership of its founder. Moreover, although his failures of leadership involved all four elements in our comprehensive framework, Ford never understood the importance of a capable supporting organization, and his pivotal mistake was the willful destruction of the team that had been critical to the company's early success. It was replaced by a highly dysfunctional organization, a mistake that was rooted in Ford's self-centered stubbornness, insecurity, and need for control.

As noted earlier, James Couzens was the key hire at the founding of Ford Motor Company in 1903. He was an exceptionally able manager and businessman who freed Ford to single-mindedly pursue his vision. For most of the next 12 years, Couzens was vice president and general manager of the company with wide responsibilities for finance, purchasing, advertising, and sales. Among many other achievements, he built and closely controlled Ford's dominant dealer network, and he developed its innovative dealer financing program and sales incentives. He also convinced Ford to institute the Five Dollar Day and the Sociological Department, created in 1913 as a well-meaning if intrusive and paternalistic way to help employees to improve themselves. Couzens was as strong-willed as Ford, according to Bak, and "a lot of industry observers, then and now, felt the Ford Motor Company would not have survived, much less prospered," without him.[31]

With Couzens managing the business, Ford was an effective—perhaps even exceptional—leader during this period. His insightful *vision* for the Model T and mass manufacturing had a transforming impact on the company, the auto industry, and industrial economies worldwide. Although he was shy and a poor public speaker, he *communicated* by embodying his enthusiasm and passion for his vision in these years. He attracted a large number of talented people who enjoyed working with him and whom he inspired to help him achieve his goals. Wills, for example, was an important collaborator in the development of the Model A and the Model T, and Charles Sorensen played a critical role in the development of the continuously moving assembly line. These and other capable people, together with the relative simplicity of the business in these years, made the *organization* effective, despite its growing size. And at the apex was Ford himself, a determined but generous, friendly, and seemingly *selfless* leader, who often walked through the plant, joking with the workers, and occasionally even helping them.

With the achievement of his vision, however, Ford's behavior began to change, a change Bak attributes to the celebrity he had suddenly and unexpectedly achieved after the announcement of the Five Dollar Day. Ford, Bak writes, "started believing his press clippings, and in short order his head got too big for his bowler."[32] In Ford's mind, the credit for what his company had achieved belonged to him and his ideas, not Couzens and others whose reputations were also growing. Biographers Peter Collier and David Horowitz add that Ford "began to believe that he, the representative of the common man, had a responsibility to speak out on... topics that his Midwestern populism defined as important."[33] Ford started with a quixotic effort in 1915 to broker a peace between the warring powers in World War I. He then waged a losing campaign for the US Senate in 1918. During the 1920s, he used the pages of his own newspaper, the *Dearborn Independent*, to promote his extremist views, including vicious anti-Semitism. After the passage of the Wagner Act in 1935, he resorted to both rhetorical and physical violence to resist efforts to unionize Ford Motor. All of these activities resulted in a barrage of criticism.

Perhaps his most painful public experience was his 1919 slander suit against the *Chicago Tribune* for an editorial three years earlier. Criticizing a Ford policy that employees who bore arms as National Guardsmen against the Mexican revolutionary, Pancho Villa, would lose their jobs, the *Tribune* had written, "If Ford allows this rule of his shops to stand, he will reveal himself not as merely an ignorant idealist, but as an anarchistic enemy of the nation which protects him in his wealth."[34] Defense lawyers exposed Ford's lack of education during the trial and made him appear ridiculous to many who had admired him. Under remorseless questioning, he testified that the American Revolution took place in 1812, that Benedict Arnold was "a writer, I think," and that chili con carne was a "large mobile army."[35] While he won the suit, the jury awarded him only six cents in damages. Humiliated by the ordeal, Ford "would never again," state Collier and Horowitz, "be the sunny optimist who had captivated America a few years earlier."[36] Couzens had earlier concluded that Ford "was not one man but two men,"[37] and the second, highly suspicious, callous, and even brutal Ford began to dominate at this time.

An apparent result of Ford's relapse into such *self-centered* behavior was his determination to gain even more control over both the shares of the company and its management. He acquired the former through a stock manipulation scheme, by depressing the value of the company's shares with an announcement that he would step down as Ford's president at the end of 1918. He intended, he said, to start a new company that would sell a better car than the Model T for half the price. Unwilling to call his bluff, the minority shareholders all sold out to him by mid-1919, giving him 100 percent control of Ford Motor. "Of course," his son Edsel told the press, "there will be no need of a new company now."[38]

Ford secured control over management by purging the senior executive ranks of all those with strong wills of their own. First to go was Couzens in late 1915, ironically over his refusal to publish an antiwar editorial by Ford in the company magazine. He was followed out between 1919 and 1921 by Wills, Couzens's replacement Frank Klingensmith, and a rising young star, Bill Knudsen, among others. Ford's motivations were again transparent, as his explanation for Knudsen's ouster illustrates: "This is my business. I built it, and as long as I live, I propose to run it the way I want it run." He let Knudsen go "not because he wasn't good, but because he was too good—for me."[39] The purged executives would be replaced by less talented and more subservient managers. Any future strong young talent would face the same prospect. Beginning in the early 1920s, only Ford's name was allowed to appear in company press releases.[40]

The result of the management purge was twofold. First, Ford provided highly talented staff to many of his competitors. For example, Bill Knudsen became the head of Chevrolet, which went on to overtake Ford's market share during the 1920s. And Harold Wills worked as an award-winning engineer for Chrysler for the next two decades. Second, the departure of men like these together with Ford's contempt for formal *organization*,[41] constitutional indiscipline, and growing paranoia led to the gutting, as Bak puts it, of "the administrative infrastructure of the world's largest automaker... The company would become as disorganized as its founder, filled with waste, corruption, and competing cliques."[42]

One of the casualties of this dysfunction was labor relations, beginning soon after the introduction of the Five Dollar Day. Workers were expected to be more productive immediately in exchange for their higher pay. Assembly lines were sped up and job safety declined. Even worse was Ford's increasing cynicism and its corrosive impact on working conditions. His attitude was that "the vast majority of men want to... be led. They want to have everything done for them and to have no responsibility."[43] The solution, as implemented by his hirelings, was to treat workers like cogs in a machine. "Time-study men set unattainable production stan-dards for each job," Bak writes. "Anyone who couldn't keep up with the killing pace was let go."[44] Some 20,000 Ford employees were let go any-way in 1920–1921, the workforce slashed to 50,000, when Henry Ford was struggling with a postwar economic downturn as well as the tens of millions in debt that had financed his buyouts of minority shareholders.[45] After the Sociological Department was abolished in 1921, the Service Department, an internal security unit run by the infamous Harry Bennett, set the tone in the company. By the 1930s, this thuggish force was spying on workers, firing them on any pretext, and violently suppressing any attempts to organize a union. Ford's support for Bennett, whom he once pointed to as the greatest man he had known[46] and who called himself "Mr. Ford's personal man,"[47] *communicated* Ford's elevation of his own interests and his simplistic beliefs about the evils of unions above the needs of his workers. Indeed, he only capitulated to unionization in 1941 after the Supreme Court refused to review a lower court decision against the company and under pressure from his wife, years after every other auto-mobile manufacturer.

Moreover, his public statements early in the Depression, for example, that the nation's economic collapse was "a good thing" and that "the aver-age man won't really do a day's work unless he is caught and cannot get out of it," convinced most of his remaining admirers of what his work-ers already knew.[48] He was out of touch and indifferent to the needs and interests of those who worked for him. His personal reputation plummeted as he went from a folk hero to a man who was despised by most of his employees and an object of public derision. Meanwhile, wages for Ford workers had declined from the Seven Dollar Day announced in 1929 to less than five dollars per day by 1933.[49]

Ford now had no strong senior executives around him. The survi-vors, as one up-and-comer had boldly observed to him in January 1926, "when with you, hesitate to say what they think."[50] That left Ford free to make business decisions over the coming decades that almost bankrupted the company. For example, as the market and competitive environment changed during the 1920s, he stubbornly refused to alter his *vision*. Other automobile companies, led by General Motors, began to offer annual styl-ing changes, new features, and different models, colors, and price points. Ford, however, stubbornly stuck to his original formula of offering an ever cheaper, simpler Model T, which he himself famously said was avail-able in "any color [the customer] wants, so long as it is black."[51]

Paradoxically, the great innovator became resistant to introducing new technology. While General Motors invested significantly in research and development, Ford "had nothing—no engineering laboratory, no proving grounds."[52] For example, only in 1919 was an electric starter offered as an alternative to the hand-crank on the Model T, seven years after Cadillac.[53] As late as 1938, Ford refused to adopt hydraulic brakes in any of his cars, even though they had been invented in 1918 and General Motors had long made them standard equipment. He dismissed them disdainfully as "air in a bottle."[54]

In an almost obsessive effort to control all of the factors of cost and production, Ford's strategy was to vertically integrate everything from raw materials through the manufacturing of a finished vehicle. While this brought costs and prices down, it wasn't enough to keep the company competitive with an increasingly sophisticated and demanding car-buying public. Although Edsel Ford, now a senior executive himself, struggled mightily until his premature death in 1943 to convince his father to change his business model, it was largely in vain, despite the indisputable evidence offered by General Motors' success.[55] Ford trusted no one's judgment over his own.

★　★　★

In summary, in the early years of Ford Motor, Henry Ford was an effective, if one-dimensional, leader. A mechanical genius, he had an inspired vision for manufacturing a reliable family car via a standardized process that would make it affordable for the average American, thereby creating a huge new market and revolutionizing both manufacturing and American life. Moreover, compensating for his poor communication skills was his infectious enthusiasm, inspiring others who were excited by the adventure and promise of a better life offered by the advent of the automobile age. Thus he was able to attract talented people, to whom he in turn gave the room they needed to create a capable supporting organization. A number of factors, however, conspired to make Ford increasingly ineffective over the last 30 years of his career. His intellectual rigidity, poor education, and lack of judgment did not allow him to adapt his vision to the changing realities of the consumer market. Indeed, he seemed to become a reactionary, frozen in 1908 with an *idée fixe*. His suspicion, intolerance, and lack of openness overwhelmed the attractive aspects of his personality, especially after his much-criticized forays into public life, and made him increasingly reliant on coercive and unethical methods to get his way. Most importantly, his need for control and his personal insecurities caused him to purge strong executives who had balanced his weaknesses, thereby destroying the capability of his supporting organization. And of course, underlying these actions was a self-centered set of motivations that attributed his success entirely to his own efforts, unsupported by colleagues or an organization, and that valued his own interests and views beyond those of anyone else, even his cherished family. As Ford raged when asked to rescue a floundering bank group during the Depression in which Edsel was the major shareholder, "Let them fail! Let everybody fail! I made my fortune when I had nothing to start with, by myself and my own ideas. Let other people do the same thing."[56]

Soichiro Honda

> He was a great person who played the leading role in this drama.
> So those of us who played supporting roles had to build a grand
> theater—a corporation—that would suit the leading actor.[57]
> —Takeo Fujisawa on his partnership with Soichiro Honda

One wonders whether any of the young Honda's relatives and neighbors might have predicted his future success when, for weeks after first seeing an airplane at age seven, he rode around his village wearing cardboard goggles on a bicycle equipped with bamboo propellers.[58] Honda's first view of an automobile was even more galvanic. "Forgetting about everything else," he recalled, "I went running after the car . . . I was deeply stirred . . . I think it was from that moment, even though I was a mere child, that the idea originated I would one day build a car myself."[59]

Born to a poor family in 1906 in a village 150 miles from Tokyo and with little formal education, Honda's dream seemed unlikely to come true. In the early twentieth century, Japan was a rigidly hierarchical society with duty and obedience to one's superiors as supreme values. The only path for someone with Honda's background was to become an apprentice in his chosen field and hope that his master was accomplished, a good teacher, and willing to let his apprentices blossom. Accordingly, at age 15 Honda went to Tokyo and became an apprentice in auto repair at Art Shokai, or the Art Automobile Service Station, where he spent his first six months babysitting the owner's young child.[60] At last, however, he was given the opportunity to assist with auto repairs. After thoroughly learning the craft, he was encouraged by the owner, a racing fan, to use his use free time to build a racing car. Honda did so, making every component himself, other than the engine. Then he raced the car and won a number of events.

After six years at Art Shokai, in 1928 Honda finally opened his own business in Hamamatsu, near his home village.[61] Soon he established an excellent reputation for repairing cars. He also continued to build racers on the side and demonstrated impressive mechanical genius in the process. Indeed he obtained the first of what eventually became more than one hundred patents, in this case for cast metal automobile spokes.[62]

Honda's racing career ended in 1936 when he injured himself seriously in a crash while setting a national speed record of 120 kilometers per hour in the All-Japan Speed Rally. From here on he would invest all of his energy in his businesses, beginning with Tokai Seiki Heavy Industry, which he founded later the same year to manufacture piston rings. The first test was to learn how to cast metal and then create a successful prototype. Displaying his characteristic persistence, capacity for hard work, and willingness to flout convention, Honda spent virtually all of his waking hours for nine months at the factory and in a classroom at the Hamamatsu High School of Technology, which he attended part-time in his search for an answer. According to the author of a history of Honda Motor, Tetsuo Sakiya, Honda "became a hermit, and his wife had to come to the factory to cut his long, straggling hair... Honda says he worked harder in those few months than at any other time in his life."[63] When Honda was solving a problem, he was intensely focused and egoless. He did whatever needed to be done and sought the advice and involvement of whoever could help. These characteristics would attract and inspire many in the future.

Tokai Seiki became successful, and World War II made it even more profitable. In September 1945, a month after Japan's defeat, Honda cashed out, selling the company to Toyota Motor, a major customer. Then, flouting convention again, he took what he called a "human holiday," a year off from work.[64] He bought a drum of medical alcohol; the whisky he produced fueled many parties with his friends.[65]

The rate at which Honda generated business ideas and new ventures suggests that his drinking and partying were a sound investment. In 1946, he founded the Honda Technical Research Institute in Hamamatsu and before long turned to the manufacture of motorbikes. With gasoline rationing and supply shortages during the Allied Occupation of Japan, motorbikes were a useful and prized mode of transportation. Honda began by buying small army surplus engines and using hot water bottles as fuel tanks. He attached them to bicycles, and sold the result at high profit margins.[66]

Honda soon began to think about developing a motorcycle that would be much faster and more capable. Although his first one, the Dream Type D, would not be completed until August 1949, the company was renamed Honda Motor in 1948 and began its evolution into one of the world's most successful motorcycle and automobile companies.

A key component of that success was the quality of people with whom Honda surrounded himself. One notable early hire was Kiyoshi Kawashima in 1947. This young engineer played an important role in assisting Honda in the design of his first motorcycle engines and more than 25 years later succeeded him as head of the company. The most critical hire was that of Takeo Fujisawa in 1949. An ambitious younger businessman, he had run a small manufacturing company during the war and a sawmill afterward. Honda was looking for an investor, and a mutual acquaintance introduced him to Fujisawa, who had no capital himself, but had the ability to raise it from others. Honda liked him right away "because he possessed a personality totally different than mine." He also perceived him as a businessman with a practical bent. "If he had been a man who did nothing but chase dreams, I would not have been impressed." For his part, Fujisawa said that while he had no strong first impression, he soon decided that "I had never met a terrific person like [Honda]. Nor had I read any novel or history book describing such a man."[67] They decided to become partners and proved to be an exceptional team, with Honda focusing on research, development, and manufacturing, as well as "teaching plant employees and engineers about technology, while Fujisawa devoted himself to sales and corporate management."[68]

Honda's motorcycles were soon a great success. Although the Dream Type D's sales were disappointing, Honda learned from its design weaknesses in engineering its 1951 successor, the Type E. The key was his invention of a revolutionary overhead valve engine that boosted the compression ratio, doubled horsepower, and made the Type E the best-performing product on the market.[69] Soon it was also one of the best selling. Between 1952 and 1954, the company filled out its product line with a motor scooter, a motorbike aimed at the low-income market, and a high-performance motorcycle. In addition, Fujisawa ingeniously distributed Honda's products through bicycle retailers. This enabled him to quickly establish a network of 13,000 dealers rather than compete with other manufacturers for the attention of Japan's 400 motorcycle distributors. Moreover, among these dealers he established a separate distribution network for each model, ensuring that dealers would go all-out to sell their assigned product. This spurred sales across the Honda line and generated the cash required for a risky investment of 1.5 billion yen in three new plants to keep up with demand.[70] Those developments led to a dramatic increase in Honda's market share and forced more than two hundred competing companies to go out of business.[71]

In 1958, Soichiro Honda's masterpiece, the Super Cub, was introduced.[72] Powered by a small but strong 50cc engine, with an automatic clutch and electric starter, the Super Cub was truly a motorcycle for the masses. Simple and easy to use, it was Honda's equivalent to the Model T. Its step-through, open frame also made it more comfortable for women to ride. The Super Cub was a sensation in Japan and drove Honda's share of the domestic motorcycle market up to 60 percent by 1962; the Super Cub grabbed an astonishing 93.6 percent of small-cycle sales.[73]

The Super Cub also served as Honda's entry into the global market. Fujisawa, reasoning that if Honda could succeed in America it could succeed everywhere, insisted that the United States be Honda's international debut, even though its motorcycle market was small and dominated by large high-performance bikes like those produced by Harley-Davidson. Most Americans associated motorcycles with what Honda called "the black leather jacket set."[74] He and Fujisawa decided to go to America without the help of any *sogo-shosha*, the powerful trading groups through which the export of Japanese products was conducted at the time. The Japanese Ministry of Finance was highly skeptical and allowed the company to invest only $250,000 in the American Honda Motor Company, which was established in Los Angeles in 1959. Four years later, behind the advertising slogan "You meet the nicest people on a Honda,"[75] Honda alone was selling 90,000 motorcycles in the United States, more than the 60,000 sold to Americans by all manufacturers combined in 1960.[76] The company's American push opened the door for global expansion and Honda was soon exporting its motorcycles to 135 countries, selling 2.7 million bikes abroad by the end of 1967.[77] By 1972, Honda was the largest motorcycle manufacturer in the world, building close to 2 million bikes a year, or nearly a third of global production.[78]

From the mid-1950s Soichiro Honda also had been thinking about entering the automobile market. Beginning in 1958, prototypes were developed for a small sports car and a mini-truck. But he was in no hurry. He stated in a 1959 company newsletter, "We shouldn't rush into auto production...until we conduct thorough research and are absolutely confident that every requirement has been fulfilled, including the performance of our cars and production facilities."[79] In 1961, however, a policy paper from the powerful Ministry of International Trade and Industry (MITI) proposed to strengthen Japan's international competitiveness by closing the car market to new manufacturers. This forced Honda's hand. He needed to establish himself as an automaker before the Japanese Diet converted the recommendation into law. Honda had three vehicles ready for display at the Tokyo Motor Show in 1962, and a sports car and mini-truck went on sale in 1963.

The proposed bill never passed the Diet, but Honda Motor's momentum and determination continued. As it had so successfully for its motorcycles, Honda used racing in the Formula I circuit as a means of developing its auto technology and garnering publicity. After carefully adapting its motorcycle dealer network to the sales, financing, and servicing of automobiles, it launched its first passenger car in 1967, the N360 mini-car.[80] This was followed by the Honda 1300 in 1968, a "full-featured" passenger car that the company hoped to market worldwide. Each had its problems. The N360 had an innovative front-wheel drive system and was immediately popular in Japan, but when reports reached Japan in 1969–1970 about Toyota and Nissan recalls of 27,000 cars sold in the United States, a headline blared: "Is Honda Next?"[81] The "defective car" scandal led to hearings in the National Diet. Honda acknowledged nine defects in its N360, ranging from inferior brakes and carburetors to loose steering columns, but the company's voluntary recall of 200,000 cars did little to stem the public relations damage.[82]

Meanwhile, the company was losing money on the sale of every Honda 1300. It was Soichiro Honda's personal project and a highly controversial one within the company. Like the N360, it featured an air-cooled engine, which the founder, to the dismay of many of the company's engineers, insisted upon developing, rather than a conventional water-cooled system. Air cooling resulted in a car that was heavy and inordinately expensive to produce. The 1300 never had a chance in the global market. Once the Clean Air Act of 1970 was passed, it could not be exported to the United States because it wouldn't meet new emission control standards. Only when Fujisawa became involved in the controversy and convinced Honda that he had to choose between continuing "to serve as the president of our company, or...join[ing] the engineers" did Honda reluctantly agree to allow the development of water-cooled engines to proceed.[83] The company never put another air-cooled auto engine into production.

The introduction of the Civic in 1972 marked the company's return to form, its breakout moment in the global auto industry. The Civic was a small, reliable family car that won Japan's Car of the Year award for an unprecedented three straight years. Its pioneering water-cooled, low-emission engine met American environmental standards and the car secured Honda's foothold in the tough US market. Honda's sales in the United States leapt from 4,000 cars in 1970 to 102,000 in 1975.[84] By 2006, 16.5 million Civics had been produced worldwide,[85] and the model's eight generations had won Car of the Year awards not only in Japan but also in the United States, Canada, Brazil, and South Africa.[86] While Honda did not personally lead the development of the original Civic engine, the 20 engineers involved had all apprenticed under him and included the next three presidents of Honda Motors, Kiyoshi Kawashima, Tadashi Kume, and Nobuhiko Kawamoto. At the press conference introducing the Civic, Kawashima, now the head of R&D, also paid tribute to the twenty-first engineer on the team, "our president, Soichiro Honda, who guided us with his unceasing belief that it was possible to create a low-polluting engine without using any additional devices."[87] The Civic was a worthy crescendo to Honda and Fujisawa's careers, who retired together in 1973.

★ ★ ★

Unlike Henry Ford, Soichiro Honda left a strong company as his legacy. With Kiyoshi Kawashima and his successors in charge, Honda Motors built on the success of the Civic to become one of the world's great automakers and a fierce challenger to the Big Three in the American market. It was the largest maker of internal combustion engines, eventually producing 14 million a year.[88] Part of the company's success was clearly due to the founder's vision of a technology-driven company where profits were the result of creating great products. Honda also was effective in inspiring others to follow his vision based on his passion, his dedication, and his example. However, the key to his success—and the company's success following his retirement—was the highly effective organization that Honda built with Fujisawa's help, an organization that was animated by his own selfless and caring behavior.

A central example of his *selflessness* of course was his partnership with Fujisawa. Not only was he comfortable surrounding himself with and sharing the spotlight with other strong people, he recognized his own weaknesses and was willing to delegate. As he said about dividing responsibilities with Fujisawa,

> Each of us is only half a person, and only by combining the two can you get one real executive...Nobody in the world is perfect. A good thing, and an important thing in any organization, is for the individual to seek assistance from others for what is missing in him and what he cannot do, and at the same time spare no effort for maximum utilization of what he has.[89]

Yet there was no question in anyone's mind, including Fujisawa's, whose company it was. He himself had "total responsibility for the management of the company," Fujisawa once remarked, but Honda, as president, "is like the sun; he is bright and magnanimous."[90]

Fujisawa's characterization of their roles was accurate. He primarily served as a manager in their partnership. He could never have led as Honda led; in the end, crucial as he was to the company's success, he was replaceable while Honda was not. Fujisawa superbly implemented Honda's vision in the areas of marketing, sales, finance, and organization. In John Kotter's terms, he brought consistency and order to the company through his ability to plan and budget, to structure and staff the organization to achieve those plans, to monitor progress, and to solve problems as they arose.[91] It was, however, largely Honda's vision that he implemented. It also was primarily Honda's passion, charisma, and embodiment of that vision that communicated it to employees, distributors, and other key constituencies. Thereby he gained their commitment and inspired them. Finally and critically, it was Honda's selflessness and recognition of his own limitations that gave Fujisawa, as well as Kawashima and many others, the opportunity to make the vital contributions that they did.

Even in the areas of Honda's personal expertise, he was open to the opinions of others and generous in sharing opportunities and credit. As noted earlier, Kiyoshi Kawashima played a key role in designing the company's early motorcycle engines. In the mid-1950s, two other young engineers, Tadashi Kume and Kimio Shimmura, developed the original design for the racing engine that was to be used in a crucial motorcycle race on the Isle of Man. While most Japanese companies would never give such significant assignments to junior staff, Honda again flouted convention. However, he himself was no figurehead. When Kume and Shimmura's original design experienced troubles operating at high speeds, it was Honda who solved the critical problems over the next two years, while still praising the two young engineers. He also encouraged research on ways to maximize the energy produced by combustion, which led to further improvements in the engine's design.[92] Indeed, Honda was the principal architect of many of the company's most successful motorcycles, as well as its early automobiles.[93]

Honda also was willing to admit his mistakes, something Ford was never able to do. Even though he agreed only reluctantly to allow the development of water-cooled automobile engines, effectively abandoning the air-cooled engine, he did it and later acknowledged wistfully, "Air-cooling was the limit of my technology."[94] Indeed, in accepting an honorary degree, he once said that over his career, "I feel that I have made nothing but mistakes." However, he noted, "I am also proud of an accomplishment...my mistakes or failures were never due to the same reason."[95]

Finally, Honda cared deeply about his employees, and again he had a nontraditional view of their role. Instead of expecting unquestioning loyalty to the company, he believed "[e]veryone must work for himself. Even I work because I like working. I must create a workshop where everybody will enjoy working."[96] Reflecting the philosophy he expressed when receiving his honorary degree, he would also tell new employees, "All I want of you is to be generous enough to be able to sincerely say [when you retire], 'Although I have made many mistakes during my career, on the whole I accomplished a tremendously great deal.'"[97] He made it clear as well that Honda Motors did "not belong to the Honda family," and he and Fujisawa would not allow their sons to work for the company.[98] He wanted the employees to work hard for the sake of themselves and the company, not for his family or personal interests. True to his word, when he retired he remained on the board for ten years, but was careful not to meddle in company affairs. Still, he once remarked to his secretary, "I know I'm not supposed to comment on how to run the company anymore, but I wonder if it would be okay to make comments as a consumer?"[99]

Honda's caring was not confined to employees, but extended to the company's customers and distributors. Indeed, his *vision* came to be summarized as "The Three Joys." "The name may sound odd," said Hiroyuki Yoshino, president of Honda America, in 1991, "but the principle behind the three joys is really very simple. Our goal is to provide joy for those who buy our products, sell our products and produce our products. In other words, our main concern is for people."[100] Moreover, as Honda himself observed pragmatically, "Ensuring all three...are delighted encourages production and the development of new technology, which allows our business to grow."[101] Honda's goal was to produce "world-best" vehicles that would provide "worldwide customer satisfaction."[102] To do so, the company had to put "technology first," as Fujisawa phrased it, not "money first."[103] If the company produced great products, the money would follow.

While Honda was likeable and even charismatic, no one would describe him as a great oral or written *communicator*. However, his passion was inspiring, he embodied his vision, and he led by example. He "came to the factory in the morning before anyone else," said Nobuhiko Kawamoto, the young engineer who later became president, "and would be working alone at something that could not be figured out the day before. When we saw the sight of him sitting there struggling alone, there was nothing we could do but try harder."[104] Moreover, he would ask nothing of others that he wouldn't do himself. A story is told of him climbing into a latrine to retrieve a foreign guest's false teeth in the early days of the company. "That was the embodiment of my belief," said Honda later, "that the man at the top of an organization must personally do things that others would hate to do most."[105] He was also highly visible. Biographer Sol Sanders notes that Honda shunned the corporate office, "ate in the company cafeteria...and was often seen smeared with grease as he worked side by side with his development engineers."[106] His example and genuine caring allowed him to be demanding, even outrageously so. He was known for his fierce temper, and he would berate or even hit employees who made mistakes. One employee, whom Honda had struck for supervising the production of a bolt that protruded three centimeters further than designed, was about to quit "but when I raised my head to glare at the boss, I saw that his eyes had welled up with tears. When I saw that, I couldn't say anything."[107] That employee and many others received exactly the message intended, as Honda believed that "[w]e are selling things that can affect customers' lives...I never make any compromise."[108] Even after his retirement, he was an inspirational role model throughout the company. During a plant visit in Ohio in 1989, he insisted upon shaking hands with every employee. When a plant manager remarked on his "energy and enthusiasm," Honda replied, "That is my job. I must inspire people—and it should be your job too."[109]

Most critically, the result was a collegial and collaborative, but also an innovative and risk-taking *organizational* culture, unlike most other companies whether Japanese or not. Kume and Shimmura's recollections of their early days exemplified the environment, "We were told to start designing racing engines right after we joined the company. Nothing could have been more interesting, and we were both very excited."[110] And the heart of that culture was Honda himself, who another young engineer said was "a company president who is not like a company president at all" but rather a "person with whom we can have an 'on-the-same-level' dialogue.'"[111] Such a culture attracted talented people—as exemplified by the three presidential successors Honda recruited to his engineering team. It also allowed constructive dissent and debate to take place around important issues such as air-cooled versus water-cooled engines, and it facilitated a relatively smooth unionization process and good labor relations. For example, in the construction and ongoing operation of the Suzuka plant, where Honda oversaw the "implement[ation] of a make-to-stock, mass production system for the Super Cub,"[112] he insisted on a large budget to encourage employee "improvement suggestions" during and after construction, which eventually grew to 30,000 annually.[113] It helped, too, that people were well-paid, working conditions were good, and beginning in 1955, stock options were offered for purchase by any employee at a discount from the market price.[114]

The culture enabled Honda and Fujisawa to create a highly effective organization overall. Their innovations were many. For example, much authority was vested in lower levels of the company in keeping with the desire to motivate employees. In developing the Super Cub, Honda broke with the Japanese corporate tradition of rigid adherence to hierarchies and set up task forces composed of men drawn from various parts of the organization to tackle different parts of the development process.[115] Fujisawa championed an independent R&D organization in order to allow engineers to devote their careers to becoming experts in their specialties, rather than having to become managers to achieve career success. This was also a way to avoid the problem of overdependence on the creative engineering of Soichiro Honda, which Fujisawa recognized as the greatest long-term threat to the company. "We cannot be assured of continued corporate activity unless we have not just one but many Soichiro Hondas."[116] Fujisawa also created a "directors' room" in which he housed all of the most senior executives in the company except for himself and Honda in an effort to create more Fujisawas by exposing them to all the functions in the company and encouraging trust and cooperative behavior. Perhaps Honda's and Fujisawa's greatest contribution was mentoring and giving space to the next generation of company executives, as they did during the "defective car" crisis when, said Fujisawa, "neither Mr. Honda nor I said anything to the four senior managing directors about their handling of the crisis, because we thought they had to be trained and to gain experience to prove themselves as being capable of running the company in the future. They did a very good job indeed."[117] The company's record over the past four decades suggests that so did Honda and Fujisawa.

★   ★   ★

At first, the similarities between Ford and Honda seem striking. Honda has been described as "the world's single most brilliant and successful entrepreneur of mechanical engineering since Henry Ford."[118] Both were passionate about their visions. Both had volatile tempers, but could be jocular and charismatic as well. Both too had little formal education and placed little value on a university degree. And of course, both experienced great success after persisting through difficult times.

However, their differences were far greater and explain why Honda built a great company and Ford almost destroyed one. Honda was self-aware and secure, while Ford was close-minded and suspicious. Honda was adaptable and willing to listen and share credit with other strong people, while Ford was inflexible and eventually purged all who threatened his unchanging vision or his control. Honda cared about others—his employees, his customers, and his distributors—while Ford seemed to care only about himself and his company, which he viewed as an extension of himself. As a result, Honda was able to build a strong, adaptable organization that could extend his vision of a superb technology-driven company long after he and his partner Fujisawa were gone. Ford, in contrast, dismantled his initially capable supporting organization and might have ruined his company had he not finally retired. For all these reasons, Honda was an exceptional leader, while Ford was a failed one.

PART III

Powers of Persuasion

Persuasive communication is commonly associated with leadership. Through soaring oratory, artful writing, inspirational embodiment, and imaginative use of mass media, leaders motivate us to follow them, to take action, and ideally to rise above our normal human capabilities. Of course the same skill can be used to manipulate, mislead, and exploit followers, as demagogues have done for millennia. Still, without the ability to persuade, a leader will be ineffective regardless of his ability to manage or the quality of his vision.

The following three chapters spotlight leaders who possessed a unique ability to persuade, albeit in very different ways. The impact of their communication skills on their effectiveness as leaders was widely variable, largely due to their degree of selflessness or selfishness. Insincere or inauthentic messages can succeed for a while, but followers will eventually detect them and desert leaders who place their personal interests first. We first analyze G. Stanley Hall and William Rainey Harper, contemporaries who led Clark University and the University of Chicago, respectively, to very different positions in the firmament of great American universities. We then assess the impact of two scientists on modern life, the controversial physicist Edward Teller on nuclear proliferation and the universally beloved Sir William Osler on the practice of medicine. Finally, we contrast Napoleon's meteoric rise and equally spectacular fall with the success of Augustus in retaining power over six decades and establishing the Roman Empire.

CHAPTER SIX

G. Stanley Hall and William Rainey Harper: University Presidents

Granville Stanley Hall and William Rainey Harper were leading figures in one of the most transformational periods in American higher educa- tion, the era that began just after the Civil War and extended into the early years of the twentieth century. During that time, American higher education gradually, and often with much struggle and debate, broke the grip of the Oxbridge ideal of classical learning on which it had been established since colonial times. Passage of the Morrill Act by Congress in 1862 led to the creation of a system of universities funded and endowed by large grants of public lands, providing that each state would have at least one institution with major responsibility for research and instruc- tion in such practical fields as engineering, agriculture, and manufactur- ing. The aim was to produce a new class of highly competent specialists who would lead the way in developing the material potential of a vast continent. At the same time that the Land Grant institutions were being established, there was a parallel and sometimes overlapping movement to build new universities and to transform existing ones into institutions where pure research—the creation of intellectual capital—would be at least as important as teaching, just as in the German universities that led the world in the nineteenth century.

In this exciting era in higher education, G. Stanley Hall and William Rainey Harper rapidly became principal figures. Each was the founding president of a new institution that held the promise of ranking with the elite German research universities. At the University of Chicago, Harper led the way in creating a preeminent example of the type. Yet while Hall was at the helm of Clark University far longer than Harper led Chicago, at the end of his presidential tenure Clark stood in the shadow not only of Chicago, but also of Johns Hopkins, Stanford, Cornell, Columbia, the University of Michigan, the University of Wisconsin, and other exem- plary American research universities. What accounts for the difference between the fortunes of Chicago and Clark?

G. Stanley Hall

> There are no more fatal errors than those of ambition by which we reach too far, and attempt too much.[1]
>
> —G. Stanley Hall in his student years

Hall was born on February 1, 1844, in the small village of Ashfield in western Massachusetts. While in his mid-teens, he excelled as an elementary school teacher for a year before entering Williston Academy to prepare for admission to Williams College, some 40 miles away. The president of Williams during Hall's time there was the legendary Mark Hopkins, whose personal style of instruction gave rise to the aphorism voiced by one of his former students, President James A. Garfield, that the ideal education was Mark Hopkins on one end of a log and a student on the other. It was principally Hopkins who set the evangelical tone at Williams that influenced Hall.

In 1863, halfway into his freshman year, and amid great student awareness of the Civil War and its horrors, Hall wrote his parents that he had undergone a religious conversion. Moreover, for much of the nineteenth century it was common for revivalist fervor to flare during the late winter season. Hall's religious zeal was short-lived, and he soon began to feel self-conscious and somewhat embarrassed. Still, religious emotions and interests would continue to stir Hall to some extent throughout his life. In 1866 he wrote an article for the *Williams Quarterly* titled "The Student's Sin," which purported to be a description of a general condition of Williams students but also read as Hall's own confession. He lamented his failures and made the statement about overreaching ambition quoted in the epigraph. If this was self-description, it was also prophecy, as Hall's relentless drive would prove damaging to his most cherished goals.

As he looked beyond college, Hall hoped to study philosophy in Germany but lacked money for it. Somewhat reluctantly he turned to preparation for the Christian ministry. As a student at Union Theological Seminary in New York, he luxuriated in the cultural and intellectual resources of the metropolis. He joined the Brooklyn church of the acclaimed Henry Ward Beecher and through him realized his dream of foreign study when Beecher wrote a letter of introduction to Henry W. Sage, a merchant and later a major benefactor of various colleges and universities. Sage presented the surprised young man with a check for $500 as an interest-free loan that helped to fund a period of study in Germany.

Despite his theology degree from Union and education abroad, Hall had difficulty acquiring a college teaching appointment when he returned to the United States in the fall of 1870. Eventually, in 1872, Antioch College in Ohio hired him as professor of rhetoric and English literature, in which capacity he was responsible for instruction not only in English literature, but also in French, German, Anglo-Saxon, and later philosophy. Through enterprise and imagination of the sort that marked his entire career, Hall almost immediately became a presence of almost whirlwind force at Antioch—directing and acting in plays, preaching in the chapel, serving as librarian, directing the college choir. As a teacher he was known as a kind and helpful mentor who nonetheless demanded much of his students. But after four years it was increasingly clear to Hall that Antioch was struggling financially and, as a trustee acknowledged, had "too few pupils...to offer a man like Hall enough to do."[2] Hall wrote to President Daniel Coit Gilman at Johns Hopkins in the hope of landing a position, but he had done virtually none of the research or publishing the university required.

So in 1876, only four years after Harvard began to offer doctorates, Hall decided to enter its PhD program in philosophy, a choice he hoped would eventually bring professional security. In fact, Hall's main interest now was "the application of scientific methods in psychology."[3] At the time, psychology was considered a branch of philosophy. His principal mentor at Harvard was William James, then a young assistant professor of physiology. Only two years older than Hall, James was already on his way to becoming the foremost psychologist in the United States. His new student would eventually be second only to him. Almost immediately, Hall felt a rivalry with James, one that persisted throughout the years, though James was more bemused than threatened by the periodic potshots that Hall launched in his direction.

In June 1878 Hall received the first doctorate in psychology granted by an American university. He hoped to teach but few institutions were even aware of the new field of scientific psychology. Hall knew that President Gilman wanted to recruit William James to Baltimore, a development that might lead to an appointment for himself at Harvard. Nevertheless, he chose to head off to Germany once more and soon he was established in a laboratory in Berlin, the world center of research in physiological psychology, with special emphasis upon the physiology of the senses. Working among the world's elite in the field confirmed his growing conviction that philosophy should be grounded in the new scientific psychology. While at Harvard he had published a short but pungent piece in the *Nation* under the initials G. S. H. urging that philosophy as taught in American colleges be emancipated from its thralldom to theology. On other occasions, though, when lacking anonymity and with professional advancement possibly at risk, Hall seemed much more deferential to the Christian theology that remained at the heart of American education and thought. Throughout his long life, Hall threw off conflicting signals about his fundamental beliefs. The resulting confusion and distrust among those who looked to him for leadership weakened his effectiveness.

Back from Germany after two years and now 37 years old, Hall urgently needed a teaching appointment. A fortunate break came when his friend Charles Eliot Norton, an eminent literature professor at Harvard, arranged for him to give a series of public lectures on psychology and pedagogy there in March 1881, which proved almost sensationally successful. Norton kept up his good work on behalf of Hall by writing President Gilman to suggest a similar series at Johns Hopkins. Hall's ten lectures on the "new psychology," delivered in January 1882, provided a timely introduction to the Hopkins community. Almost immediately, Gilman offered Hall a three-year appointment, a foothold in a university setting that he regarded as ideal.

Two years later, in April 1884, Hall, now 40, at last won the secure and prestigious position that he had long sought: a full professorship in the philosophy department at Johns Hopkins. Yet instead of taking advantage of the opportunity to inspire his colleagues and contribute to a strong and stable department, he exhibited what became a career-long characteristic of duplicitous behavior and a need to maintain control. He had been friends with a part-time departmental colleague, George S. Morris, since they were students together at Union Theological Seminary. Though the two collaborated at Johns Hopkins and Hall praised Morris's work to his face, not only had he outmaneuvered Morris for the professorship, but the negative evaluations he sent to Gilman were a large factor in Morris's failure to win another permanent appointment. Hall impeded not only Morris but every other likely candidate and the chair was never filled.[4]

Biographer Dorothy Ross attributes such behavior to Hall's insecurity, that "he felt safer without strong intellectual challenges around him and set about to eliminate them."[5] He apparently found even graduate students threatening. John Dewey and James McKeen Cattell were departmental fellows whose stipends financed their graduate work, but they left Johns Hopkins after Hall objected to the renewal of their fellowships. Both became renowned leaders in psychology, and Dewey also won recognition as one of the era's most creative philosophers. Yet when, a few years later, Gilman suggested to Hall that one or other be hired at Hopkins, Hall dismissed them as incompetent.[6]

When Hall received an invitation in 1888 to assume the presidency of the newly chartered Clark University in Worcester, Massachusetts, he suggested to President Gilman that he might agree to remain at Johns Hopkins if he could have greater support for his psychology laboratory and receive funding for a significant new venture, the *American Journal of Psychology*. When Gilman failed to respond favorably, Hall set off to Worcester to head an institution that still lacked a faculty and student body. Because of his intolerance of rivals, as well as his recruitment of several Hopkins colleagues to follow him to Clark, Hall left Johns Hopkins with a greatly weakened philosophy faculty, while a pioneering psychology department that had seemed so full of promise was thoroughly decimated. It was no surprise that many at Johns Hopkins wondered whether Hall was the right person to establish and lead a new university. Even his wife expressed doubts, warning him that he was "untried in administrative work."[7]

At the heart of G. Stanley Hall's success or failure as the founding president of Clark University was the relationship between Hall and Jonas

Clark. While Hall's tenure lasted three decades, the essence of his story encompassed surprisingly few years.

Jonas Clark was born in 1815 about 20 miles outside Worcester. First a peddler in his home region, he moved to California with a wave of gold-digging migrants from the east. Starting as a supplier of miners' needs, he became one of San Francisco's most prominent merchants. Declining health led him to sell his California businesses in 1860 and return East a few years later to invest his wealth in real estate and securities. When he moved back to Worcester in 1880, he began to think about the legacy he wished to leave behind. Though he had not attended college, he valued higher education, and extensive European travel provided him with some knowledge of universities there. He wrote and spoke of a university that would offer instruction and research in the full range of such classical subjects as theology, philosophy, and arts and letters, as well as the laboratory sciences and mathematics. His vision showed the influence of the Johns Hopkins and Cornell models: an undergraduate college would serve as the foundation and supply enrollments to a later emergent graduate program. Moreover, he wanted Clark University to be "in and for Worcester."[8] His focus on an undergraduate college was not merely a strategy for funding graduate study but a means for educating the young people of the region. He envisioned a symbiosis in which the city and region would benefit economically and culturally from the new institution and in turn support it financially and otherwise.

When the Massachusetts legislature granted a charter for Clark University in 1887, Jonas Clark immediately set about constructing two buildings. He knew about construction and felt that he needed little advice in this aspect of developing his institution, though the resulting buildings looked like factories, or, as local citizens joked, prisons. Still, the faculty and students who were their first occupants thought they worked marvelously well. But whatever his architectural competence, Clark knew that he needed help defining the new university's academic mission and leading it through the challenging early years.

In the spring of 1888 Stanley Hall formally accepted the invitation to become president. The assumption had been that operations would begin in the coming fall but Hall immediately demonstrated his persuasive powers by convincing Jonas Clark that it would be advantageous if the opening of the new university could be delayed until the fall of 1889, thus allowing the president to spend several months inspecting European universities. His European trip was a rousing public relations success, so much so that Clark University was seen as a beacon of American higher education before a single student had been enrolled.

Returning to Worcester from Europe, Hall took charge in no uncertain way. He persuaded Clark to launch the new school as a purely graduate university, with the promise that the undergraduate college would open within two years. Clark also agreed that the academic core of the new institution should consist of just five subjects, all sciences: psychology, mathematics, biology, physics, and chemistry. Some latitude was allowed in setting the boundaries of the disciplines; Franz Boas, for example, a cultural and physical anthropologist, was among the initial appointees in the psychology department. Hall had gathered a faculty of stunning accomplishment and reputation. Tapping his international network of distinguished academics, Hall convinced scholars who shared his dream of a university devoted to pure research to leave established schools and accept lower salaries. Money, he knew, was not their principal incentive. While he assigned himself the generous salary of $6,000, he bargained relentlessly with potential recruits. As Ross notes, Hall knew better than other college presidents of the day that what mattered most to creative scholars was "minimum teaching obligations, maximum free time for research, and all the research equipment they needed."[9]

Clark University opened its doors in the fall of 1889 with 18 faculty members and 34 graduate students. Of these, 15 had studied or taught at Johns Hopkins, and 19 had done graduate work at various European universities. Also, 12 of the graduate students had already earned their PhDs elsewhere. They were what later came to be called postdoctoral fellows. Faculty members lectured no more than two hours a week and there were no formal rules of instruction. Inside those two ugly brick buildings the atmosphere was electrifying as colleagues shared and created knowledge, devised experiments, and planned articles and books. They were all passionate scholars doing exactly what they loved. Their work together was a calling, a religion. As professor of anatomy Franklin Mall explained, "[T]he highest duty of a scientist is to add to knowledge. This place is founded on such an idea...On account of much freedom here, in spite of our trouble (confidential), we cling to our ideals."[10] For a period, Clark University was a scholar's paradise. But "our trouble" would reveal it as a fool's paradise.

Amid the exciting and heady success of the early months, it was easy for the new president, the trustees, and the citizens of Worcester to overlook what Jonas Clark had said when he announced the appointment of President Hall—that his own further financial support was contingent upon the financial participation of the Worcester community. Local excitement over plans to establish the university gave way before long to speculation, controversy, and even derision. The university was a strange and alien place, an impression reinforced by the foreign origins and connections of a substantial number of the professors and students. In early 1891 sensational and often inaccurate newspaper stories about vivisection in Clark's biology laboratories stirred up a storm, and Hall was besieged by inquiries from people whose pets had disappeared. Franz Boas's proposal to take physical measurements of local schoolchildren brought further ridicule and suggestions that prurient foreigners were not to be trusted with Worcester schoolgirls. President Hall and his colleagues were too preoccupied with what was going on inside those two buildings on the edge of town to overcome misconceptions and prejudices by joining clubs or attending parties or engaging in what they may have regarded as hucksterism.

President Hall danced around the fundamental questions of precisely what the university's funding needs were and his specific plans for its future. His grand rhetoric about the university initially impressed Jonas Clark, but the ambitious young president soon gave him and others plenty of reason to wonder whether those dreams were grounded in reality. In his first president's report, published in 1890, Hall made the euphoric and clearly false claim that on the foundation of the initial five graduate departments there could be established—with little time, effort, or expense—an undergraduate college, a medical school, and a technical school. The reality was that, before the university's first year was out, there was talk of retrenchment, even as Hall began to renege on his extravagant commitments to the faculty.[11]

Clark's own initial pledge for the university was $1 million and after the cost of buildings and equipment had been met, $600,000 was left as permanent endowment. While that was a generous provision, it did not match his ambitions, nor did it compare favorably with the $3 million available to Johns Hopkins or Harvard's $5 million endowment. Clark could afford to give more money, but he was waiting for the Worcester community, especially the trustees, to demonstrate a commitment. He had appointed a truly distinguished founding board of trustees dominated by Harvard alumni, including John Washburn, Clark's neighbor, a Harvard overseer as well as graduate, who became one of the principal voices in the effort to define the new university's academic mission. Another was Stephen Salisbury, also a Harvard graduate, an unmarried gentleman who was reputed to be Worcester's richest citizen. Salisbury, however, was singularly unresponsive to the financial needs of the fledgling university. All too typical of Clark trustees, he gave little money from his own ample resources while his fund-raising efforts came to virtually nothing. When he died he left $100,000 to his housekeeper but nothing to Clark University.[12]

President Hall's own contribution to fund-raising was scarcely more rewarding. In view of the prodigious efforts of presidents at Harvard, Columbia, and elsewhere, his neglect of this imperative was irresponsible and destructive to the school's prospects. But Hall, as historian and former Clark University archivist William A. Koelsch notes, "took a perverse pride in never having 'hinted at a donation' to anyone in Worcester in his first 25 years as president."[13]

Jonas Clark felt betrayed both by his president and by his trustees. It was understandable that he initially deferred to Hall's judgment on educational matters. But in retrospect it is clear that Clark's instincts regarding the character of the new school were far sounder than Hall's. He watched with deepening dismay and disillusionment as the university that carried his name and his dreams developed into an institution built on grand but unsustainable illusions. Some of the blame, though, might be laid to Clark himself. As his disappointment grew and his health declined, he withdrew, spending less time in Worcester and neglecting the board. He was reluctant to tell trustees how much he intended to invest in his new venture and his general lack of communication kept them uncertain of his own long-term commitment to the school. Perhaps he should have been more present, more insistent, and more persistent. But what he needed even more—and should have had—was a president who would be the interlocutor between Clark and the university's trustees and also between the founder and the general population of Worcester. Stanley Hall shirked that role. Far from being Clark's ally, he was subverting the founder's dream.

The bitterest blow was the failure to open an undergraduate college. Not only did that betray Clark's hopes of giving local youth a first-class education, but it denied the university a major source of income and virtually guaranteed that it would operate under continuing budget constraints. Johns Hopkins apart, university research in the United States flourished most successfully in such large multipurpose institutions as Harvard, Chicago, Michigan, Cornell, and other schools that emulated those models. In the fall of 1892, Clark tried to revive the original understanding regarding the new institution's development. He urged Hall and the trustees to reallocate resources to establish the undergraduate college that had been promised. The board, prompted by Hall, rejected Clark's appeal, insisting falsely that the original plan for the college had been only tentative and that to open Clark to undergraduates would wreck it as a research university. Hall had once assured Clark that a college could be started at little expense; now he and his trustees insisted that the cost would be ruinous.[14]

For Clark, that was the last straw. He ceased making financial contributions and, though he remained a trustee, he withdrew from participation in the governance of the university. Desperate for the founder's money, Hall and the trustees persisted in trying to "bamboozle" Clark, as Koelsch puts it, "into thinking they would follow his wishes without actually moving to implement them."[15] In 1897, the ailing old man even fell into negotiations again with Hall about the establishment of his beloved college. But once more, Hall betrayed him, urging proposals that, as Clark wrote, were "totally different from those which I had supposed we had both agreed to."[16]

Jonas Clark died on May 23, 1900. Though he had lived in alienation from the university and from most of Worcester for almost a decade, Clark left half of his residual estate to the support of the graduate school and the university library, the first addition to the endowment principal since 1891. His will stipulated that the other half of his residual estate would be used to establish a three-year undergraduate college "as originally intended and proposed as the principal feature of Clark University."[17] He could have left no clearer message that he felt betrayed by President Hall than with the provision that the undergraduate college

would have its own president and faculty. The graduate school and the undergraduate college essentially operated as separate institutions until 1920 when they merged their operations following Hall's retirement from the presidency.

Hall's duplicitous behavior toward Jonas Clark was part of a pattern that was discernible at least as far back as his time at Johns Hopkins. At Clark, a series of arbitrary and capricious decisions and broken promises relating to faculty made the university vulnerable to what would be the single most devastating event in its history. By the third year of the university's existence, faculty mistrust of Hall had grown so rank that rebellion loomed, with professors demanding a greater role in the university's governance, while Hall evaded, bluffed, filibustered, and deceived to fend them off. He was, thought one professor, a "Jekyll and Hyde personality," while another described him as a "pseudomaniac." A third termed him a plain and simple liar.[18] The fight reached a boiling point early in 1892, when seven faculty members resigned because of "lack of confidence in the President."[19] The trustees intervened, first on Hall's side, then on the faculty's, but for weeks Hall refused to discuss faculty governance. Finally, early in April the president turned aside most of the faculty's proposals in an announcement that sounded conciliatory but conceded nothing. It was, one faculty dissident snorted, "a huge joke."[20]

Into the middle of this crisis arrived William Rainey Harper. After he assumed office as the University of Chicago's founding president in April 1891, Harper had set about recruiting faculty members with the training and promise to make important contributions to the store of human knowledge. In his first year he appointed 147 faculty members, an astonishing achievement. The capstone was Harper's catch from a recruiting trip to Worcester that began eight days after Hall's rejection of the faculty's proposals. By the time Harper was ready to return home, he had persuaded over a third of Clark's faculty to join him in Chicago, a testimony not only to his powers of persuasion, but to the depths of disillusion with Hall's leadership. The bonanza of Clark's talent insured that Chicago would immediately have world-class standing across the sciences. The heads of its new departments of biology, chemistry, and physics were all defectors from Worcester. Clark University never recovered from this blow. Altogether, Hall's war with his professors saw the departure of two-thirds of the faculty and 70 percent of the student body. The institution had been stripped down to just one truly distinguished department, psychology, where Hall himself was the mainstay.[21] He remained as president until 1920, another 28 years. By that time his institution was markedly less distinguished than the University of Chicago, or the university that he himself had long ago envisioned. He had failed to bring to fruition the bright promise that had marked Clark's founding.

Why this gap between promise and performance? What kind of leader was Hall in his role as a university president as measured by the criteria that we have developed?

With regard to the clarity and consistency of his *vision* and the *communication* of that vision, Hall's record is seriously flawed. He articulated his overarching educational purpose only sporadically and even then to audiences that he had reason to believe would be receptive. Hall's grand dream had been that new research universities modeled on Clark would create a new unifying vision that would replace the Christian worldview. In truth, he was not the first American university leader to proclaim this goal. Almost a quarter century before Hall assumed Clark's presidency, Andrew D. White became the first president of Cornell University in 1865. For some 30 years, White enlarged and refined his direct challenge to the Christian aims and presuppositions of such universities as Yale and Princeton, pointing to the long history of Christian resistance and repression in the face of advancing scientific knowledge. And despite what many would regard as White's heretical views on religion, Cornell prospered under his leadership, in part because the people of New York and far beyond understood what Cornell had to offer them. Founder Ezra Cornell and President White spoke with a single voice in representing the university's purpose and plans. In contrast, to the people of Worcester and the surrounding region, Clark University and President Hall seemed remote and irrelevant.

Moreover, Hall was so lacking in candor that it was virtually impossible for anyone to know what his vision actually was. "He hates clearness," said his old mentor, William James, "...and mystification of some kind never seems distant from what he does."[22] In his early relationships with Jonas Clark he ostensibly agreed with Clark's intentions for the new university. But his subsequent failure to take any initiative in creating programs for undergraduates revealed a fundamental misalignment of the visions of founder and founding president and drove a wedge between the two that crippled the new institution. Frustrated and stung by Hall's duplicity, Clark withheld further support and essentially disengaged from the enterprise in which he had invested such great emotion and appeared ready to back with far greater financial contributions. As a crowning absurdity, years later, after Clark's death, Hall would claim that at the time of the final showdown in late 1892, he had *forgotten* about his 1888 promise to open an undergraduate college.[23]

Did Hall build an *organization* that not only capably managed its current operations but also promised the perpetuation of Clark University beyond his tenure as president? We find that he did not, above all because of his failure to put in place systems that ensured equitable treatment and orderly ways of making decisions. Instead, he was an autocrat who relied largely on ad hoc decisions arrived at, in too many cases, capriciously. Such a simple structure as a faculty executive committee, or a faculty senate, could have prevented the grief that ensued when Hall imperiously reduced the pay of faculty members or graduate fellows upon the slightest of excuses, such as missing days because of the illness of family members. Indeed, Hall's problems with Clark faculty and students often escalated from such everyday matters as his pettiness and arbitrariness regarding appointment and budget questions. Desperately short of money, he never honestly confronted the university's financial problems or the people most directly affected by them, his faculty members. His dealings with trustees also show a pattern of false assurances regarding costs and failure to persuade them of their obligation to give and get money for the new institution. Hall's defenders excused what they called his "artistic mendacity," but as a result Clark University, during his long tenure, never became a "normal" institution.[24] It remained an extension of G. Stanley Hall. It was, as he said at its 25th anniversary, "not a structure but...a state of mind."[25]

Finally, was Hall *selfless* as a leader? He was not self-aggrandizing in that he attempted to enrich himself and there was a core of decency in the man. He suffered a terrible blow when his wife and one of his children died of asphyxiation during his first year as president of Clark, a family tragedy he handled with grace. Still, as Ross argues so persuasively, Hall was essentially a prophet in the field of psychology, and prophets can be exasperatingly sure of themselves and irritatingly insistent that the rest of the world march to their music.[26] Confident that both psychology and Christian theology should align themselves instead with the emergent experimental scientific movement of which he was a part, Hall saw Clark University in very personal terms as a proving ground for the vision that made him a great pioneer and entrepreneur in helping to establish psychology in the United States as a full-fledged, independent academic discipline. Toward that end, he founded the American Psychological Association and the *American Journal of Psychology*. However, he found it difficult to share control over those instruments and often became acrimonious in disputes. While he shunned face-to-face conflict, Hall often spoke disparagingly and indiscreetly behind the backs of colleagues. He seemed deficient in the empathy that would have made him appreciate the feelings and thinking of other people, as most particularly revealed by his relationship with Jonas Clark. In summary, his own peculiar self-centeredness blurred Hall's vision, muddled his message, alienated his followers, and seriously undermined his effectiveness as a leader.

His former Hopkins graduate student James McKeen Cattell, in an 1895 letter to the editor of *Science*, well summarized Hall's ego problem from another point of view as an impediment to effective leadership: "It seems a pity that President Hall, who has accomplished so much for the advancement of psychology in America, should claim...that he has accomplished nearly everything...Even those who have done the most are representatives of such a movement, not causes of it."[27] Cattell astutely enunciated the insight that successful leaders embody or symbolize their movements, causes, or organizations. Flawed or failed leaders, by contrast, seek to delineate and separate themselves from their followers and colleagues by titles, power, special knowledge, and special perquisites. In the end, successful leaders make themselves prototypes of their movements, companies, or governments.

William Rainey Harper

> He had the mind and manners of a captain of industry, but he had the heart and soul of a scholar and a sage.[28]
>
> —Joseph H. Beale, Jr., founding dean, University of Chicago Law School

William Rainey Harper was born on a farm in the small village of New Concord, Ohio, on July 24, 1856. New Concord's population was some six to eight hundred, mostly Presbyterians who insisted upon a strict code that was especially intolerant of alcohol. In many respects its pious Protestant ethos was similar to that of Ashfield, Massachusetts, Stanley Hall's birthplace.

Harper's parents recognized the precocity of their son, a voracious reader by the age of three, and they made schooling arrangements that suited his needs. At the age of eight he was enrolled in a college preparatory school, and at ten he entered nearby Muskingum College, where the average age of his classmates was twenty-four. Graduating at thirteen, Harper and his parents dreamed that he would go to Europe to continue his studies, but financial realities prevented it. Instead, he spent more than three years at home, where, surviving a serious illness, he clerked in his father's store, studied languages, learned to play the cornet, and led the village band. At sixteen, he taught a course in Hebrew at Muskingum.[29] One of his first students recalled that Harper's teaching "created an enthusiasm in his pupils such as they had never experienced in any of their studies."[30] It was an observation that many others would make throughout his career.

In 1873, Harper entered Yale to pursue a PhD, emerging less than two years later with his degree in ancient languages. After a year as the principal of Masonic College in Macon, Tennessee, young Dr. Harper, with his new bride Ella Paul, daughter of the president of Muskingum, relocated in September 1876 to Baptist-affiliated Denison University in Granville, Ohio. This appointment in ancient languages was significant for his future not only because it represented a move up the status ladder, but also because Harper became a Baptist.

When a faculty position in Hebrew opened in 1878 at the Baptist Union Theological Seminary of Chicago (also commonly known as the Morgan Park Seminary), Denison's president recommended Harper. Despite his growing experience and success as a teacher, Harper was, at 22, still a very young man, young enough in fact to warrant hesitation about appointing him. But as he was finally able to teach the language he loved most, his employers soon realized that they had found a special talent. In his first year, he completed so much of the curriculum as a special student that the seminary awarded him the degree of bachelor of divinity and promoted him to full professor. In the next two years he not only published several Hebrew textbooks and founded a new journal, the *Hebrew Student*, but he also created a Hebrew correspondence course and began a summer school in Hebrew. Harper saw no reason why an institution's outreach should stop at the campus walls and he viewed the summertime hiatus in college calendars as wasteful and inefficient.[31]

His Yale mentors took note of his prodigious productivity in Chicago, and in 1886 he was offered a newly endowed professorship in New Haven. Morgan Park pulled out every stop in its efforts to keep him, including a visit with the vice chair of the board of trustees, John D. Rockefeller. After Harper made his decision to go to Yale, he received a letter from Morgan Park trustee Thomas Goodspeed urging him: "Hold yourself ready to return here some time as President of a new University."[32] In 1887, Augustus H. Strong, president of Rochester Theological Seminary, informed Harper that John D. Rockefeller was planning to help build a great university in New York and he wanted Harper's assistance.

The references to the university planned for New York or Chicago reflected the debate that Rockefeller was having with himself, assisted by such advisers as Goodspeed, on where he should apply the millions he was prepared to invest in higher education. John D. Rockefeller, the fabulously rich oil magnate widely castigated as a "robber baron," was a shrewd, calculating businessman who surveyed the terrain carefully and used the help of experts before he made important decisions. He was also a pious Baptist who saw himself as God's steward in the use of his wealth. In Goodspeed and later Frederick T. Gates, Rockefeller found kindred spirits who understood and largely shared his religious faith as well as his mindset regarding business decisions.

The original University of Chicago was a struggling little Baptist college whose financial difficulties had forced it to close in 1886. Because denominations used their colleges to compete for adherents and influence, the failure of the Old University, as it came to be called, in so strategic a location as Chicago was a large defeat for Baptists, who could look enviously at nearby Northwestern University, a Methodist institution, and Lake Forest, a Presbyterian college. The great majority of the colleges founded in the Colonial era were church-sponsored and all were private, and although the growth of public higher education accelerated following passage of the Morrill Act in 1862, church sponsorship of higher education continued to be robust until well into the twentieth century.

Because they believed in the autonomy of each congregation, Baptists lacked a hierarchal organizational structure. This was a disadvantage in the race to build colleges, since it meant they required the voluntary cooperation of groups of local churches. They needed effective leadership too. Eventually, in 1888, the American Baptist Education Society was established to plan for the founding and development of new colleges. Frederick Gates, pastor of a Minneapolis church, was chosen to lead it, and he set about almost immediately to assemble the facts about Baptist higher education and how it compared with that of the other major denominations.[33] His conclusions were disquieting. Although the Baptists could take pride in such institutions as Bates, Colby, Brown, the University of Rochester, Colgate, Vassar, and others, their record did not compare favorably with that of other denominations. In particular, Baptist colleges west of Chicago were few and undistinguished despite the rapidly growing population in that part of the nation. Gates's analysis underscored the message that Thomas Goodspeed was already proclaiming: Chicago, the gateway to the West, needed a major Baptist university. Goodspeed, an alumnus of the Old University who had left the pastorate to raise money for the Morgan Park Seminary, was perhaps the most successful fund-raiser of his time. Even as the Old University was in its death throes, he had set about to recruit John D. Rockefeller to the cause of building its successor. Rockefeller served with Goodspeed on the board of Morgan Park, and thus was acquainted with the history of the Old University.

Frederick Gates's job was to promote Baptist higher education throughout the nation, and initially he held no special brief for Chicago. But his investigation converted him to the cause, where he partnered with Goodspeed. That, in turn, brought Gates to the notice of Rockefeller, who was attracted by his sharp mind and sound judgment and soon made him his principal business and philanthropic adviser. Gates's remarkable executive talents would be demonstrated through decades of work on enterprises that included the General Education Board, the Rockefeller Foundation and the biomedical institute that would become Rockefeller University. He would serve as the principal interlocutor and negotiator in the complicated but magnificently fruitful partnership between Harper and Rockefeller.

Rockefeller, Gates, and Goodspeed were so impressed with Harper after several meetings with him that the decision to found the new University of Chicago was concurrent with their mutual conviction that Harper must lead it.[34] No sooner was the university incorporated in September 1890 than the new—and exceptionally distinguished—board of trustees elected Harper as president. He asked for time to consider the offer. Yale did not make it easy for him, raising his already abundant salary by about 50 percent and providing a generous leave arrangement. Rockefeller urged Harper not to rush his decision, even suggesting that he might make a commitment to remain at Yale for at least a short transitional period. This nervous counsel was based on worries that Harper might actually choose Yale. Meanwhile, the whole of American academia as well as many newspapers were caught up in the drama of Harper's quandary. Letters of advice poured in, with most urging him to go west. Meanwhile, friends at Yale were suggesting that Chicago was a bubble that would eventually burst.

For his part, Harper was deeply troubled by an accusation that his religious beliefs were not consistent with those of the Baptist mainstream. The university's bylaws stipulated that its president must be a Baptist, as Harper had become years earlier. As a biblical scholar, though, he was an advocate of the Higher Criticism, a methodology that treated the books of the Bible as texts written by human hands reflecting the issues, needs, and conflicts of the cultures in which they originated. Thus, Harper believed that the scriptures conveyed important spiritual messages but not that they were literally the word of God. He asked Rockefeller for an investigation to decide whether he was orthodox enough to serve as president and teacher at Chicago. Gates, who thought Harper "morbid on the question of his own supposed heresy," understood that a trial of his faith would be extremely destructive to Harper and imperil plans for the university.[35] The efforts of Gates and Goodspeed, and Rockefeller's silence, had a settling effect on Harper. In February 1891 Harper, at age 34, informed the trustees that he was ready to become president. Meanwhile, he had been planning the new institution, and the blueprint was virtually complete.

Harper had sketched out the broad outlines of his plan for the University of Chicago on a train trip from Chicago to New Haven in September 1890, five months before he accepted the appointment, and by December, he had the plan worked out in detail.[36] The trustees approved it as offered, even though Harper had not yet agreed to accept the presidency. His overarching concept pictured the university as the hub of a system of Baptist-affiliated colleges and college preparatory academies, with the university in effect setting standards for the schools, helping to upgrade the professional qualifications of their faculty, and training new teachers. The affiliated colleges would send their graduates to Chicago for graduate and professional education. The academies would prepare students for admission to the university's undergraduate programs. Ultimately the private academies proved unnecessary because of rapid growth in the number and quality of public high schools, while the system of affiliated colleges never attracted the required financial support. Still, the university did draw many faculty members from colleges in the Midwest and Northwest to its graduate programs, and those same institutions appointed to their faculties many degree holders from Chicago.

Before the university admitted its first student, Harper issued a series of reports that told the wider world what kind of institution it would be. Its general organization was to include five divisions: the University Proper, the University Extension, the University Press, the University Libraries, Laboratories, and Museums, and the University Affiliations. Theologian and author Lyman Abbott observed that Harper's university could be distinguished from those in England and Germany by its emphasis on service.[37] Harper saw the extension, the affiliations programs, and the press as vehicles for expanding and multiplying the service of the university. The extension program, which was somewhat modeled on English examples, was two-pronged. One consisted of faculty lecture courses in and around Chicago for working students who could progress toward degrees on evenings and weekends. The other, correspondence courses, an innovation Harper brought with him from Morgan Park, flourished after a slow start and eventually enrolled thousands of students throughout the world.

Though Harper knew that he was to build a university, not a college, he aspired to create an institution—which he sometimes referred to as the "Yale of the West"—that would be hospitable to undergraduates.

Demanding admissions standards ensured that the students would be capable and serious. At the same time, he wanted them to enjoy their college experience. Toward that end, he would encourage a plethora of student clubs, among them fraternities and sororities—although the Greek-letter organizations operated under tight university rules. So much was going on at the University of Chicago that it was commonly and good-naturedly referred to as "Harper's Bazaar."[38] Harper also encouraged intercollegiate athletics. One of his earliest faculty hires was Amos Alonzo Stagg, whom he brought from Yale to teach physical culture and who became a legendary football coach at Chicago. The school would be a founding member in 1896 of the Western Conference, which later became the Big Ten, and football played a role in helping a broad base of the population in Chicago and far beyond to identify with the great university that the team represented.

Harper addressed his long-standing concern about wasted time in the traditional academic calendar by putting his university on year-round footing, with four quarters and a week's vacation between them. As at Morgan Park, Harper made the summer quarter an integral part of the academic year. Closely related to the new calendar was the practice of admitting students at the start of any quarter and holding graduation exercises at the end of every quarter. Moreover, undergraduate students were not divided into the usual four classes but were ranked as members of the Junior College in their first two years and of the Senior College in their final two years.

Before any of Harper's vision could be realized, money had to be raised, buildings built, and faculties appointed. The trustees decided that the new institution needed a start-up base of a million dollars. Rockefeller agreed to give $600,000, with $400,000 to come from other sources. Gates and Goodspeed immediately mounted a brilliantly conceived fund-raising campaign,[39] focusing first on the Baptist community of Chicago, then the Chicago business community, and then the national population of Baptists. The effort caught the imagination of people around the world, and gifts came in from throughout the United States and many other countries. Within a year they had met the campaign goal. The response of citizens of Chicago, urged on by the city's newspapers, made it clear that this institution had already transcended its denominational character. The Jewish community, with many alumni of the Old University, contributed significantly to the campaign and was represented on the board of trustees and the faculty. Additionally, because the University of Chicago admitted women on the same basis as men from the beginning, and the faculty and administration included women, the list of major donors in the University's founding years included a strikingly large number of women.

The national and international publicity attending the fund-raising campaign had the unanticipated but happy effect of attracting thousands of applications for admission, making it unnecessary for the university to recruit students. Those applicants faced a rigorous admission test; good high school grades and a diploma were not enough. Harper was determined that the quality of students in his institution would be comparable to that of the dominant East Coast universities. When classes began on October 1, 1892, 742 carefully sifted students were enrolled, more than a quarter of them women.[40]

As Harper began to recruit a faculty, he chose people who were suitable for a research university. His strategy was to appoint head professors for the various departments and then rely on those individuals to recruit and hire for the remaining slots. He quickly learned that $6,000, the going rate for a head professor at Yale, Harvard, and Johns Hopkins, was insufficient to lure comparable talent to Chicago. However promising and exciting the new university might seem, it was also a risky venture for professors who would give up secure positions in long-established institutions in the East. Consequently, a salary of $7,000 was necessary to attract head professors.[41]

The university's first year of operation coincided with the nation's worst financial crisis to that time, the Panic of 1893, which brought a four-year-long depression. The money necessary to sustain the university's development slowed to a trickle. Harper sank into a mood of deep despair and confessed to his closest colleagues that he felt that he was not the person for the job and would resign if he could. The pattern of turning to John D. Rockefeller to make up deficits began at that point and would persist long after the nation's economy righted itself. Rockefeller suffered considerable anxiety over the university's budget deficits throughout the Harper years and he would convey through Gates his concerns about the lack of orderly budget planning. He feared that deficits would eventually destroy both the quality of an institution and public confidence in it, as the demise of the Old University had demonstrated. Even though Rockefeller poured unprecedented wealth into the university, gifts that eventually amounted to $35 million,[42] and the university before and after the depression had splendid success in raising money from thousands of other sources, William Rainey Harper was in a hurry, and there was never enough money. His goal was to build a great university, and he was convinced that in a single generation the University of Chicago could earn comparison with Yale, Harvard, and Columbia. In fact, the unexpectedly large enrollment continued to grow, and within five years, Chicago was larger than Harvard and Yale.[43] It was necessary to increase the faculty and staff. New buildings had to be constructed and equipped. Harper essentially proved his point, but the cost was large deficits year after year. Rockefeller had such great confidence in Harper's leadership that he stepped forward again and again to solve budget crises. He knew that Harper was temperamentally incapable of patience and that his vision for the university was sound. Moreover, the university's board of trustees included many highly successful business leaders who reached deeply into their own pockets to help meet costs. They did not wish to destroy the ardor that drove Harper's success.

Still, the deficit had become so large by the winter of 1903–1904 that Rockefeller sent to Chicago a tough attorney by the name of Starr J. Murphy. Murphy was tremendously impressed by the university's vitality and readily credited it to the genius of President Harper. Nonetheless, he urged a period of consolidation of programs and finances after the university's rampant growth. Perhaps inevitably, his report had little impact, and so the next year, when Murphy returned for a new inspection, he was less forgiving. Probing deeply into the university's operations, he produced a report that, in Thomas Goodspeed's offended view, effectively characterized them as a "scheme to plunder the founder" of his wealth.[44] Goodspeed accused Murphy, the graduate of a small college, of not understanding the nature and purpose of a university. Murphy's recommendation that there be a resident overseer representing Rockefeller's interests led to such consternation among the trustees that there was talk of resignations. Some doubted that John D. Rockefeller knew what Murphy was up to, but that did little to allay the apprehension about the threat that now appeared to hang over the university. Then another, almost simultaneous, event shoved Murphy's report into limbo.

In a letter to Gates dated February 3, 1905, William Rainey Harper announced that he had incurable cancer. Rockefeller wrote to Harper: "You are constantly in my thoughts. The feelings which I have always cherished towards you are intensified at this time ... I have the greatest satisfaction and pleasure in our united efforts for the University, and I am full of hope for its future. No man could have filled your place."[45] President Harper lived on until January 10, 1906. During those remaining months he continued to invest all of his waning energy in the development of the University of Chicago while his close colleague Harry Pratt Judson, dean of the General Faculties, performed many of the presidential duties. Following Harper's death, in a move that met overwhelming approval within the university community, the trustees named Judson president. He knew that his primary task was to consolidate the magnificent growth of the university and balance its budget, and he succeeded admirably in a presidency that lasted until 1923.

In December 1910, John D. Rockefeller wrote a warm and gracious letter to President Judson and the trustees in which he announced a final gift of $10 million. He stated that it was far better for the university that it have a broad base of financial support and not be overly dependent upon a single donor. He expressed deep satisfaction with the development of the university and praised the citizens of Chicago and the western regions of the country generally for their financial generosity.[46]

★   ★   ★

As we measure Harper against our criteria for effective leadership, we must be mindful that the *vision* that guided him is more easily described in the language of engineering and architecture than philosophy. He thought in concrete and pragmatic terms, paid great attention to details that were easy to picture and group, and made little use of abstract language. In effect, his vision was a set of blueprints. It embodied no philosophical statements about the unity of all knowledge. As historian of higher education Laurence R. Veysey describes Harper's style of thinking and his remarkable power to persuade others, he represented "charisma without ideology."[47] Harper viewed the university as a kind of educational laboratory, and he did not expect every feature to work out exactly as planned.

In assessing Harper's effectiveness in *communicating* his vision for the university and telling its story to the wider world, we need to note how he used public events. He loved ceremonial occasions, including the four annual commencements. He devised convocations, which also occurred quarterly, as another kind of university-wide assembly. Harper explained that their purpose was to review the university's progress and achievements, recognize the contributions and achievements of individuals, and speak about plans for the future. To enhance public recognition and knowledge of the university, ceremonial events were sometimes held away from its downtown Chicago campus. By contrast, commencements at Clark University were private affairs closed to the general public. William Rainey Harper himself was one of Chicago's best-known citizens. A member of the public school board, superintendent of his church's Sunday school, and a man with an outgoing personality who was comfortable with all kinds of people, he was seen making his way around campus and along city streets on a bicycle. He did all he could, in a workday that typically stretched from 5 A.M. to close to midnight, to insure that everyone knew about his university. Unlike G. Stanley Hall, Harper was astutely aware that public support depended critically upon its familiarity with the new university's purposes, practices, and people.

Although Harper was the architect and driving force behind the academic plan for the university, his plans became official policy only after the trustees and the faculty senate approved them. Winning their support was a test of his communications and interpersonal skills. The senate consisted of head professors, a distinguished, strong-willed collection of veteran scholars who came from a variety of institutional backgrounds and had their own ideas about what the university should be. Harper had to persuade them that his proposals were sound and practicable. And persuade them he did, often after prolonged and strenuous debate. The faculty followed Harper in part because of his passionate convictions and reasoning powers and in part because of his eminence as a scholar. Comfortable with his faculty, he respected them, believed deeply in their work, and celebrated their accomplishments. He was also one of them; he too was a head professor who carried teaching and research responsibilities along with the task of building a great university from scratch. They all worked hard, and he worked alongside them, but on far less sleep and with much more stress. A few faculty members regarded him as too much given to Midwestern boosterism and as something of a boyish braggart who wanted everyone to know that he mapped out every day in 15-minute segments. But the overwhelming sentiment among his colleagues was that he was a great leader and a splendid human being.

Indispensable to Harper's success as the founding president of the University of Chicago were his relationships with Rockefeller and his key associates. Goodspeed served as secretary of the board of trustees, and in time he became registrar of the university, a key adviser to President Harper, and in his later years, a principal chronicler of the university's early history. Gates was a usually sympathetic ambassador from Rockefeller's court who shared the founder's admiration for Harper.

As for the magnate himself, Rockefeller had declined to serve as a trustee and expressed no interest in having the university named for himself. He did agree to be known as founder. Harper frequently sought Rockefeller's opinion on various issues, especially in the early years. But Rockefeller steadfastly refused to weigh in on matters that he regarded as the proper business of the university's officers, faculty, and trustees. In an impromptu speech at the celebration of the university's fifth year since its founding, Rockefeller recounted that at the beginning of his relationship with President Harper they came to an understanding that he was to serve as a "silent partner" in the enterprise of building the university.[48] He adhered to that role with remarkable fidelity, even when he found some developments disquieting. Unlike Hall, Harper never lost the founder's support. Nevertheless, the interlocutory messages that passed from Rockefeller through Gates to Harper and the board contained some persistent themes that represented the founder's deep convictions. One theme was that the fundamental character and quality of an institution depended largely upon the character and quality of those who did its principal work.

Harper shared this view, understanding that *organizations* were no greater than the men and women who worked for them. He undoubtedly was anticipating many more years at the university's helm when he received the news from his physicians that his life would soon end. But he was prepared for that unexpected eventuality. In the university's very small general administration, he had created an exceptionally effective team, a cadre of executive and leadership talent that would sustain the momentum of the university after he was gone. Judson had been with Harper from the earliest days of the university and was well prepared to step into the presidency. Although dramatically different in temperament from Harper, he was just the right leader to succeed him. His presidential successor, in turn, was Ernest D. Burton, another veteran from the original faculty cadre that Harper had hired.

In summary, Harper was a very capable executive, who many thought could manage any large enterprise. As Marvin Hughitt, one of Chicago's most prominent industrialists, said to him, "The fact is, Dr. Harper... you ought to be president of the North Western Railroad in my place; you could run it better than I can."[49]

Finally we come to the test of *selflessness*. Harper was certainly imbued with ego strength. Though he was self-assured, at the same time he was as free of arrogance as one could be. The kinds of spats that occupied far too much of Stanley Hall's time were unimaginable in the case of Harper. The first two head professors that Harper hired were William G. Hale and J. Laurence Laughlan, both from the Cornell faculty. As they learned more about Harper's plans for the university that was still largely a dream, they became more anxious about the momentous step they were about to take. In somewhat imperious fashion, they demanded that Harper come to Ithaca to discuss their concerns. In the middle of his frenetically busy life, and without any sign of irritation or bruised pride, Harper made the arduous trip. The two men never forgot the conversation that ensued, including Harper's suggestion that a faculty senate be a central component of the governance structure.[50] They became Harper stalwarts as well as key faculty leaders who saw to it that important decisions always were thoroughly aired. When things went wrong, Harper blamed himself, not others. At moments of discouragement he sometimes referred to the wonderful life of a scholar and teacher that he had left behind at Yale. Still, despite such occasional bouts of ambivalence, he gladly subordinated personal interests to the larger service that he rendered as the university's founding president. As his health declined and he approached death, there was much speculation that he had shortened and sacrificed his very life in that service. Whatever the medical evidence may be on that point, he surely would not have hesitated to make such a sacrifice.

Recognizing that Harper had some very human flaws and foibles and that he took extraordinary, perhaps even reckless, risks relative to the financial management of the university, our verdict is still that he was an exceptional leader.

★   ★   ★

Both Hall and Harper were talented academics who had visionary ambitions for their new institutions at a turning point in American higher education. Each also had the ability to excite and inspire their founders and faculty about their visions of a new form of university. Because of Hall's duplicity, autocratic style, and unwillingness to share credit, however, he soon lost the trust of Jonas Clark, and many of his most talented colleagues abandoned him. Nor was he capable or even interested in persuading potential donors or the community of the worthiness of his vision for Clark University. Harper, in contrast, built enormous trust, confidence, and enthusiasm for his vision through his transparency, inclusive style, and supporting actions over time. While he clearly had a strong ego and ambition, no one questioned that he was motivated by the best interests of the University of Chicago. In short, Harper embodied his message, while Hall did not.

CHAPTER SEVEN

Edward Teller and Sir William Osler: Scientific Leaders

If the human race survives another thousand years, textbook summaries of the nineteenth and twentieth centuries may well label that era as the Age of Science and Technology. Much as the Renaissance is associated with the revival of humanism and the Enlightenment with the growth of rationalism in the conduct of human affairs, the last two centuries arguably were defined principally by the explosion in scientific knowledge and its technological impact on humankind. Much of that impact has been enormously positive, including unimagined advances in health care, information technology, transportation, industry, and the average quality of life throughout the world. But there have also been unintended negative consequences, ranging from the development of weapons of mass destruction to global climate changes. New technologies contributed to the deaths of over 110 million people in World Wars I and II alone.

The seminal leaders in the domain of science have been primarily *indirect leaders* in Howard Gardner's definition of the term. That is, they have led through the power of their transforming ideas and insights to inspire other scientists, rather than by organizing and moving a group of followers directly toward a mutually agreed upon goal. Indirect leaders included geniuses such as Albert Einstein, Louis Pasteur, Marie Curie, Francis Crick, and James Watson. Often, however, the *application* of scientific discoveries has been the work of *direct leaders*, who understood but did not make the foundational discoveries. For example, after physicist Richard Feynman discussed the theoretical possibilities of nanotechnology in 1959, others, like Gordon Moore, the cofounder of Intel, used Feynman's insights to build an industry that produced ever-more-powerful semiconductors. These in turn have powered the personal computing revolution that has transformed modern life.

The two leaders treated in this chapter were unusual in being both direct and indirect leaders to different degrees. One was associated with the positive impact of science and the other with its potentially catastrophic implications. Sir William Osler was the most admired physician of the late nineteenth and early twentieth centuries. He provided critical, direct leadership to the effort to base the clinical practice of medicine upon science, primarily through embodying his vision and the force of his personality. But as an indirect leader, he also used his powerful skills as a communicator to reach an international audience of professionals with books and lectures on the principles and practice of medicine, along with innumerable papers on a wide range of diseases, conditions, and treatments.[1]

The theoretical physicist Edward Teller, best known as the "father" of the hydrogen bomb, also contributed significantly to the field of nuclear physics as an indirect leader, especially in the first half of his career. In addition, through his tireless lobbying efforts he became an unusually effective direct leader—too effective, according to his detractors—of the political and military camps determined to sustain the United States' lead over the USSR in the nuclear arms race of the Cold War era.

In this chapter, we focus on the direct leadership of Teller and Osler. Each was exceptionally persuasive in communicating his vision to other experts and to laypersons, despite the complexity of the science undergirding that vision. Osler was universally admired during his lifetime, and he is still lionized by physicians more than a century later. Teller, in contrast, was highly controversial during his career and evoked strong divided opinions among physicists, nuclear policy experts, and laymen long after the end of the Cold War. Was this difference due solely to the degree of controversy inherent in their respective visions? Or did their communication of their visions also suggest something about their respective motivations and sincerity that contributed significantly to these differing reactions?

Edward Teller

Aggression is wrong whether carried out by bow and arrow or by the hydrogen bomb. Defence is right, whether it uses a stream of particles or the concentrated energy locked in the atomic nucleus. Without such an agreement [on the morality of self-defense] we cannot count on the survival of the society that holds moral values so strongly that it calls them human rights.[2]

—Edward Teller

The controversy over Edward Teller's leadership during his Cold War heyday was as starkly polarizing as his own worldview. Some saw his persistence in championing the hydrogen bomb and the US nuclear arsenal as exemplary genius and patriotism in the face of great odds. Others saw him as blinkered, obsessive, ruthless, and possessing suspect motivations. To this group, Teller was a real-life Dr. Strangelove, the twisted genius in Stanley Kubrick's brilliant 1964 black comedy, *Dr. Strangelove, Or How I Learned to*

Stop Worrying and Love the Bomb. Did Teller fit either of these caricature-like portraits, or was he a more complex combination of some features of both? And if the latter, was it this combination of features that was the source of both his effectiveness and his limitations as a direct leader?

★ ★ ★

Teller was born in Hungary in January 1908. Growing up in a prosperous Jewish family, he encountered many of the upheavals of World War I and its aftermath. Dissolution of the Austro-Hungarian Empire brought the brutal communist regime of Béla Kun to Hungary. Food was scarce; soldiers were quartered in private homes (including the Tellers's); and the legal practice of Teller's father was greatly diminished.[3] When the short-lived communist government was overthrown, Hungary's Jews were blamed for its excesses because Kun and a number of his chief lieutenants were Jewish. The ensuing anti-Semitic reign of terror targeted what had been one of the most assimilated Jewish populations in Europe and led to the executions of thousands of Jews. Later in life, Teller wrote: "During my first eleven years, I had known war, patriotism, communism, revolution, anti-Semitism, fascism, and peace. I wish the peace had been more complete."[4]

An awkward and socially immature child, Teller was a mathematics prodigy who was teased mercilessly until he won over fellow students by tutoring them in math. In the view of biographer Peter Goodchild, "This thirst for acceptance—with the hurt and anger he felt when it was denied—was to become a defining feature of his life."[5]

When he graduated from high school, Teller's future path was far from certain. Despite his passion for mathematics and physics, he followed his father's urging to take up a more "practical" subject, leading him in 1925 to Budapest University to study to become a chemical engineer. At the same time, though, he entered Hungary's prestigious Eotvos competition, winning the physics prize outright and sharing the math prize with two other students. This success convinced his parents that he was gifted enough to study abroad. In Germany's Karlsruhe Technical Institute he became the star pupil of Herman Mark, a chemist who was investigating the potential applications of quantum mechanics. Mark eventually interceded with Teller's father, convincing him to allow his son to switch focus from chemistry to physics.

The next decade or so took Teller to the pinnacle of his new field, despite a serious accident that slowed his progress. He had only begun at the University of Munich in 1928 when he lost most of his right foot in a train accident. When he recovered, almost a year later, Teller transferred to the University of Leipzig to study under Werner von Heisenberg, the quantum mechanics pioneer.

His education at Leipzig was crucial to Teller personally, scientifically, and politically. He learned that he could compete intellectually with the brilliant young physicists working with Heisenberg. Only 20 years old when he arrived at Leipzig, Teller received a PhD at 22. Despite his youth, he found that he was well-received socially by his peers. His stature in the emerging field of quantum mechanics benefited greatly from a doctoral dissertation that is still viewed as the most accurate quantum mechanical description of the hydrogen molecular ion. Politically, he had his first adult exposure to totalitarian injustice. In his postdoctoral year at Leipzig, a friend from Hungary, Lazlo Tisza, joined him to collaborate on a research project for a few weeks. Like many students at that time, they debated the relative merits of communism and fascism. Teller recalled that he was "confused and undecided," while Tisza was sympathetic to the communists, although not a party member. But upon Tisza's return to Budapest, where the communist party had been outlawed, he was arrested and beaten for carrying a message to party members. "I was deeply distressed by Laci's imprisonment," Teller later wrote. "If, as my father believed, the basis of all good government was *audiatur et altera pars* (letting the other side also be heard), Hungary was badly governed. Laci, unfairly, was paying the price; serving even a short prison term in Hungary meant that his career was ruined."[6]

Following his postdoctoral year, Teller accepted a job offer from another prestigious German center of physics, the University of Göttingen, where he was to spend the next three years. He had the chance to work there with international luminaries, including a new mentor, the eminent Italian physicist, Enrico Fermi. Soon, however, harsh political realities intruded again with Hitler's appointment as German chancellor in January 1933. Nazi propaganda directed at Jewish scientists convinced Teller that he had no future in Germany. A Rockefeller Foundation fellowship enabled him to study for a year in Copenhagen with Niels Bohr, the Danish pioneer in describing the structure of atoms. In Copenhagen, Teller also married his childhood friend, Augusta Maria ("Mici") Harkanyi-Schutz, a marriage that would last over five decades. After a year in London at University College and still only 27 years old, Teller received an offer for a full professorship at George Washington University, and in 1935, the Tellers emigrated a final time.

Teller's first few years in the United States were marked by intense scientific creativity as he became an increasingly influential indirect leader in his field. In addition to teaching, he published or coauthored dozens of papers in the fields of quantum, molecular, and nuclear physics. Teller's preferred mode of operation was collaboration. He would come up with a question that interested him and then search for an intellectual partner. Indeed, according to Goodchild, "there was a generosity about Teller at this time that was widely appreciated. He only needed to be excited about an idea or a problem and he would offer his time and effort freely. He was also always generous in the credit he gave to others."[7]

At the same time, Teller could not ignore the storm clouds gathering over Europe as fascists and communists strengthened their grip on power and destroyed the lives of many that he knew and loved. In the summer of 1936, he and Mici made their last trip to Hungary for 50 years. Many of Mici's family would die in the Holocaust as would Edward's sister's husband and his closest childhood friend. Teller was also profoundly affected by the imprisonment of his friend and colleague from the Leipzig years, Russian physicist Lev Landau, during Stalin's purges of the late 1930s, and by Tisza's disillusionment with communism in the Soviet Union, where he had emigrated following his imprisonment in Hungary.[8] Finally, Teller was shaken by Fermi's worries in 1937 about growing anti-Semitism in Mussolini's Italy and the safety of his Jewish wife.[9] Together these experiences reinforced the revulsion Teller felt for all forms of tyranny and strengthened his bonds to his newly adopted country, where he and Mici became naturalized citizens in early 1941.

Teller's major opportunity to help the American war effort came through his participation in the top-secret Manhattan Project, the massive military-civilian effort to develop an atomic bomb at Los Alamos laboratory in New Mexico. In 1939, the theoretical possibility of nuclear fission, or splitting the atom and producing an enormous amount of energy, had been confirmed experimentally only weeks after its discovery in Germany. Nuclear physicists immediately recognized the potential for creating an awesomely powerful bomb. In Germany, the Nazi government launched an effort to develop such a weapon under Heisenberg's leadership. In the United States, a group of émigré physicists that included Fermi and Teller tried to alert the American government to the danger of a nuclear-armed Germany but it was only when they recruited Albert Einstein to send a letter to President Roosevelt outlining the German threat that they were able to get the government to act. The eventual result was the creation of the Manhattan Project under the overall leadership of Brigadier General Leslie Groves and the scientific leadership of Robert Oppenheimer.

Older than Teller by four years, Oppenheimer, too, was a gifted physicist. The elder son of a wealthy American Jewish businessman, he also had studied at Göttingen and won acclaim for his contributions to quantum physics. One major difference between these professional peers, however, was Oppenheimer's cultural and social sophistication. A man of refined and eclectic tastes, ranging from literature to fine wines to eastern philosophy, he moved within a circle of friends from many fields. Teller, in comparison, was still socially awkward and intellectually narrow, and his friends tended to be other physicists.

Another difference was that Oppenheimer had been a communist sympathizer. While never a party member, he had attended meetings, given money, and been under surveillance for almost two years because of his contacts. Groves ignored the objections of the FBI and the US Army's security arm. He got along well with Oppenheimer and felt the worldly physicist was able to understand the military's needs for secrecy and discipline and yet manage the quirky scientists on whom ultimate success depended.

When Oppenheimer became head of the Manhattan Project, he sought out Teller, who had spent much of 1941 working on a nuclear reactor project with Fermi at Columbia University. Suddenly Teller was enlisted in the feverish quest to develop the world's most destructive weapon. This was to mark the beginning of an entirely new phase in his career, from which he would emerge as a much less generous and congenial scientific colleague, but as a quite effective direct leader of an aggressive, nuclear-based defense policy. The roots of both appear to lie in his thwarted personal ambition and an increasing obsession with the threat posed by communism.

Even before the war, some colleagues had observed that Teller's enthusiasm for physics was often paired with a great desire to have his own way. He was a generator of ideas, and whether those ideas were practical or not, Teller insisted on pursuing them. As Manhattan Project colleague Rudolf Peierls noted, "[T]his makes him act at times like a prima donna."[10] That insistence was on display almost immediately in the Manhattan Project as Teller became fixated on the idea of developing a hydrogen bomb, or the "Super" as he termed it. Provoked by Fermi's casual comment that a fission weapon might be used to trigger an even larger nuclear fusion reaction, Teller convinced himself that it was possible and became obsessed with pursuing the idea. His rationale was ostensibly economic. A fusion bomb would deliver far more bang for the buck.[11] Years later he admitted that he was motivated by the Super's novelty.

> Not knowing how it would influence the future, I wanted both as a scientist and also for practical reasons to know how it would work. Some will perhaps consider this as irresponsible because they pretend to be able to see into the future...[I]f you are a little more modest about the influence that a scientist can have on the course of events, then I believe it is not irresponsible to try to work out those technical developments which can be worked out.[12]

Yet because the problems in building the fission bomb were proving much more difficult to solve than anticipated, work on the Super was sidelined. Teller's disappointment was compounded by being passed over for head of the Manhattan Project's theoretical division in favor of his friend Hans Bethe. According to Bethe's wife, Rose, this rejection echoed those Teller had experienced in his school days. As she remarked years later, "It's from this point on you get those extreme reactions to people and situations which cause so many problems."[13] Bethe himself noted that "Edward essentially went on strike. Well, he didn't literally. He continued to work, but from then on he seemed rather disinterested in working on the direct business of the laboratory."[14] Indeed, Teller's refusal to do any of the theoretical calculations needed for the implosion of the fission bomb damaged his close friendship with Bethe, and led to his replacement by Peierls on that part of the project. Moreover, even though Oppenheimer allowed him to continue to explore the feasibility of the Super and agreed to spend an hour per week discussing whatever Teller wished, "not even this extraordinary gesture satisfied Teller, who thought that his friend had become a 'politician.'"[15]

Teller's relationship with Oppenheimer deteriorated further after the war when Oppenheimer was credited as the "father" of the atomic bomb. Moreover, Oppenheimer used this prestige to try to persuade senior politicians in Washington that there was no need to continue research on the hydrogen bomb.[16] Teller, though, was even more convinced that developing the Super was vital. Bethe would recall a conversation not long after the war when he first heard Teller describe himself "as terribly pessimistic about relations with Russia. He was terribly anti-communist, terribly anti-Russian." Research on nuclear weapons had to continue, Teller insisted to Bethe. "The war was not over and Russia was just as dangerous an enemy as Germany had been."[17] In his memoirs, Teller claims that reading Arthur Koestler's novel *Darkness at Noon* in the summer of 1943 was a critical event in shaping his worldview. The book "brought together and crystallized the objections to the methods of control used by Russian communism, which had been forming and accumulating in my mind for fifteen years."[18] Personal experience, thwarted ambition, strong ideological and strategic beliefs—these combined to make Teller uniquely forceful among scientists in pressing for the continued development of nuclear weapons.

Following the war, Fermi, Bethe, Oppenheimer, and most of the other senior scientists returned to their university teaching posts. Teller, however, stayed on at Los Alamos hoping to pursue the development of the Super. Only when it became clear that neither Norris Bradbury, the new head of the lab, nor Oppenheimer, would support his ambition did he return to the University of Chicago. Despite his many frustrations, traces remained of the prewar Teller who had been known among his peers as an enthusiastic and generous colleague. British physicist Freeman Dyson, who met him in 1946, wrote, "He seemed to do physics for fun rather than glory. I took an instant liking to him."[19] And Goodchild adds that "[c]olleagues coined the term 'Teller' as a unit of enthusiasm. Finer degrees of positive thinking were measured in 'micro-Tellers' or millionths of a Teller."[20]

Yet as one of his Chicago colleagues recalled, "Talk about physics and Edward was inventive and enthusiastic...However, talk about politics and it turned to one thing. The Russians are coming."[21] Indeed, the intensifying Cold War was turning the political tide in Teller's favor. In 1949, China fell to the communists and President Truman announced that the Soviets had successfully tested their own fission bomb. Both events fed an increasing paranoia in the United States that would set the stage for the poisonous McCarthy era of the early 1950s. Pressure for exploring the possibility of a fusion weapon became irresistible. Teller was named chairman of a committee to do so, and his leadership was critical in President

Truman's approval in March 1950 of a crash program to develop the hydrogen bomb. Teller recruited old friends and former students to join the effort, and he lobbied the powers in Washington indefatigably. After years of frustration, he was determined not to let this opportunity elude him. The triumph was largely his. "I was enormously impressed by the fact that one man could have that impact on policy," a colleague recalled. "He was everywhere."[22]

Despite this victory, the battle over the Super's future was hardly won. One big problem was that Teller's working design was not feasible, as mathematician Stanislaw Ulam demonstrated in a report the day before Truman's announcement of the crash program. Teller was apoplectic and accused Ulam of sabotage, though Fermi soon confirmed that the design would not work. Teller was also convinced that Oppenheimer and his ally, Norris Bradbury, were scattering obstacles in his path. Though Teller had returned to Los Alamos in 1948 at Bradbury's invitation, he would accuse the director in his memoirs of not letting him pursue an alternative design and of putting an enemy of the Super in charge of its development.[23] Even Teller recognized his own obsessiveness. "There can be no doubt that having discussed, worked on, and worried about the Super for almost ten years, a part of me wanted it to work. Many find that desire, at the very least, improper." But, he continued, the calculations showed "that fusion failed only by a narrow margin. What if we had given up and the Soviets hadn't? What if they had succeeded?" Convinced that "had I abandoned the attempt, the chances for successful development during this period would have been exceedingly small," he acknowledged that "to say that I was committed is an understatement."[24]

The search continued at Los Alamos for a workable fusion bomb design. The breakthrough came in 1951 when Teller built on an idea of Ulam's to come up with what became known as the Teller–Ulam design. Credit for the discovery even now remains mired in controversy, but Bethe and other scientists believed Teller's intellectual contribution to have been crucial and his relentless determination the key to realizing the design. Teller eventually became known popularly as the "father" of the H-bomb.[25] Nonetheless, Bradbury would not name him to a leadership role in the program to develop Mike, the first bomb to use the Teller–Ulam design. One relieved colleague at Los Alamos described Teller during the development process as "hostile...really nasty, second-guessing people, and there were an awful lot of people, they wouldn't have worked for him for anything."[26]

Teller became convinced that the solution to the frustrations he faced at Los Alamos was to establish a second, competing lab, and he threw himself into lobbying key government officials for it as tirelessly as he had lobbied for the Super itself. After teaming up with the politically connected physicist Ernest Lawrence, the inventor of the cyclotron and winner of the 1939 Nobel Prize for physics, they persuaded the Atomic Energy Commission (AEC) to recommend in June 1952 the establishment of a second lab, near San Francisco, what became the Lawrence

Livermore Laboratory. As Teller described it, "Oppenheimer accused Ernest Lawrence and me of being experienced 'promoters'... In connection with the second laboratory, I earned the title: Over the next several months, I went to talk with everyone who would see me."[27] He would pay a steep price. By siding with a fierce right-winger like Lawrence and his anticommunist allies, Teller became embroiled in a new, highly political world and sacrificed many remaining friends. Fermi warned that he was making a serious mistake, asserting that the people involved with Lawrence Livermore "are not like us. We think about science as science. They are political plotters."[28] As Teller purportedly told a friend of fellow physicist Isidor Rabi, "I have quit the appeasers and joined the fascists."[29] Yet as he would write in his memoirs, "Come what might, I felt that I had to turn my deeply felt advocacy of a second laboratory into reality and see the hydrogen bomb through to a more mature state."[30]

But when Lawrence Livermore Labs (LL) opened in September 1952, Teller's frustrations continued. First of all, Herbert York, not Teller, was named the director.[31] Even worse was the absence of a thermonuclear weapons design group in LL's proposed organizational chart, since that was the reason that Teller had promoted a second lab. Only after Teller declared that LL was "all a fake" and threatened to quit was a compromise reached that ensured a place for his work.[32]

Undermined and marginalized not only by his former, "liberal" colleagues at Los Alamos but even by his new right-wing allies, Teller became ever more controlling, manipulative, and isolated. His isolation only increased with the testimony he gave against Oppenheimer at a 1954 AEC hearing that cost Oppenheimer his security clearance at the height of the Red Scare. Though he said he assumed that Oppenheimer was loyal to his country—"and I shall continue to believe it until I see very conclusive proof to the opposite"—when asked whether he considered Oppenheimer a security risk, Teller testified that in "a great number of instances" he had seen Oppenheimer act "in a way which for me was exceedingly hard to understand," actions that "frankly appeared to me confused and complicated. To this extent, I feel that I would like to see the vital interests of this country in hands which I understand better and therefore trust more."[33] Former colleagues were outraged by testimony they saw as motivated by resentment and frustration and from then on, Teller was ostracized by many of his peers.[34]

The removal of Oppenheimer's security clearance left no comparably high-profile scientist to oppose Teller in the political arena, and with LL, he now had his own platform. For the next 40 years, he used it brilliantly to accelerate and perpetuate the Cold War's nuclear arms race. In convincing a series of presidential administrations that continued heavy investment in nuclear weapons capability was a necessity, he was ingenious—devilishly so in the view of detractors—in marshalling every argument possible. Rabi saw Teller as "an enemy of humanity" who was "brilliant in inventing excuses" to thwart arms control.[35]

His advocacy during the Eisenhower presidency serves as a good example. The explosion of the first Soviet hydrogen bomb in 1953 made the necessity to stay ahead of the USSR easy to sell. Over the next few years, dramatic improvements in the size and yield of weapons were achieved by both Los Alamos and LL. Soon, though, the dangers of nuclear fallout from atmospheric tests as well as the apocalyptic implications of the actual use of such weapons created enormous public pressure and by early 1957 led Eisenhower to favor a test ban treaty. In response, Teller and Lawrence lobbied Congress and the president himself with moral and practical arguments for continued development and testing. Morally, they argued, smaller, "cleaner" weapons—ones with less fallout—would kill far fewer people if they ever had to be used. They might even have beneficial uses in peacetime, in oil mining, for example, or for blasting a new Panama canal or a deep-water harbor in Alaska, or changing global weather patterns. Moreover, they pointed out, the Soviets could hide underground and upper atmosphere tests from detection, and thus violate any test ban unless intrusive verification were possible. An undetectable LL test in September 1957 two thousand feet under a mountain demonstrated the point. Eisenhower was impressed with their arguments, and the launch of Sputnik in October 1957 exacerbated concerns that the Soviets might be dangerously ahead, especially in missile technology.[36]

Against Lawrence and Teller, Rabi, the new chair of the AEC's General Advisory Committee, and other scientists continued to push for a test ban, arguing that detection of violations was feasible. Realizing that the scientific community was divided and in an effort to get an objective view, Eisenhower appointed an 11-man committee, chaired by Bethe and including Teller, as well as representatives from the AEC, the CIA, and the Department of Defense. Over Teller's objections, the committee report concluded that with a mixture of techniques detection would be possible, and in the summer of 1958 a conference of US and Soviet scientists led to an agreement on detection methods. As a result, Eisenhower announced that a one-year testing ban would begin on October 31, and Soviet Premier Khrushchev accepted his proposal to begin negotiations on a permanent ban. Teller, now fully in charge of LL following Lawrence's death in August, unleashed an intensive effort to show that effective monitoring would require four times as many inspection stations and onsite visits as the scientists' conference had agreed upon. There was little chance that the Soviets would have approved such intrusive inspections under any circumstances. When they shot down an American U2 spy plane in May 1960, all hopes of negotiating a permanent test ban during Eisenhower's presidency vanished. In his final speech as president, Eisenhower warned of "the acquisition of unwarranted influence, whether sought or unsought, by the military-industrial complex," and of the "danger that public policy could itself become the captive of a scientific-technological elite." The technological elite he had had in mind, Eisenhower told Herbert York later, were Teller and Werner von

Braun, another scientist who shared Teller's talent for doom-mongering super-salesmanship.[37]

In 1960, Teller stepped down as head of LL, but he remained with the lab, and to the end of the Cold War, continued to be a forceful and effective advocate for continued weapons development and testing, including the space-based missile defense system known as Star Wars. Teller allied himself with a series of like-minded, conservative organizations and individuals, becoming a savant and totem to the American right wing. His final obsession was the shaping of his legacy and reputation, never voicing any uncertainty or regrets over his role in the nuclear arms race. In 2003, he received the Presidential Medal of Freedom from George W. Bush only two weeks before his death.

★   ★   ★

Clearly Teller was an effective direct leader as the successful advocate for the hydrogen bomb, the establishment of LL, and the development of generations of nuclear weapons over five decades. Why was he effective, and could he have been even more so? Was he, in fact, exceptional, as some of his admirers would argue?

Evaluating the effectiveness of Teller's *vision* is complicated by the controversy that continues to surround it. Should we judge its effectiveness by whether it was the best and wisest vision for the long-term good of his country and humankind, or by whether it proved to be compelling to the audience of decision-makers, young scientists, and general citizenry whose support he needed in order to pursue his goal of winning the nuclear arms race? We believe the latter criterion is most appropriate and in that respect, Teller's vision was highly compelling. Many key figures in Congress, the military, the AEC, the intelligence community, and the American public shared Teller's distrust of communism and feared that the Soviets would stop at nothing to achieve their goal of world domination. Moreover, the political views of younger generations of scientists were shaped by the prevailing sentiments in the country, and many were highly sympathetic to Teller's view of the need for continued development and testing of thermonuclear weapons as a means of protecting the free world.[38]

The key, however, to Teller's success in persuading his audience to support his vision was his extraordinary effectiveness as a *communicator*, in particular his mutually reinforcing skills as an advocate and educator. From early in his career, he was known as an outstanding teacher, and while he was a professor at George Washington University, students would often commute 40 miles from Johns Hopkins in Baltimore to hear him lecture.[39] As York later put it, "Edward is charismatic in the true, simple sense. He's enthused, he does have a thorough grasp of the basic ideas, whether they're his or not, he's a teacher and he knows how to explain," and, of course, "he's strongly ambitious to have his way."[40] When these skills were combined with the credibility of his scientific credentials, he made a very persuasive advocate for his convictions: that a fusion bomb was feasible, that the Soviets would soon develop their own, that detection of Soviet testing was nearly impossible, and that the United States therefore needed to continue testing. He also possessed the raw, relentless energy and political instincts to become a highly effective lobbyist. Over the years, his network of political and military allies became extensive both within and outside the government through influential conservative organizations and individuals. Indeed, for decades, he succeeded in frustrating the efforts of liberal scientists and politicians to slow development and testing. For example, during the Kennedy and Johnson administrations he successfully lobbied for the 1963 Nuclear Test Ban Treaty to allow underground testing and for the 1968 Non-Proliferation Treaty to allow an exception for the "peaceful" uses of nuclear explosives. And during the 1980s he persuaded President Reagan to fund the creation of the Star Wars program, even though its feasibility and strategic wisdom were as controversial as Teller himself.

To his detractors, another reason for Teller's persuasiveness was his disingenuousness and dissembling. For example, as early as 1946, he exaggerated the theoretical progress that had been made in order to promote the Super. An old colleague, Robert Serber, wrote that he found Teller's report "really incredible. The conclusion was that it was almost certain that it would work." He worked with Teller to eliminate "some of the more extreme statements" but "a couple of months later when the report came out, none of the changes were made that we had agreed on."[41] In 1956, to win a US Navy contract for developing the Polaris missile, Teller made the completely unsupported claim during the final negotiations that LL would be able to triple the blast yield of warheads in five years.[42] Three decades later he grossly oversold the technical feasibility of Star Wars.[43]

Were all of these simply byproducts of his enthusiasm and optimism, even a means of challenging himself and his colleagues to greater levels of creativity? After all, the fusion bomb was successfully developed, as was the Polaris missile. Or more darkly, was this tendency an indication of his willingness to delude others and perhaps even himself in order to achieve his goals? To Bethe, Teller crossed an ethical line when he persisted in advocating the Super despite strong evidence that his proposed design would not work. In Bethe's view, Teller was guilty of leading the country "into an adventurous program on the basis of calculations which he himself must have known to have been very incomplete."[44]

Similarly, Teller would tailor his argument for pursuing development and testing to whatever audience he was addressing. To those fearful of the Soviet menace, he would emphasize the difficulty of detection. To those with moral objections to the use of nuclear weapons, he would focus on the need for clean bombs or a missile-defense shield. To the young scientists who were essential to further development of any weapons, he would appeal to the pursuit of knowledge for knowledge's sake. In many cases, he would use some combination of all of these points. In this, he was of course not different from any advocate. The question is whether he deceived his audience in the process. Whatever his intentions, our view is that Teller's exaggerations and dissembling were driven largely by his obsession with building weapons to counter the threat of Soviet imperialism.

In contrast to his communication skills, Teller's *organizational capabilities* were mixed at best. On the one hand, his behavior at Los Alamos during the Manhattan Project and the later development of the hydrogen bomb (Mike) demonstrated that he was not a team player. When thwarted he would sulk or misbehave. Nor was he a capable and steady manager. Indeed, most agreed with Robert Serber that Teller was "a disaster to any organization."[45] As a result, his superiors consistently avoided naming Teller to a senior managerial position. Oppenheimer passed over him to appoint Bethe as head of the theoretical division at Los Alamos; Bradbury refused to make Teller head of Mike's development; and Lawrence named York, not Teller, the first director of LL. York later described how at LL he worked around Teller's erratic style: "We established a small steering committee and made him a member of it without responsibility for any specific part of the laboratory or its program, but with a personal veto authority for the first year... This arrangement enabled him to participate as he wished in whatever part of the program took his fancy."[46] Bethe explained, "Nine out of ten of Teller's ideas are useless. He needs men with more judgment, even if they be less gifted, to select the tenth idea which often is a stroke of genius."[47]

On the other hand, Teller did recognize the importance of having a supportive, well-functioning organization to realize his vision. When it became clear to him that Los Alamos was unlikely to provide that support, he lobbied vigorously to establish LL. And his approach to organization during the brief period when he was LL's director from 1958 to 1960 suggests he was aware of his own managerial weaknesses. "I [adopted] the advice Herb York had given me shortly before he left," Teller wrote in his memoirs. "'Leave as many of the details of the job as possible to other people. Delegate!' Had I not followed his advice, my directorship would have been a failure."[48] To one executive he assigned responsibility for LL's operations; to another, fusion weapon development; and to a third, fission development. This left Teller free to focus on his main goal—resistance to Eisenhower's drive for a test ban treaty—for which he knew the laboratory needed to have "as effective a spokesperson as possible to explain the importance of continued testing to our national defense."[49] While Teller's organizational capabilities were weak overall, they proved adequate. He understood the critical importance of a strong, supporting organization in realizing his vision and reluctantly agreed to accept a limited managerial role within that organization. In his brief tenure as LL director, he proved capable of delegating to others.

While judging the degree of Teller's *selflessness* is also difficult due to the complexity of his motivations, we believe it to be the weakest element of his leadership. At one level, we see no reason to question his genuine distrust and fear of totalitarianism. From his childhood onward, he had witnessed the havoc that fascists and communists had wreaked on his family, friends, and the civilized world. Similarly, his strategic belief—that knowledge once discovered will be pursued and that limiting one's own development and testing of weapons without appropriate means of detecting violations by others would be foolhardy—is credible. At the same time, though, along with his vision he appeared to have other equally strong motivations related to his personal insecurities, especially a need for recognition and a resentment of others like Oppenheimer who had either achieved such recognition or thwarted his ambitions. These insecurities were stoked by rejections and disappointments he had experienced, ranging from early childhood onward. In addition, the seeds of obsessive behavior appear to have been present in Teller's personality from an early point as indicated by his determination to have his own way once he became fixated on an idea. Arguably it was the combination of these personal, psychological motivations and his legitimate political and scientific beliefs that led to Teller's obsession with developing the Super. Did that obsession lead to a nuclear arms race that was far longer, riskier, and more expensive than it could have been? Did it contribute to greater proliferation of nuclear weapons than would otherwise have occurred? It is hard to answer these questions definitively, although clearly many, including his former colleagues, felt that it did. Bethe spoke for many of his peers when he argued in 1954 that the United States' lead in fission weapons had provided an adequate defense against the Russians, that by not developing a thermonuclear weapon ourselves we would have left open the possibility that the Soviets would not do so, and that if the Soviets had secretly developed such a weapon, we would have detected any test immediately.[50]

What is more certain is that Teller's obsession changed his behavior from that of an enthusiastic and generous colleague in his prewar scientific career to an increasingly difficult and isolated person over the balance of his life. It is also clear that his behavior led many of his former colleagues and the liberal public to conclude that Teller's vision was motivated as much by his own needs and interests as by the best interests of the nation and humankind. Whether or not this judgment was fair, it certainly prevented Teller from being as effective a leader as he might have been.

In summary, Teller was a moderately effective leader overall because his outstanding skills as a lobbyist enabled him to sell his vision of the Soviet threat to a group of like-minded senior government officials and influential advisors over a period of five decades. While his organizational skills were poor, they were sufficient for the support of his vision. Unfortunately, however, the self-centered insecurities that appear to have fueled his obsession and his willingness to bend the truth in pursuit of that obsession led many to lack confidence in his judgment, vision, and ethics.

They cause us as well to conclude that he was not an exceptional leader. In our view, scientific leaders have a special responsibility for being honest in their communications and selfless in their motivations, given their specialized knowledge and the stakes involved. When the outcome could be nuclear holocaust, none of us should be comfortable with having Dr. Strangelove at the controls.

Sir William Osler

Osler did more than any other man of his day...to teach all men that the study and pursuit of disease is a pursuit which a properly trained mind can follow with as keen enjoyment and uplift as an artist can study great pictures or a musician can hear great Masters.[51]
—A student of Osler's

While Edward Teller was a polarizing figure through much of his life, William Osler was a man beloved throughout the international medical profession and within the communities where he lived, taught, and practiced. By the early twentieth century, he was the best-known physician in North America, credited with helping to achieve enormous advances in medical science, in the practice of clinical medicine, and in public health. Upon his death in 1919, he was universally mourned, and 18 of that year's articles in the *Bulletin of Johns Hopkins Hospital*, where he had worked from 1888 to 1904, were devoted to his life and work. Indeed, as his biographer, Michael Bliss, states: "Everyone loved the Chief...To a modern biographer searching for the feet of clay that make subjects credible, the remarkable unanimity of the sources is disconcerting...No one thought ill of the man."[52]

Why was the support for Osler and his vision so universal, while that for Teller was sharply divided? One reasonable hypothesis might be that improving health care and thus the quality of life is inherently less controversial than a nuclear arms race. Yet in the late nineteenth century, health care reform was often resisted vociferously by conservative elements of the medical establishment, by politicians and community leaders indifferent to improving public hygiene, and by poorly educated physicians, homeopaths, and other types of practitioners who saw their livelihoods threatened. What then was it about Osler's leadership—about his vision, his ability to persuade others, his organizational capabilities, and his motivations—that enabled him to have such exceptional impact?

★ ★ ★

William Osler was born in July 1849 in remote western Ontario. His father, an Anglican priest, and his mother had emigrated reluctantly from England a decade earlier when the church sent them out as missionaries.

Despite the hardships they endured, they became deeply committed to ministering to their widely scattered, backwoods congregation. From his parents, Osler's patient and biographer Edith Gittings Reid claimed, originated a number of William's core values: "[T]he philosophy of their lives was service, kindness, faith and works... with initiative to undertake almost any work and power to complete once undertaken."[53] William was the eighth of nine children, and until the Oslers moved closer to Toronto in 1857 for the sake of their children's education, he and his siblings lived in the harsh frontier forest. Nonetheless, William remembered very little about these years other than being happy.

During his school years, Osler's positive demeanor, good nature, and kindness drew others to him. A contemporary at the boarding school Osler attended near Toronto remembered that "his consistent high qualities were such that in every scope of activity he was recognized without bitterness or jealousy of any kind, as the head."[54] It was at boarding school that Osler met the two teachers through whom he would discover his life's passion—Rev. W. A. Johnson, who introduced the boy to nature studies and the new world opened up by the microscope, and Johnson's friend, Dr. Richard Bovell, a naturalist, physician, and teacher at Trinity College in Toronto, who exposed Osler to the field of medicine.

After boarding school, Osler matriculated at Trinity College, and by his second year, he had decided to follow Bovell into medicine rather than follow his father and Johnson into the clergy. From then on, he directed all his energies to that "single idea," devoted to "doing the day's work before me just as faithfully and honestly and energetically as I could."[55] His family's philosophy of life had clearly taken root.

In the late 1860s, the practice of medicine was quite primitive and unsophisticated. Despite numerous scientific breakthroughs in the diagnosis of disease, corresponding advances in treatment lagged greatly. Moreover, there were many types of medical practitioners—homeopaths, hydropaths, and others—in addition to physicians and surgeons, and almost anyone could get a license to practice, if a license was even required.[56] Similarly, medical schools varied widely in curricula, practices, and requirements.

Osler was lucky that he spent his first two years at Trinity College working closely with Bovell, a leading physician and medical teacher who was remarkable for his scientific literacy.[57] Outside of the lecture hall, much of Osler's time was spent dissecting, which honed his powers of observation and his skill in using the microscope.[58] In addition, Bovell gave him the free use of his extensive library, which inspired Osler to establish scientific libraries wherever he taught and practiced.

When Bovell moved to the West Indies in 1870, Osler transferred to McGill College in Montreal, which offered the best medical education in Canada. Closely affiliated with the Montreal General Hospital, it had relatively high admissions standards and a four-year curriculum rather than the typical two or three.[59] At McGill, Osler met his third key mentor, Dr. Robert Palmer Howard, with whom he developed an "almost

filial" relationship and who urged Osler to get a generalist scientific training rather than become a specialist in ophthalmology as he had originally planned.[60]

His time at McGill also reinforced the practical focus imparted by Osler's family values. According to Reid, his exposure to Howard influenced Osler "to feel that he must add to his equipment the functioning power of the executive, one who, once knowing his work to be right, would also put it over."[61] And through his reading during this period, he discovered and adopted an aphorism of Thomas Carlyle's as a personal philosophy: "Our grand business undoubtedly is, not to *see* what lies dimly at a distance, but to *do* what lies clearly at hand."[62]

After receiving the degree of doctor of medicine and master of surgery from McGill in 1872, Osler began a two-year European course of study. It was here that he saw the future—for the practice of medicine, for medical teaching and training, and for public health—and the foundation for his vision as it evolved over the following decades. He first spent over a year in London working primarily with Dr. John Burdon-Sanderson, a leading experimental physiologist and pathologist, whose lab generated many medical advances. Indeed, Osler himself did important research there on blood platelets.[63]

In the fall of 1873, Osler went for several months of study in Berlin and Vienna, the recognized centers for advanced medicine and medical training. He was extremely impressed, especially with the emphasis on research and clinical teaching. In Berlin, he was excited to observe the great pathologist Rudolf Virchow, who "performs a post-mortem on Monday morning making it with such care and minuteness that three or four hours may elapse before it is finished. The very first morning of my attendance he spent exactly half an hour in the description of the skull cap!"[64] Virchow was a model for the physician, scientist, and teacher that Osler aspired to be.

By the spring of 1874, Osler was ready to return home, where McGill offered him a position as lecturer in the Institute of Medicine. Though younger than many of his students, he became a well-regarded teacher, and at the end of the 1874–1875 academic year, he was promoted to professor.

Despite his success, he needed to earn more than his modest teaching salary if he was to live comfortably, much less adequately equip his students to realize his pedagogical vision. In 1874, he became a physician in Montreal General Hospital's smallpox ward and in 1876 was named the pathologist for a new smallpox hospital in the city. He took these opportunities to study the processes of this dreaded disease in detail and thus began his career as a great clinician and a prolific contributor to the literature of clinical medicine.[65]

Osler soon became the leader of a "renaissance" at McGill, spearheading improvements in clinical training and revising the curriculum. Starting with the introduction of an optional course on microscopy and histology based on teachings from Burdon-Sanderson that used student microscopes he purchased with his small salary from the smallpox ward, he followed it with another course on practical pathology performing autopsies at Montreal General. Sharing his clinical findings with the Medico-Chirurgical Society of Montreal, publishing them, and consulting for colleagues, he quickly became a respected pathologist in the city's medical community.[66] In 1878 he was appointed an attending physician at Montreal General and there, too, he soon made his mark. A colleague described the impact of the young reformer when he took over a section of the hospital while older doctors "looked at him with bated breath, expecting disastrous consequences." But Osler turned his ward

> from a sickroom into a bright, cheerful room of repose. Then he started in with the patients. Very little medicine was given. To the astonishment of everyone, the chronic beds instead of being emptied by disaster, were emptied rapidly through recovery... The revolution was wonderful. It was one of the most forceful lessons in treatment that has ever been demonstrated.[67]

Osler's travels gave him fresh exposure to developments in medicine and education, causing his vision to evolve further. On short trips to Harvard in 1876 and 1877 he examined President Charles Eliot's educational reforms and the quality of Harvard's medical facilities. Longer journeys to the International Medical Congress in London in 1881 and to Berlin in 1884 allowed him to keep up with the latest advances in medical science, such as bacteriology. With his prolific publications on a wide range of human pathological conditions, Osler's reputation in the international medical community steadily grew, as evidenced by his being named a fellow of the Royal College of Physicians in London.

How was Osler so productive? "The secret of successful working lies in the systematic arrangement of what you have to do," he told McGill students.[68] Indeed, a housemate described Osler as "more regular and systematic than words can say; in fact, it was hardly necessary, living in the house with him, to have a timepiece of one's own... He always had a day's work laid out before the day began," and was "always deliberate in every movement, never rushing, never hesitating."[69] Osler's day always concluded with an hour's reading of classical literature, after which his light switched off at 11 P.M. It was a routine that enabled him to be extraordinarily productive (and literate).

Despite the renaissance Osler led at McGill, he yearned for the opportunity to work in a more sophisticated environment where he might have a broader scope in which to realize his emerging vision. Thus, when the University of Pennsylvania offered him the chair of Clinical Medicine in 1884, he accepted after much thought, telling colleagues, "I must admit that I am leaving McGill for a larger field through *ambition*."[70]

Penn was one of the leading medical schools in the United States, but Osler was soon disappointed. The school was much more bureaucratic and conservative than McGill, and Osler was a youthful dynamo among many entrenched, change-resistant senior professors. Consequently, his ability to lead a reform of the medical school or of the university hospital was highly limited. He instead concentrated his energies on teaching and research, most notably a study of malaria, as well as presenting his work to local professional societies and to similar groups around the United States and beyond, building a network that he expanded and nurtured throughout his life.

Still, Osler wanted a platform for putting reforms into practice. Thus, in 1888, he seized the opportunity Johns Hopkins University offered to join several like-minded visionaries in building a new medical school and hospital from scratch. One was Daniel Coit Gilman, the university's founding president and an ambitious promoter of the hospital. Another was John Shaw Billings, a leading physician who designed hospitals during the Civil War. A medical reformer and advisor to the board, Billings believed that medical education needed to be redesigned to emphasize research and teaching in the clinical setting of a modern hospital. The third was Dr. William Welch, a pathologist who greatly admired German medicine and wished to emulate its emphasis on research. Hired a few years before Osler, Welch was largely responsible for attracting him to the hospital. Osler was named the hospital's physician-in-chief and professor of the theory and practice of medicine of the medical school, though the latter would not open until 1893.

It was at Hopkins, where he had the opportunity to work closely with Gilman and Welch in shaping the new institution, that Osler fully flowered as a leader. It was there that he would have the chance to create an innovative new culture and organization. As physician-in-chief, he had oversight of all doctors and used that power to hire and mold the kind of team that would help realize his vision of the scientific teaching and practice of medicine.

That *vision* had three major elements. The first was to adopt and improve on the German model he had admired in his trips to Berlin. At Hopkins, he sought to combine the best of the scientific research practices in German universities and the most effective pedagogical methods being used in Germany, the United Kingdom, and North America. To do both would in turn require a careful, innovative approach to the *organization* of the Johns Hopkins hospital and medical school, and Osler played a critical role in planning them. Shortly after joining Hopkins, he accompanied President Gilman to New York City to observe how the best hotels and department stores were run, an approach that Gilman wished to emulate in organizing the hospital. Osler agreed with his view, and wrote that the new departure in medical education at Johns Hopkins "was not the hospital itself, as there were many larger and just as good; it was not the men appointed, as there were others quite as well-qualified; it was the organization. For the first time in an English-speaking country, a hospital was organized in units—each one in charge of a head or chief."[71] That head in turn had real accountability for the performance of his department.

As physician-in-chief at the hospital, Osler worked hard to recruit strong department heads, who would chair those same departments within the medical school when it opened. While a number of these men were mediocre teachers, they were outstanding researchers and thus on the German model excellent catches.[72] He also mimicked the Germans in supporting department heads with strong senior resident physicians who were long-term. Osler personally chose the interns or junior residents and they reported directly to him, rather than rotating through the various departments as was the custom. Finally, Osler introduced the clinical clerkship in the fourth year of medical school, a practice long established in Canada and Britain, which enabled students to rotate through the wards and gave them some minor responsibility for patients. It was the last piece of Osler's pedagogy, of what he called "the natural method" of teaching medicine, with students launched as practitioners. "The best teaching," Osler held, "is that taught by the patient himself."[73]

All told, when combined with tough admissions standards and the superb equipment and facilities enabled by the Hopkins endowment, Osler's model gave medical students, interns, and senior residents an unprecedented education, and it provided patients with exceptional care. As Osler, Gilman, and others hoped, the Johns Hopkins Hospital became a place where one went to be cured, not to die.

Osler played an important role in aligning other factors to optimize Hopkins' effectiveness. He was instrumental in creating a set of shared research and teaching values based on a caring, collegial, and inspiring culture. Osler embodied these values and, as Bliss observed, "was always encouraging his staff to give papers and publish, or advising them on career opportunities and personal problems."[74] With colleagues, he founded a journal club, a medical society, and an historical club. And the *Johns Hopkins Hospital Bulletin* and the *Johns Hopkins Hospital Reports* were started as outlets for sharing their work and excitement with the medical community.[75] The flood of papers and articles that the research culture engendered quickly enhanced Hopkins' institutional skills and its medical reputation, which then attracted other qualified students and staff.

It is worth noting that Osler also promoted an egalitarian culture, one open to gender equity. At the time, no top-tier medical school in America would accept women students. Osler had observed in Europe that coeducation worked well. Thus when several daughters of Hopkins trustees offered in 1890 to raise $100,000 toward the $500,000 endowment required to open the medical school under the condition that coeducation be made available, Osler and others advised the university trustees to accept the offer. They did, despite severe opposition. Osler vigorously defended the board's action in *Century Magazine*, writing, "This is right: if any woman feels that the medical profession is her vocation, no obstacles should be placed in the way of her obtaining the best possible education."[76] More than a year later, Osler's enlightened stance was rewarded when the daughter of a trustee contributed the additional funds needed to reach the school's required endowment. As a result, instruction began in the autumn of 1893.

After the creation of the Hopkins model for medical education and practice, the emphasis turned to the second component of Osler's vision, his dream of establishing far more demanding standards for medical training and licensing in general. Late in the nineteenth century, licensing in states was haphazard or nonexistent, and medical school standards varied dramatically. Of the five other medical schools in Baltimore, the best ones offered only two years of instruction before awarding diplomas, and few students had undergraduate degrees. In addition, the rivalry between regular physician practitioners and other types of practitioners, especially homeopaths, was fierce. Osler became one of the foremost proponents of more rigorous medical education and state licensing, arguing that otherwise most medical degrees would become meaningless bits of paper.[77]

The third and final element of Osler's vision was to improve public health. He became an advocate in Maryland, using the new insights into the causes and spread of diseases to lead campaigns against typhoid and tuberculosis.

Persuading others of the wisdom of his vision required superb *communication skills*, skills that did not come naturally to Osler. As he himself recalled, "My first appearance before the class filled me with a tremulous uneasiness and an overwhelming sense of embarrassment."[78] It was only through diligent work on his speaking style as well as his students' appreciation of his knowledge of and enthusiasm for the material that he became the popular and masterful teacher generations of medical students so admired.[79]

Similarly, his writing style also evolved and improved over the years, in part as a result of the ongoing literary education he received from his hour of reading classical literature each evening and in part from the sheer volume of writing practice involved in his prolific correspondence and publishing. Osler's monumentally influential textbook, *The Principles and Practice of Medicine*, was issued in 16 editions and stayed in print from 1890 through 1947. Osler achieved "medical textbook writing at its best," according to Bliss, distinguished by "its extreme clarity, Osler's straightforward style, and the sense he conveyed that medicine was anything but cut-and-dried."[80] Indeed, in both his written work and in his lectures, he became a master of the memorable phrase, or what he called "burrs that stick in the memory."[81]

Perhaps the most important aspect of Osler's communication skills was how he embodied his message and vision. By the time he got to Hopkins, he had been an active advocate and, to the extent feasible, a successful practitioner of his proposed model of the scientific practice and teaching of medicine. Indeed, this was a major reason he was hired. Osler's embodiment of that aspiration proved to be critically persuasive in shaping and maintaining a caring, inspiring, and collegial culture. He lived by the golden rule, modeled a passion for research and teaching, and artfully nudged violators of those norms back into line.

For the second and third elements of Osler's vision to be realized, however, all of his communication skills were critical, especially as there was no formal organization supporting his efforts in the public arenas toward raising standards and improving public health. For example, in the battle to raise licensing standards, he was able to broker a compromise between homeopaths and regular medical practitioners in Baltimore that led to agreement to ask for state supervision in certain areas. In his advocacy of public health measures, he reached out to a number of factions in the Baltimore community—from politicians to the media to local practitioners—and regularly urged them to take more active steps. Indeed, his fierce insistence at a public meeting catalyzed the Baltimore authorities into finally taking the steps required to prevent the spread of typhoid fever.

Finally, it is difficult to separate Osler's embodiment of his vision from his caring *selflessness*. Literally everyone seemed to like him, and he was often referred to as "Christ-like." While he demonstrated personal ambition with his move to Hopkins, his central concern was to promote the worthiest of causes, the improvement of health care and human welfare. Although his private practice at Hopkins eventually made him an affluent man—a status he appreciated all the more because of his marriage to Grace Lindzee Revere in 1892, a widow with whom he had a son in 1895—he would always sacrifice financial gain for the benefit of those he was leading. When the Hopkins Hospital suffered serious damage from the Baltimore fire of 1904, Osler stepped forward to offer ten years of his salary to meet the need. Nor did building his personal reputation appear to be a major motivation for him. Although he was showered with honors over the course of his career, none seemed terribly important to him. His first duty was always to his students and patients. His habitual concern and kindness evoked enormous affection and respect. As one student at McGill said, "Once Osler shook his hand, the student had found a friend for life and he knew it."[82] Yet Osler did not develop these relationships by being undemanding. As a Hopkins colleague wrote, "His criticisms of students and their work were incisive and unforgettable, but never harsh or unkindly; they inspired respect and affection, never fear."[83]

His patients, too, felt that he was fully invested in their well-being. Edith Gittings Reid directly observed Osler at Hopkins, where she, her husband, and her children were his patients. "In a room full of discordant elements," Reid wrote, "he entered and saw only his patient and only his patient's greatest need, and instantly the atmosphere was charged with kindly vitality, everyone felt that the situation was under control, and all were attention... The moment Sir William gave you was yours."[84] His colleagues responded similarly. As Reid added, "Three times in my life have I seen him, when in consultation, smash the attending physician's diagnosis and turn the entire sick-room the other way about; but he left the room with his arm about the corrected physician's neck," and the reason, she wrote, was "perfectly evident: every physician felt himself safe in

Sir William's hands...that if, with the tip of his finger, Sir William gaily knocked down his house of cards, he would see to it that the foundation was left solid."[85]

What were the sources of Osler's caring selflessness? One appeared to be the core values that his parents imparted. Another was his positive outlook on life and his fellows that may have been the legacy of a happy childhood and adolescence. A third was likely the support, kindness, and role-modeling he experienced from his three mentors, Rev. Johnson, Dr. Bovell, and Dr. Howard. Still another was his own discovery of the virtues and satisfactions of working hard and focusing on the work at hand, as Carlyle's aphorism advised.

Even Osler, however, could not keep up the hard and focused work of his years at Hopkins indefinitely, and by 1904, he was exhausted. Consequently, when offered the prestigious, remunerative, and less demanding position of Regius Professor of Medicine at Oxford, he decided to take it. The reaction at Hopkins was both dismay and appreciation, with many believing that, as one colleague told Osler, "the success of the Hospital and Medical School has been largely your achievement."[86] Osler himself thought that American medicine was rapidly gaining. "I think at last we have got the Germans stirred up to the conviction that there is good work being done on the other side."[87]

Although his position and age limited his impact at Oxford, Osler remained true to form. He sought to modernize the pathology laboratory and facilities and expand the university's medical library. He started clinics to realize his vision for medical education.[88] And he entered fully into the broader British medical community and such public health issues as the fight against TB. In recognition of his lifetime contributions—and despite his initial reluctance—a hereditary baronetcy of the United Kingdom was conferred on him in 1911 by the new king George V and a knighthood in 1912. He was now Sir William Osler, Bart. Characteristically, he chose to attend a patient rather than the investiture ceremony for his baronetcy.[89]

During World War I, he became an honorary colonel in the Oxfordshire Regiment and a consulting physician to two hospitals. Among other activities he led a campaign for typhoid vaccinations in the army, prompted by the awareness that disease could cause more fatalities than combat. The war took a terrible toll on Osler and his family. His own efforts to support the troops exhausted him physically, and the loss of his son in combat was a severe blow emotionally. Perhaps in part as a result of these stresses, in late 1919 he succumbed to pneumonia.

Testimonials to Osler's life and work poured in from the international medical community. One contemporary, George Adami, pathologist and vice chancellor of the University of Liverpool, captured the impact of Osler's leadership, writing that among the great physicians, "those who by their lives, their practice, their teaching, and their writings, have exercised the greatest influence over the greatest number of their fellows...Osler must be awarded the first place." There was, Adami went on, "no one individual who has done so much to advance the practice of scientific medicine...no one, in short, who has combined in the same degree the study, practice, and teaching—the science and the art of medicine."[90]

★   ★   ★

In summary, while both Teller and Osler were effective direct leaders in the domain of science, only Osler was exceptional. His vision for improving the clinical practice and teaching of medicine was a splendid contribution to humankind. He also was uniquely able to promote and embody this vision, both within the institutions where he worked and throughout the international medical community, with his tireless teaching, writing, speaking, and networking. Importantly, he pursued his vision in an entirely selfless manner through his actions and habitually demonstrated that personal credit and acclaim meant little to him. As a result of this selfless motivation, both his colleagues and students trusted him completely and in many cases even revered him. Finally, Osler was able to leverage his personal impact through the practical, organizational abilities he demonstrated, most notably at Johns Hopkins.

Teller, of course, presents a very different profile. His vision remains controversial at best and potentially catastrophic for humankind at worst. His motivations were suspect and, many would argue, disturbingly self-interested. Indeed, he appeared willing to bend the truth on numerous occasions to present his vision more forcefully. His highly effective lobbying and communication skills, however, brought him impressive success throughout his career. Finally, while his organizational skills were limited, they were just good enough not to undermine his effectiveness.

In short, while their communication skills were key to both men's effectiveness, what made Osler exceptionally persuasive was the caring selflessness evident in his embodiment of his message. What made Teller so polarizing, in contrast, was in significant measure the suspect motivations and disingenuousness, including occasional dissembling, that underlay his message.

CHAPTER EIGHT

Napoleon and Augustus: Empire Builders

The subjects of this chapter, Napoleon Bonaparte and Caesar Augustus, were world-historical figures. Each came to power in the wake of a violent period of civil unrest and turmoil, and each ultimately chose to abandon nominally republican forms of government and establish authoritarian empires. Their motives were complex and their levels of success were distinctly different. Napoleon enjoyed a meteoric rise and experienced great military and political success initially. Yet he soon fell from power as the French Empire dissolved. Augustus, in contrast, seemed to have been the far more successful leader in light of his transformation of the Roman Republic into the Roman Empire. Still the question remains, was Augustus an exceptional leader?

We will argue that while both men were effective, only Augustus was exceptional, in important measure due to his greater skill in persuasively communicating his vision to others. For six decades, he consistently communicated a vision of Rome restored to its former glory and values. His message deemphasized his own interests while promoting the benefits his leadership brought to most citizens. Napoleon's evolving message, in contrast, increasingly identified the future of France and its empire with Napoleon himself. This vision grew less and less compelling as his self-interest became ever more evident and his seeming invincibility proved an illusion.

Napoleon

The natural spirit of man is the wish to dominate.[1]
　　　　　　—From an essay by the young Napoleon titled
　　　　　　　　　　　　　　　　"Réfutation de Roustan"

I love power...as a musician loves his violin, for the tones I can bring forth, for the chords and harmonies.[2]
　　　　　　　　　　　—Napoleon I, emperor of the French

Snow fell all night, and then December 2, 1804, dawned clear and cold in Paris. Shortly, Napoleon Bonaparte would depart the Tuileries in a magnificent procession to the Notre Dame Cathedral. Once there, in an elaborate ceremony attended by the pope he would crown himself emperor of the French. It was a spectacular achievement for someone who, at the beginning of the French Revolution only 15 years before, had been a 19-year-old junior officer in the army of King Louis XVI. The rise was to be accompanied by an equally dramatic fall not a dozen years later, ending with a final defeat at Waterloo. To what extent can the short life of the French Empire be attributed to the failure, or at least the limitations, of Napoleon's leadership?

Rise to Power

Napoleon Bonaparte was born on the island of Corsica on August 15, 1769, the second of eight children. The Bonapartes were a respectable family of Italian stock and modest means who, critically for Napoleon's future, were granted French patents of nobility during his childhood years. This allowed him to aspire to a career as an officer in the army. Thus, in 1778 Napoleon was sent to France to attend a series of elite schools until his graduation from the prestigious *École Militaire* in Paris at age 16. He excelled in school and in 1785 became one of the youngest (and the only Corsican) to be appointed a lieutenant in the Royal Artillery. Still, he chafed at the disdainful treatment he received from his snobbish, aristocratic classmates, becoming "taciturn, distant, irascible...famously disliked and feared."[3] Given these feelings of second-class citizenship and his family's historical involvement in the Corsican independence movement, Napoleon responded readily to the revolutionary impulse of 1789.

Economic mismanagement and social injustice were the primary causes of the challenge to King Louis XVI's absolute monarchy in the late 1780s. As France slid close to financial ruin in 1789, the king desperately convened a meeting of the Estates-General to address the problem. This meeting quickly spun out of his control. The First and Second Estates, the nobility and the clergy, were exempt from paying taxes. Each had a single vote, which they were unlikely to cast in favor of taxing themselves to solve the kingdom's financial crisis. Yet the far larger Third Estate, representing the tax-paying French public, also had only a single vote. When the king refused the Third Estate's demand to reform the voting rules, its delegates decided to meet separately as the National Assembly, thus touching off a revolution. At first, the Assembly's goals were relatively modest. It established a constitutional monarchy and reformed the privileges held by the nobility and clergy. However, in June 1791, Louis XVI tried to flee the country and other European monarchies threatened war to return him to the throne. The king was arrested and the monarchy abolished. The new National Convention, which replaced the National

Assembly, proclaimed France a republic. In April 1792, it also declared war on Austria and Prussia, and early the next year executed Louis XVI for treason.

Six years of civil turmoil and violence followed. The radical Jacobins seized power in 1793 and began a reign of terror to crush their domestic opposition. After more than 15,000 executions by guillotine in little more than a year, they were overthrown, and their leader, Robespierre, was guillotined in July 1794. A new constitution was written, and the government was restructured along more conservative lines. Executive control was given to a five-member group known as the Directory, and a new bicameral legislature was created.

Though he aligned himself fully with the Revolution, Napoleon spent more time during its first few years in Corsica on leave from the army than in France on active duty. It was only after returning to his regiment in 1793 that his star began to rise. At the time, the new French Republic's fortunes were at a low point. Civil war raged throughout the south of France, inflation soared, and food riots racked the major cities. Political factions were fighting to the death for control of the Revolution, and royalists at the major French naval base at Toulon turned the port over to the British. The Republic was starved for good news when Captain Bonaparte paid a call in September 1793 on Antoine Christophe Saliceti, a Corsican ally who was now the Jacobin representative to the republican army besieging Toulon. Through Saliceti's intervention, Napoleon was named to replace that army's wounded artillery commander. This was the junior officer's great opportunity, and he would not miss it. Napoleon devised a simple but effective strategy for taking Toulon and tirelessly promoted it. As biographer Steven Englund summarizes: Napoleon "thought more quickly, rose earlier, went to bed later, and talked more than anybody else."[4] The plan worked, with Napoleon bravely leading a number of the assaults. On December 17, Toulon fell, and soon thereafter, Napoleon was promoted to brigadier general and appointed artillery commander for the Army of Italy. By the age of 24, his rise to power had begun in earnest.

The next two years displayed Napoleon's political as much as his military skills, as he had to navigate the chaos created by the fall of the Jacobins in July 1794 and the interregnum that followed. In this turbulent but brief period, Napoleon was arrested, cleared, promoted to general, and then struck from the list of general officers in September 1795. A month later, however, he played an important role in suppressing a royalist insurrection. As a reward, he was named commander-in-chief of the Army of the Interior.

This promotion opened important opportunities to him. He met and soon married the aristocratic Josephine de Beauharnais, the one great love of his life. Then, in March 1796, he was given command of the Army of Italy. A series of stunning victories over the Austrians during the following year swelled his reputation as a military genius.

While Napoleon was in Italy, the situation in Paris remained tumultuous. The Directory, almost as badly mired in financial problems as Louis XVI had been, found itself under renewed attack from royalist and other conservative elements. The right-wing press targeted Napoleon too, accusing him of treason and characterizing the war in Italy as imperialist. Consequently, when the Directory staged a coup d'état against the legislature in September 1797, Napoleon sent one of his officers to lead the army investing Paris and help purge the legislature of the Directory's opponents. For this support, the Directory gave Napoleon command of the Army of the Orient formed to conquer Egypt.

As was almost expected by now, Napoleon swiftly achieved his military goal. To the conquered Egyptians, he offered himself as a revolutionary liberator and "lover of Islam."[5] The scientists and scholars who accompanied him founded the *Institut d'Égypte* to study all aspects of the country and discovered the Rosetta Stone. Yet the French grip on Egypt never was secure. Nationalist uprisings were brutally suppressed; the army's ranks were dangerously thinned by battle and disease. The British and Ottomans allied and finally drove out the decimated Army of the Orient in 1801.

Napoleon was long gone from Egypt by then. He had returned to France in October 1799 as a conquering hero, wearing "not his military uniform, but 'Egyptian' dress, complete with scimitar."[6] The oriental campaign had captured the popular imagination at a time when the political situation at home and abroad remained chaotic. The army was still entangled with Britain and the European monarchies in a war that showed no signs of decision. Domestically, the Directory clung to power only through such measures as forced loans to the state by the wealthy, mass military drafts, and controls on the freedom of the press.

The opportunity was ripe for a strong hand to seize the helm of the French ship of state. On November 9–10, 1799, Napoleon and an ally, Emmanuel Sieyès, staged a coup d'état. They overthrew the Directory and formed a three-person consulate with Roger Ducos. One of their first acts was to draft a new constitution, which placed the primary power of the government in the consulate, instead of the legislature. Moreover, within the consulate, the first consul was invested with the real authority while the other two held only consultative power. Not surprisingly, Napoleon was named first consul.

The next three years were a whirlwind of activity and achievement for Napoleon. Through a series of military victories and treaties with Britain and its European allies, he brought a short-lived peace to France for the first time in a decade. And by signing the Concordat with the pope, he created peaceful relations with the Catholic Church as well.

Domestically, Napoleon was equally busy. He instituted a series of civil and administrative reforms known collectively as the "blocks of granite," aimed at modernizing the system of civil government and achieving social peace. They included the establishment of the Bank of France to restore order to public finances; the reorganization of civil administration around a system of prefects and subprefects, which enabled top-down governmental control; the creation of a new educational system of state-supported high schools and universities; and the enactment of the Civil Code, a comprehensive body of laws that covered persons and property and, above all, guaranteed equality before the law. Many of these reforms still endure today and constitute Napoleon's legacy to the French nation.

Thus, within a decade, Napoleon had risen from a captain in the army to the pinnacle of power in the French Republic. In August 1802, he engineered his election as consul for life based on his enormous popularity. Why was his leadership during this period so effective?

In the first place, it is important to distinguish between Napoleon's military leadership and his civil, or political, leadership. His effectiveness in the former was, of course, the foundation for the latter. His *vision* for the army was twofold. He saw it as defending the French Republic from its external and internal enemies and spreading the Revolution to the rest of Europe. But the army's purpose was also to achieve victory and glory for both the *patrie* and the individual soldier. Unlike most commanders of the time, Napoleon saw in his soldier "not a machine to be put in motion but a reasonable man to be directed." He thought men should be ruled by the "stimulus of honour," motivated by emulation and the opportunity to rise in the ranks.[7]

Napoleon *communicated* his message in a variety of ways. In the first Italian campaign, for example, he published two newspapers, *France Seen from the Army of Italy* and *The Mail of the Army of Italy*. They enabled him to convey his story as well as interpretations of events at home to both the army and the French public. He also issued inspiring proclamations summoning his soldiers to pride and glory: "All of you want to be able to say, when you return to your villages one day, I was in the conquering Army of Italy."[8] He was a master at adapting himself to different audiences. With his generals, Englund notes, Bonaparte was all military in style and speech, and he exercised extraordinary authority over them: "[T]hey became his men to a degree they were never anyone else's."[9] With the common soldiers, he employed a variety of gestures to demonstrate his concern for their well-being, which earned their respect and often their love. For example, Napoleon's secretary told of how the general would be briefed on the background and service record of a soldier in the ranks before each troop review. On the day of the review Napoleon would go up to the soldier "as if he recognised him, address him by his name, and say, 'Oh! So you are here! You are a brave fellow—I saw you at Aboukir—how is your old father? What! Have you not got the Cross? Stay, I will give it to you.' Then the delighted soldiers would say to each other, 'You see the Emperor knows us all; he knows our families; he knows where we have served.'"[10] During the Egyptian campaign, he personally cared for some of his soldiers stricken with plague. He said in Egypt: "I shall always be disposed to do for my soldiers what I would do for my own son."[11]

The civil aspect of Napoleon's vision was to achieve social peace and lasting glory through the reestablishment of a centralized governance structure in France with a strong, stable ruling hand. Not a surprising vision for a military man, it also resonated with a public that was weary of civil turmoil and violence and was willing to trade some of the theoretical benefits of democracy for social peace.

Once again, Napoleon artfully communicated both aspects of his vision using a variety of means, unapologetically adapting his message and even his persona to his audience. "It was by making myself a Catholic," he said at the time of the Concordat, "that I won the war in the Vendée, by making myself a Moslem that I established myself in Egypt... If I were to govern a nation of Jews I would rebuild the Temple of Solomon."[12] He also intuitively understood the power of propaganda and symbols and the intoxicating effects of victory. He rode the wave of his military success into the position of first consul, artfully combining his vision of a new, strong, and centralized civil order with its revolutionary antecedents. As he declared when presenting the new constitution in December 1799, it "is founded on the true principles of representative government, on the sacred rights of property, equality, and liberty." He added, "Citizens, the Revolution is established on the principles which began it. It is finished."[13]

His genius extended to creating effective civil *organizations* and institutions as well. The achievements of his first three years as consul—the "blocks of granite," the Concordat, an amnesty for returning French émigrés, and the 1802 Peace of Amiens with Britain—led to the first real stability experienced by the French Republic. Although the new civil government was not a perfect meritocracy, it nonetheless came far closer than any prior regime and included many with real experience regardless of their political sympathies. Similarly, he chose very gifted officers to serve under him in the army, and he drove them and his civil subordinates mercilessly, although no harder than he drove himself. Finally, he created the Legion of Honor, an award for military or civilian excellence that was open to all. The results were effective supporting organizations in both the military and civil spheres, all reporting to him alone.

Why did the French people allow this accumulation of personal power only ten years after revolting against the absolute monarchy of Louis XVI? Partly, of course, because they wished for stability. In part, too, because Napoleon's military victories intoxicated them and led them to hope he could achieve the same success domestically. But he kept and even increased that power primarily because his reforms appeared to be in the best interests of the French people, even if they were clearly in his interests as well. Indeed, through the entire period to this point, the degree of his *self-interest* was not tested seriously by a clear conflict with the people's best interests. That test, however, was soon to come.

Empire and Fall

The dramatic pace did not slow once Napoleon assumed sole power. The resumption of war in 1803, continuing royalist plots, and Napoleon's own initiatives combined to make the next decade as fast-paced as the first one. But somewhere in the transition from first consul to life consul to emperor, Napoleon's balance shifted from working more for the best interests of the French people to working more for his own personal glory.

A royalist conspiracy early in 1804 gave additional momentum to the movement, nurtured by Napoleon, to reestablish a hereditary monarchy as a means of providing stability to the state in a time of war. It was rationalized as importantly different from the former monarchy since Napoleon had earned the position on merit, not by birth, and because he would be the emperor of the French, not France. Thus, in May 1804, the French Empire was proclaimed and in December, Napoleon crowned himself emperor in Notre Dame Cathedral. Quickly, he recreated the pomp and panoply of an imperial court, complete with a new aristocratic class, an elaborate official hierarchy, and costumes to boot. Later he would appoint various family members as kings and viceroys in conquered lands, including Italy, Spain, and Holland.

The French people supported the new imperial regime enthusiastically because they shared in the material and psychological benefits of Napoleon's continued success. After decisively defeating the Russians and Austrians at Austerlitz in 1805, Prussia at Jena-Auerstedt in 1806, and Russia at Friedland in 1807, the French controlled much of Europe, either directly or as satellite states. Moreover, during this period of "high" Empire, the French economy prospered. As Englund notes, "The great majority of *le peuple* were fervent fans of *l'Empereur*, in whom they saw a justiciar and a champion, the leader who assured (more or less) bread and jobs."[14]

In the conquered territories, however, discontent mounted. France claimed to be "liberating" subject peoples even as they faced forced conscription into the French army, repressive government, and steep taxes. Nationalist stirrings contributed to renewed warfare between France and the allies.

Nonetheless, the tide turned very slowly as Napoleon's success continued with victories in Spain and Austria, as well as annexations of the Papal States and Holland. He also worked hard at ensuring his dynastic succession. Despite his great love for Josephine, he divorced her because she had not borne him a male heir, married an Austrian archduchess, Marie-Louise, in the spring of 1810, and sired Napoleon II, who was born in 1811.

But Napoleon's ill-fated decision to invade Russia in 1812 exposed the weak foundations of his empire. Fighting through to Moscow, he arrived in September to find the city abandoned and in flames, with insufficient resources to supply his army through the winter. In the resulting retreat, the French army suffered catastrophic losses—of men, of materiel, and of its aura of invincibility. More setbacks followed swiftly as the Empire dissolved. By February 1814, Paris was surrounded by foreign armies and Napoleon was forced to abdicate. His spectacular return from exile on

Elba in 1815 concluded less than four months later with a resounding and final defeat at Waterloo. The allies exiled Napoleon to the remote island of St. Helena in the South Atlantic, while in Paris the old monarchy was restored under Louis XVIII.

What changed to make Napoleon's leadership so much less effective under the Empire than it had been before? Or perhaps a better question would be what became more apparent about his leadership during the period of the Empire? In the end his supreme self-confidence, his obsession with glory, and his belief in his own destiny proved to be fatal flaws. When combined with his unparalleled record of success through the period of the consulate, they led him to think himself the only man capable of ruling France. Indeed, he believed both that "France needs me more than I need her,"[15] and that "my domination will not survive the day I stop being strong and feared."[16] As a result, his behavior grew increasingly despotic over the years of the Empire. His self-centered melding of his own interests—indeed his own identity—with the interests and identity of France became ever more apparent through his communications and his actions.

Under the Empire, the *vision* Napoleon was communicating to the French people became far more about his glory than about the glory of France. The tag lines of defending the Republic and spreading the Revolution atrophied. The army's battle cry changed from *"Vive la Republique!"* to *"Vive l'Empereur!"* And in 1811, Englund notes, "the year of the birth of Napoleon's son, they swore to be faithful to the dynasty as well as the Sovereign and the State."[17] This shift in the balance of his message was gradual, not sudden. Much earlier, when Napoleon became life consul in 1802, his birthday was made a state holiday and his profile began to appear on coins.

As Napoleon gradually became the living embodiment of the nation, his patience with diplomacy, negotiation, and consultation grew ever shorter. In foreign affairs, he appeared to be convinced that he could do no wrong. For example, after his defeat of the Prussians at Jena in 1806, he offered draconian terms that made an irreconcilable enemy of the Prussian king. Metternich thought that if Napoleon had not sought Prussia's destruction, he might have built "a stable, solid, lasting base to the immense edifice that he had managed to raise."[18] A few months later, he compounded his error by firing his skilled foreign minister, Talleyrand, who had been urging him to rely more on diplomacy than warfare. Without Talleyrand's moderating influence, Napoleon grew ever more despotic in his relations with foreign states. His treatment of Pope Pius VII, whom he literally held hostage in an effort to replace papal power with his own, is yet another example.

Domestically, too, his willingness to consult with others and observe democratic forms, which was never great, became almost nonexistent as he came to rule by edict. Indeed, as early as his days as first consul, he had said, "When all is organized...it is natural that the work of administration should increase and that of legislation diminish."[19] Historian H. A. L. Fisher writes that in Napoleonic government, law was "derived from the administration, enforced by the administration, interpreted by the administration."[20] At the same time, Napoleon's tolerance of dissent disappeared. For example, he responded to a severe economic crisis in 1810–1811 by increasing police surveillance of potential sources of opposition and disorder. The result of this increasingly despotic behavior together with diminishing success in the field was that his *communication* began to be less persuasive to the French people. They had been willing to sacrifice all for the Revolution and for Napoleon as its guardian, but they were tired. Their country had been at war for much of the past two decades and 1.4 million French soldiers had lost their lives, including 900,000 in the wars of the Empire.[21] The economic boom of the Empire's early days had been succeeded by the crisis of 1810–1811, which would persist through the military defeats that followed. Finally, these defeats demonstrated that Napoleon was no longer invincible, nor did he seem first and foremost to speak for the people or care for their interests. Thus, it was not surprising that only 63,000 of the 300,000 drafted for the army in the spring of 1814 actually enlisted. The Senate's proclamation of Napoleon's abdication shortly thereafter made it official: Napoleon was not the state after all.

During the period of the Empire, Napoleon's supporting military and civil **organizations** also became markedly less effective. As noted earlier, by 1800 both the military and the civil government reported to Napoleon alone. While that was a highly efficient arrangement for mobilizing the military in times of war and for pushing through the reforms instituted during the Consulate, it proved to be an ineffective structure for governing an empire the size of Europe, especially when the emperor would not entrust his subordinates with any real power. Therefore, when Napoleon was leading the army abroad, the civil government was rudderless.[22] Moreover, though he chose family members to rule over conquered territories within the Empire, he kept them on a short leash and did not hesitate to intervene or even depose them when things went poorly. The army, too, was managed by Napoleon on a highly centralized basis although its structure of seven self-contained corps, each with its own cavalry, artillery, and infantry, as well as seasoned leadership, could have allowed for decentralized accountability. As he once confided, "For all the faith I have in French valor, I have equal faith in my lucky star, or perhaps in myself, and as a result I never count positively on victory unless I myself am in command."[23] The resulting dependence on Napoleon's personal presence and leadership was an increasing problem as the French Empire grew, one that perhaps even Napoleon recognized. Having just beaten the Austrian army at Ulm in October 1805, he learned of the pivotal French naval defeat at Trafalgar and grumbled, "I can't be everywhere at once."[24]

In short, the effectiveness of Napoleon's leadership ultimately was corrupted by his egotism, ambition, and inability or unwillingness to subordinate his own interests for those of the people. This *self-centeredness* came to dominate the content of his communications, which increasingly focused on himself and his achievements and values, and manifested itself in his need for personal control. He could not delegate, and when setbacks began to occur as a result, his reaction was to distrust others even more. Joseph Fouché, the commander of the Paris police, called Napoleon "perhaps the most easily offended and most mistrustful man who ever lived."[25] Indeed, because of his ego and his unsurpassed ambition, one could argue that Napoleon never really had the people's interests in mind. In a candid conversation in 1803, he claimed that he had "always known" that the Revolution's "advantages" would never accrue to the "people" in whose name it had been proclaimed.[26] Certainly no one benefited from it more than himself, driven by the ambition he articulated in 1796: "In our time, no one has the slightest conception of what is great. It is up to me to give them an example."[27] His brother Lucien saw it early, writing to another brother in 1792 that "I've long discerned in him a completely self-centered ambition that outstrips his love for the common good."[28]

Still, Napoleon was a complex man with sometimes-conflicting motivations. It may be more accurate to say that he viewed the achievement of his own ambition and the common good as one and the same. That they were not the same Napoleon himself seemed to realize at the close of the Empire. As the Allies invaded France in early 1814, he admitted, "I have made too much war...I was wrong: my projects were not in proportion to the strength and desires of the French people."[29] Even so, he retained many followers to the last, especially in the army, as his spectacular return from Elba demonstrated. He tried then to present himself as a changed man, assuring the public that "I know now what has to be avoided, I know now what has to be valued: peace and liberty."[30] Even if true, it was a lesson learned too late, as the Allied powers were determined that Napoleon would not return again.

Augustus

> Festina lente [make haste slowly].[31]
>
> —Augustus's maxim

On August 19, 14 CE, Caesar Augustus lay on his deathbed surrounded by his family and friends. He was 76 years old, and it had been more than 58 years since his adoptive father, Julius Caesar, was assassinated. He had adroitly navigated swirling and deadly political waters, risen to become the de facto ruler of Rome, ended the civil wars that had plagued Rome for almost a century, and expanded Rome's borders and influence more than any ruler before or after. All of this was done, he professed throughout his lifetime, to preserve the Roman Republic, not to found an empire. Indeed, unlike Napoleon, he never sought or

accepted dictatorial power, and he was careful to follow Roman traditions and to style himself as simply Rome's "leading citizen."[32] Yet
while he never held permanent positions of power, over the years he
had patiently appropriated all of the functions of power. And for decades
he had been grooming a series of potential successors from among his
family. So how should we interpret the comments that Suetonius tells
us Augustus made to the family and friends gathered around his bed
that day? He asked: "Have I played my part in the farce of life creditably
enough?" and added the tag:

> If I have pleased you kindly signify
> Appreciation with a warm goodbye.[33]

Was it all an act, and what does it say about his leadership?

Rise to Power

Augustus was born Gaius Octavius in Rome on September 23, 63 BCE.[34]
His father was a member of a wealthy, equestrian family, while his
mother was the daughter of Julius Caesar's sister. By the time Augustus's
father died in late 59 BCE, Caesar was already a consul, one of two who
together were the annually elected leaders of Rome. In the following
year, he became proconsul—governor and military commander—of the
province of Gaul. There his conquests would set the stage for his eventual rise to dictator-for-life and his resulting assassination on the Ides of
March, 44 BCE.

While Augustus is unlikely to have met his great-uncle until he was an
adolescent, it is reasonable to assume that Caesar's shadow loomed large over
his childhood. In 48 BCE, the year that Augustus went through the *toga virilis*
ceremony and legally entered manhood, Caesar won the battle of Pharsalus
over his great rival Pompey the Great and became the de facto sole ruler.
From this point onward, Caesar took a personal interest in the development
of his great-nephew. For example, he soon promoted Augustus's election
to one of the priesthoods, giving him his first public role. When Caesar
returned to Rome in the summer of 46 BCE after still another military campaign, Augustus became an escort and was given some minor administrative responsibilities. This amounted to a leadership apprenticeship for the
observant youth, as well as a proclamation of his special relationship with
the most powerful man in Rome. When Augustus arose from his sickbed to
join Caesar on a military campaign in Spain, he seemed to have cemented
a strong relationship with his great-uncle. Caesar soon raised him to the
aristocratic patrician class and sent him to Macedonia in late 45 BCE to
complete his education. Most importantly, according to Suetonius, Caesar
secretly wrote a will in September 45 BCE adopting Augustus and leaving three-quarters of his estate to him. Thus, when Augustus returned
to Italy shortly after hearing of his great-uncle's assassination in March of

44 BCE, he learned, possibly to his surprise, that he was a wealthy heir and very likely a marked man.

For at least 50 years prior to the rise of Julius Caesar, the Roman Republic had suffered from repeated episodes of war, civil strife, and turmoil. While many elements combined to weaken the fabric of the Republic, the most critical was the growing role of armed force in its government. As the power of Rome's generals backed by factions of the army increased, so did dangers of insurrection. The Senate, the Republic's principal legislative body, was powerless to resist these threats, including Sulla's march on Rome in 88 BCE, the first time that a Roman citizen had entered the city with an army and seized power through military force.[35]

Julius Caesar's career both contributed to the turmoil of the late Republic and pointed toward a potential resolution. On the one hand, Caesar rose to prominence and power on the basis of his brilliant military successes in Gaul and Britain, which earned him the loyalty of his troops and a large set of followers, along with the jealousy of rivals. Inevitably he became embroiled in power politics, and in 60 BCE, he became a member of the First Triumvirate with Pompey and Crassus, the other most powerful men of the period. This unofficial alliance effectively controlled the Senate until Crassus was killed and his army destroyed while battling the Parthians in 53 BCE. After that, relations between Pompey and Caesar deteriorated, leading eventually to Caesar's famous crossing of the Rubicon in 49 BCE, when he defeated Pompey in a civil war.

From that point on, Caesar was the first man in Rome and dominated its government, working hard to stabilize the city against internal and external threats. He utilized a very different model of government than the old Republic. In his years of near-absolute power, Caesar displayed little regard for the Senate and the republicanism it symbolized. When in February 44 BCE, the Senate named him dictator-for-life and awarded him the hereditary title *Imperator*, it was not hard for his enemies to imagine the next step as being the establishment of a hereditary monarchy and the end of the Republic.

Thus, when Caesar was assassinated a month later, Augustus found himself on center stage, under the spotlight, and in a very precarious position. The world and he himself only now discovered that he was Caesar's adopted son and heir, which made him a leading threat to the assassins and their goal of restoring the Republic. Likewise, he was a potential figurehead to his adopted father's followers, while Caesar's ambitious lieutenants, such as Mark Antony, would likely have viewed him as a rival. Indeed, his position was so perilous that some advised him to decline the adoption and retire to a quiet life in the countryside. But whether from a motive of duty, ambition, self-preservation, or some combination of them all, he decided to pursue his destiny. Like a good Roman, he would protect his *dignitas* (dignity, position, and authority) and honor the memory of his adoptive father by accepting his inheritance, fulfilling his legacy, and punishing his murderers. It would take 14 years for Augustus to become the undisputed first citizen of Rome and begin the transformation of the Roman Republic into the Roman Empire. Along the journey he would become masterful at "making haste slowly," in stark contrast to the impatient and impetuous style of his adoptive father—and of Napoleon.

As Augustus began his rise to power, he almost immediately began to display the signs of political genius that would characterize his long career. He quickly reassured Cicero, the elder statesman in the Senate and Caesar's fierce critic, that he had no intention of seizing power but would use only constitutional means to attain his inherited rights. He also made contact with Caesar's followers, both to assert his place as Caesar's heir and to supplement his financial resources. He then used his capital to begin raising troops and to pay the bequests to the Roman people specified in Julius's will, thus gaining much popular support. He insisted, too, upon being called Gaius Julius Caesar, his new name by adoption, in order to widely promote himself as Caesar's son and heir. Indeed, he showed himself an early master of propaganda. During a ten-day set of games to celebrate Caesar's victories that he sponsored within months of the assassination, a comet appeared each night. It became known as "the star of Julius" and was taken as evidence of the general's divinity. Ever one to seize an opportunity, Augustus had the star placed on Caesar's statues and on coins; it was useful to be known as the son of a god. Finally, he made his intention to avenge his father's murder very clear, though again only by lawful, constitutional means. Not a bad start by someone who was still a teenager.

As events unfolded, Augustus also demonstrated that he was "flexible, adaptable, shrewd, eminently realistic, and totally ruthless," as his modern biographer Pat Southern pithily summarizes his character.[36] Within a year of Caesar's assassination, he had positioned himself with Cicero's help as a protector of the Senate. He was appointed to military command by the two ruling consuls and allied with them against Mark Antony, who as Caesar's leading general was seen as the most imminent threat to the Republic. However, when Antony was defeated and both consuls killed, the Senate, again led by Cicero, quickly pivoted to view the survivor, Augustus, as the rising threat. Cicero's famous pun was that Augustus should be praised, honored, and immortalized—*laudandum adulescentem, ornandum, tollendum*—with *tollendum* also meaning removed or destroyed.

Despite this poor treatment, Augustus kept silent and bided his time, displaying the patience and ability to mask his emotions and intentions that would characterize his entire career. Within months, he seized the opportunity to become consul, outfoxing Cicero and forcing the Senate to pay his soldiers what it had promised them prior to the campaign against Antony, roughly ten times their annual pay. He then used his consular position to legalize his adoption and to prosecute and convict Caesar's assassins in absentia. Yet Augustus was keenly aware that his hold over the Senate was tenuous, and he also feared that he was vulnerable to renewed conflict with Antony and his still powerful army. An alliance with the man who was Caesar's general became imperative, and as an overture Augustus arranged for the Senate to revoke Antony's outlaw status. He then negotiated as an equal partner with Antony and another new ally, Lepidus, a powerful provincial governor, to create the Second Triumvirate. While this alliance may have been distasteful to Augustus, it also put a sufficient force behind the effort to pursue and destroy the key conspirators, Brutus and Cassius, who controlled Rome's eastern provinces. The Senate granted the three triumvirs nearly dictatorial powers, with the ability to make laws and appoint government officials. Each was also appointed to the governorship and accompanying military commands of one or more provinces. Importantly, the triumvirs also limited their appointments to a five-year term, thus avoiding Caesar's mistake of accepting his role in perpetuity.

It is during the triumviral years that we see most clearly not only Augustus's opportunism and shrewdness, but also his ruthlessness. Indeed, one of the Triumvirate's first acts was the "proscription" of all those whom they viewed as opponents. These were in fact death lists. The first, with 17 names, included Cicero, and the total number of victims ranged from Livy's tally of more than 130 senators to Plutarch's count of 300 senators and 3,000 *equites* (members of the second-ranked equestrian class). Both ancient and modern authors have attempted to excuse Augustus as a reluctant participant in these multiple executions. Still, Augustus's own efforts in later years to cast the blame for the proscriptions on his fellow triumvirs, especially Antony, and to obscure his own role, testifies to the ruthlessness of the deeds.[37] Does this purge lead us to conclude that Augustus was at his core a despot, who relied primarily on the use of force to lead? Or is this single episode in straitened times outweighed by his reliance on persuasion over most of his 58-year career? We incline to the latter interpretation, but must acknowledge that Augustus's means in this instance were immoral, even if they were understandable given his struggle for survival in a deadly political environment.

Having eliminated the immediate opposition, the Triumvirate's next order of business was to punish the principal conspirators who had fled Rome. In 42 BCE, Antony and Augustus combined to defeat first Cassius and then Brutus, with Antony properly gaining most of the glory, thus avenging Caesar and recapturing the rich, eastern provinces. For the next eight years, the Triumvirate ruled Rome through an uneasy but largely effective union with Antony responsible for the east, Lepidus for Africa, and Augustus for Italy and the west. The alliance began to crack in 36 BCE when Lepidus attempted to take Sicily from Augustus, failed, and was exiled. The fraying relationship between Antony and Augustus reached a breaking point when Antony repudiated Augustus's greatly admired sister, Octavia, whom he had married in 40 BCE to cement his alliance with Augustus. He then wed the Egyptian queen Cleopatra, Caesar's former mistress, an act that was doubly illegal under Roman law since she was a foreigner and he had not yet formally divorced Octavia.

Even worse, in a ceremony known as the Donations of Alexandria in 34 BCE, Antony asserted that Caesar's rightful heir was not Augustus but Caesarion, the son born of Julius's affair with Cleopatra. The Donations then went on to divide the eastern territories among Cleopatra and her children, three of whom she had with Antony. Despite these provocations, Augustus continued to let events unfold, waiting for an opportunity to paint Antony as a traitor and enemy of Rome. In 32 BCE, the moment arrived when he obtained Antony's will by suspect means. As Augustus read it to the Senate, the will reaffirmed Caesarion as Julius's lawful heir. It also declared Antony's wish, especially shocking to traditionalists, that he be buried not in Roman soil but in Alexandria. When Augustus made his case that Antony had become corrupted by the orient and that Cleopatra was an enemy of Rome bent on world conquest, the senators were easily persuaded. They declared war on Egypt, a war that ended with the defeat of Antony and Cleopatra at the battle of Actium in 31 BCE and their suicides less than a year later.

Thus, after 14 years of "making haste slowly," Augustus was in sole control of the Roman state, including the wealth and food supply of Egypt. How had he risen to power successfully? Certainly one reason was the attractiveness of the *vision* he conveyed to Caesar's followers in the army, the general populace, and what remained of the ruling classes. As the great man's legitimate heir, he would preserve his memory, maintain and extend his achievements, and punish his murderers. More than that, Augustus was a defender of the Roman Republic and its values. As he stated in the *Res Gestae*, his posthumously published memoirs, "I success-fully championed the liberty of the republic when it was oppressed by the tyranny of a faction."[38]

While one can quarrel with the objectivity of Augustus's own testi-mony on his motives, he did become expert at *communicating* his narrative in a variety of ways. To begin with, he could speak well, a vital skill in an era when rhetoric was valued and admired. Although over time he came to value *eloquentia* as "the skill of hiding one's eloquence rather than its public demonstration,"[39] early in his career on the public stage it was vital for him to make his case as Caesar's legitimate heir and avenger per-suasively to the army and to Caesar's followers. At the same time, he had to reassure supporters of the Republic that not only had he no intention of establishing the monarchy that they had feared from Caesar, but also that he would defend the Republic and achieve his goals constitutionally. Finally, he had to accomplish all this while convincing his rivals, includ-ing Cicero and Antony, that he was more their ally than an opponent. No wonder Suetonius reported that Augustus soon adopted the habit of writ-ing down what he intended to say both publicly and privately, "haunted by a fear of saying either too much or too little if he spoke off-hand."[40]

Equally important was Augustus's embodiment of his narrative. Although he was not a great general, and indeed was sickly throughout his life, he nonetheless demonstrated bravery in battle on several occa-sions, a vital quality in a martial period when generals led from the front.

Simultaneously, he underscored his modesty by representing his victories as being not for his glory but that of Rome and of Julius Caesar's memory. In stark contrast to many others in the period of the late Republic, he was also scrupulous about observing, while at the same time exploiting, constitutional means to accomplish his ends. For example, when a former friend became an enemy, Augustus, Southern writes, "went to considerable lengths to arraign [him] before the Senate, thus converting him from merely a personal enemy into an enemy of the entire state."[41] Similarly, Augustus patiently maneuvered the Senate into declaring war on Cleopatra, the foreigner with supposed aspirations of world conquest, not Antony, the Roman citizen.

Had Augustus relied solely upon modes of communication that depended upon his personal presence or his writing to convey his vision, he would have reached only a small fraction of the many constituents of Rome. Equally important was his mastery of the forms of mass communication. In the absence of modern media or widespread literacy, he creatively used coinage, art, and literature to glorify Julius Caesar's memory and to promote his own status as Caesar's son and heir. Shortly after the Second Triumvirate was formed, Augustus and the allies had the Senate swear an oath to uphold all of Caesar's earthly acts, and also proclaim his divinity. This enabled Augustus officially to call himself *Imperator Caesar divi filius*, or the son of a god, which he happily did. Soon new coins were issued with this inscription. Even sling bullets in Augustus's army were engraved with the words *Divus Julius*.

Given its wide circulation and pictorial format, what better way could there be than coinage to communicate to both soldiers and civilians, regardless of language or literacy? Caesar, too, had utilized the medium, becoming, according to historian Fergus Millar, the first known case of a "living Roman being portrayed on a Roman coin."[42] All three triumvirs followed his lead. Augustus issued coins showing his head on one side and Caesar's on the other to advertise his connection and dedication to the memory of the godlike hero.[43] Still others pictured Augustus wearing a beard, a symbol of grief for Caesar. Once Augustus was fully in control after the defeat of Antony and Cleopatra in 31 BCE, Millar writes, "almost every single issue of official Roman coinage, in gold, silver, and bronze, portrays Octavian-Augustus."[44] Moreover, as classicist Zvi Yavetz notes, "no longer was a young Octavian represented on coins with his face encircled by a beard...but a new idealized image of a great man and a great warrior emerged...an Augustus whose physique embodied a new political ideal."[45]

Literature also was a useful means of communicating to the literate, especially if the praise for Augustus's vision and actions came from great and widely admired poets like Virgil and Horace, who had become part of his circle when he was a triumvir. A final means of effective mass communication was through games, building projects, and other civic improvements to Rome itself. Beginning in this period Augustus encouraged his generals and other close associates who had prospered through their association with him to join him in sharing their wealth with Rome's citizens. While Augustus was patiently building his case against Antony and Cleopatra, one of his closest associates, Marcus Agrippa, became the magistrate responsible for the city's infrastructure. In that capacity, he spent a considerable portion of his own war-won fortune in constructing a new aqueduct, repairing the old ones, and putting on games for the general public.

All of this was clever propaganda. Augustus was using available forms of communication to help his cause and to hurt his enemies and rivals. But his propaganda also promoted what Augustus genuinely believed to be best for the people of Rome. Historian Walter Eder concludes that the result of the propaganda was "an increasing, self-incurred obligation on the part of Octavian's circle to act as protectors of the Roman values and traditions." What had been propaganda became "a program that, by its mere existence, achieved a reality of its own and thus no longer admitted... of any distinction between seeming and being."[46]

Augustus also displayed outstanding *organizational skills* during his rise to power, and he further refined them over the rest of his career. For example, he quickly tapped his adoptive father's many followers to build a fund-raising network. Because he understood the power of reward systems, he used his wealth and position to compensate his soldiers handsomely. Significantly, he surrounded himself with capable lieutenants and relied on them extensively, most particularly Agrippa in military affairs and Maecenas in diplomacy. Maecenas also played a critical role in attracting the circle of poets and writers associated with Augustus. Southern points out that where Augustus "lacked certain qualities he used the skills of other people to fill the gap; indeed, much of his success can be laid at the door of his associates, in whom he inspired a loyalty that scarcely ever wavered."[47]

Thus, for at least a significant proportion of the Roman people, Augustus had a compelling vision for Rome's future, which he communicated persuasively in a variety of ways. He also patiently and methodically gathered the reins of power with the support of an effective network of supporters, as well as his army.

To what degree was he at the same time *selfless*, and how did that quality affect his rise to power? If the ultimate test is sacrificing personal interests for the greater good of the group, there is no evidence that he did so. In his eyes and those of his supporters, in that chaotic period what was good for Augustus was good for Rome. If a less severe test is appearing to act primarily in the interest of Rome, then, the answer would seem to be "yes." No matter what one might believe about his underlying motives, he was careful to premise all of his actions upon the major elements of his narrative. For example, consistent with his posture as a defender of Roman values and the Republic, he dropped the title of "triumvir" once war was declared on Cleopatra in order, Southern writes, to "persuade the ruling class and the populace that not only did he intend no harm, but that he was acting positively on their behalf, with their best interests always at heart."[48] Augustus respected the Senate and was equally solicitous of his soldiers. During a demobilization after Actium, he sold some of his personal property to pay for their pensions and to purchase farmland for them. Not only did this gain him credit with his army, it also endeared him to Roman taxpayers in general and to farmers who had been subjected to land confiscations in the past. Finally, he strictly controlled his demeanor to mask personal emotions or interests. Indeed, according to Yavetz, "he very much admired the old Athenodoros [his tutor], who taught him to recite the twenty-four letters of the alphabet before saying anything in anger. Augustus learned from him the principle that silence generates wisdom."[49] Silence can also suggest detachment and the concealing of any hint of self-interest.

Was Augustus's selflessness during this period of his life purely show, ungrounded in reality? There is no question that his varied and complex motives included his personal survival and ambition as well as a desire to preserve his *dignitas*. Moreover, his posture as a defender of the Roman Republic might appear as expediency at best and dishonesty at worst in light of the Republic's eventual disappearance. Yet Augustus's dedication to Roman values and the Roman people was a genuine personal belief that had deepened with his leadership experience. This was true even when the deadly political environment forced him to focus on survival and act ruthlessly at times. Augustus's propaganda had been transmuted over time into "a program that...no longer admitted...any distinction between seeming and being." Moreover, so had his motivations. If one believes that it is difficult, if not impossible, to fool all the people, the best evidence for this transmutation is the "astonishing fact," as Eder calls it, that so soon after Actium Augustus "was able almost instantaneously to dispense with martial threats—directing the silver statues that commemorated his own career to be melted down, sending the greater part of his soldiery home, and becoming a beloved prince of peace."[50] No doubt some found it personally advantageous to side with the winning party and all welcomed peace after decades of civil strife, but the vast majority must have found his vision attractive and believable for such a transition to occur.

In summary, Augustus at age 33 had become a highly effective leader, if not yet an exceptional one. The overriding question at the time must have been: having gained power could he keep it?

The First Man in Rome

Augustus remained on center stage as the "first man in Rome" for another 43 years, with the dramatic pace slowing considerably from the tumultuous years of the Second Triumvirate. With the reins of power securely in his hands, his focus turned to maintaining civil peace, returning Rome to its rightful glory, and ultimately developing a successor to ensure the longevity of his *Pax Augusta*. In doing so, he built on and refined the leadership skills he had displayed during his rise to power. Most importantly, his known actions suggest that his motives thereafter were primarily centered on his duty to do what was best for Rome and that this enabled him to transform the fractious and arguably doomed Roman Republic into the long-lived Roman Empire.

The fundamental goals that guided him included: expanding the size of the state and focusing Rome's attention on the threats and opportunities of foreign conquest; using the spoils of these conquests, as well as his own personal wealth, to reward his followers, preserve civil peace, and improve and beautify Rome; restoring traditional Roman values; and honoring the form, if not the substance, of republican government. His success with that audacious agenda was due in no small measure to his always playing the part of the reluctant and modest leader, who would only agree to serve temporarily.

Augustus believed strongly in the manifest destiny of Rome and in the prosperity, as well as stability, achievable through conquest. During his rule, Rome grew larger than ever before, prosecuting a series of foreign wars aimed at expanding or stabilizing its borders. Importantly, these wars were conducted in a manner that created rather than destroyed wealth, which was key not only to public opinion, but also to Augustus's own position as he typically controlled all new provinces. He was not interested in war solely for glory's sake and was as content to achieve his ends through diplomacy. For example, when the border of Rome's eastern provinces with Parthia could be secured and Roman standards lost in previous wars recovered through negotiation rather than force in 20 BCE, Augustus did so and commemorated the event in both coins and art as a great victory.

Augustus also understood that the chances of civil strife would be far lower if ambitious members of the upper classes had the chance to gain glory and riches from Rome's wars of expansion. Other such outlets included the opportunity to strive for high office once Augustus stepped aside from the consulship in 23 BCE after eight consecutive years. But he recognized that another way to lessen the possibility of civil unrest was to share widely the wealth gained by conquest and domestic tranquility, and he himself set the example. Augustus was Rome's richest citizen owing to his inheritance from Caesar and other legacies, to properties confiscated in the proscriptions, and to war booty, above all Cleopatra's immense Egyptian treasure. From this fortune, he bestowed land and money on his army veterans and bought supplies of grain for the lower classes. He helped members of the senatorial class who could no longer meet the property qualification. He spent lavishly on building projects, famously finding a city of brick and leaving one of marble. In his will, he also left large amounts in cash to the people and soldiers of Rome. Indeed, an appendix to the *Res Gestae* claims that his money gifts to the Roman treasury, people, and veterans totaled an astounding 2.4 billion sesterces over his lifetime.[51]

To restore Rome's traditional values, threatened by the incursion of foreign cultures in the wake of Rome's conquests as well as by the wealth those conquests brought, Augustus undertook a program of moral regeneration. The social legislation of 18 BCE included sumptuary laws prohibiting egregious displays of wealth and luxury as well as laws intended to strengthen the patriarchal family and increase the population. A strict ban on adultery led him to banish his daughter, Julia, in 2 BCE. He also tightened the qualifications for the senatorial and equestrian classes to encourage a proper respect for rank even as he monitored them for behavior that lacked *dignitas*.

The final element of his strategy and story was his own role as the reluctant leader and defender of the Republic. In a highly symbolic act, Augustus formally returned special powers he had been granted to the Senate and people of Rome in 27 BCE, stating in his memoirs: "After this...I possessed no more official power than others who were my colleagues in the several magistracies."[52] While Augustus's contemporaries like the poet Ovid and the historian Velleius praised the action extravagantly, some skepticism was justified since in return he received the title "Augustus" and a proconsular province that included Spain, Gaul, Syria, and Egypt along with their accompanying military forces. Moreover, events continued to reinforce his own bias against letting democracy be taken too far, as, for example, the riots in Rome over a consular election during his absence from the city in 19 BCE.[53] Nonetheless, throughout the rest of his life, Augustus continued to be scrupulous about working through the Senate and the constitutional forms of government. During a famine around 22 BCE, Augustus wrote in the *Res Gestae*,

> The dictatorship was offered to me by both senate and people in my absence...but I refused it. I did not decline...to undertake the charge of the corn-supply, which I so administered that within a few days I delivered the whole city from apprehension and immediate danger at my own cost and by my own efforts. At that time the consulship was also offered to me, to be held each year for the rest of my life, and I refused it.[54]

He also shunned many personal honors, for instance, entering Rome surreptitiously at night on returning from a campaign in order to avoid the traditional ceremonial welcome.

The sum of Augustus's goals for Rome constituted a strongly compelling *vision*. Moreover, over the years he consistently *communicated* this vision and its benefits, masterfully using a wide variety of means. Through coinage, art, and the rebuilding of Rome itself, the results were visible to everyone. And so was the author of these achievements as Augustus's image was made the ubiquitous symbol of the story. Roman and provincial coins issued from 31 BCE onward portray him as a vigorous, handsome warrior, despite his advancing age and unprepossessing actual appearance. Each issue of coinage offered an opportunity to add a new and timely message about Augustus's virtues and the benefits of his regime. For example, a coin issued just after he had returned his power to the Senate in 27 BCE displayed him on one side wearing the "civic crown" he had been awarded for saving so many citizens' lives and with his new title, Caesar Augustus.[55] Another coin issued a few years later showed a kneeling Parthian returning a Roman standard circled by a message stating "Caesar Augustus: the standards recovered."[56] Still later coins pictured various members of his family that he was positioning as potential successors, who would continue his legacy.

His statues, portraying a virile, majestic Augustus, were often strategically located adjacent to the public works, buildings, and monuments he sponsored. Whether it was a new temple, an aqueduct, an improved road, or restored baths, the statues made clear who the people's benefactor was. And presumably they reminded Romans of other benefits of Augustus's rule: continued civil peace, a strong economy and steady food supply, and the entertainment of games and theater.

Last, the circle of poets and writers who had gathered around Augustus reinforced his message. Among the educated classes they certainly were influential and persuasive. Virgil in his epic poem, *The Aeneid*, linked the Julian line to Rome's legendary founder Aeneas and then pointed directly to Augustus, who had been: "[P]romis'd oft, and long foretold, / Sent to the Realm that *Saturn* rul'd of old; / Born to restore a better Age of Gold." Virgil's prophecy went on to celebrate Augustus's extension of Rome's rule "beyond the Solar Year; without the starry Way"; ultimately, "*Affrick*, and *India*, shall his Pow'r obey."[57] Augustus doubtless welcomed such praise and acted as patron to those who offered it, but there is no evidence that Rome's writers were pressured to flatter him or to mute criticism. In fact, it appears that Augustus tolerated and even encouraged free speech about Rome's problems and his own foibles, at least within limits.[58] For example, Suetonius testified that though Augustus replied "in a public proclamation to various ugly and damaging jokes current at his expense, he vetoed a law that would have suppressed speech in wills,"[59] which often were the vehicle for outspoken "last judgments" on political and social controversies.

The evidence supports the view that Augustus embodied the values he espoused. He was brave, lived simply, and gave away enormous amounts of his wealth for the benefit of Rome. He also was the master of the symbolic act. For example, one of the most compelling parts of his story was ending the civil wars and violence that had plagued the later Republic. Traditionally, Rome marked peace by shutting the door to the temple of Janus, and as Augustus himself wrote in the *Res Gestae*, "from the foundation of the city down to my birth, tradition records that it was shut only twice, but while I was the leading citizen the senate resolved that it should be shut on three occasions."[60] He also used symbolic acts in his private life to communicate his values. One famous anecdote related by several ancient writers is of the slave who accidentally broke a valuable cup at a dinner party that Augustus was attending. When the host of the party condemned the slave to a horrible death, the slave appealed to Augustus for mercy. In response, Augustus deliberately broke each of the remaining cups, thereby showing his disgust for the host's cruelty and non-Roman display of luxury. The gesture also demonstrated his concern for all people, including slaves.[61] On another occasion, a former soldier asked Augustus to represent him in court. Initially, Augustus replied that he would send a proxy. When the soldier protested that he did not send a proxy to fight at Actium, Augustus agreed to represent him personally, thus sending another clear message of caring and involvement. On the occasion of his refusal of the dictatorship at a time of famine, Augustus was said to have rent his clothes, fallen to his knees, and begged the people not to require it of him. Taking the lesser position of the official responsible for the food supply, he promptly solved the problem, thereby demonstrating his concern and competence, as well as his indifference to positions of power.

In implementing his strategy, Augustus continued to display the ***organizational and managerial skills*** that characterized his rise to power. In keeping with his ostensible restoration of republican government, he streamlined and modified, rather than redesigned, the existing infrastructure. For example, he reduced the size of the Senate on three occasions in order to enhance its prestige and the quality of its membership. He increased the government's efficiency and effectiveness through the creation of more prefects, administrative boards, and offices. He reorganized the provinces, restructured Italy into 11 departments, and divided the city of Rome into 14 regions. He conducted censuses of all Roman territories in order to make the imposition of taxes more equitable. He even revamped the fire-fighting service and established a police force for the city of Rome. Under Augustus, Southern concludes, "piecemeal government had given way to planned, co-ordinated, all-embracing influence. It would never fully return to the old order of things, and yet there was no sharp break with tradition."[62] At the same time, Augustus continued to rely heavily on close advisors like Agrippa and Maecenas until their deaths in 12 and 7 BCE, respectively. He missed them greatly and never fully replaced them.

Were Augustus's vision, persuasive powers, and organizational skills sufficient to account for his success in achieving the *Pax Augusta*, dramatically expanding the size and wealth of Rome, reigning for 43 years, and ultimately creating the Roman Empire? We believe that one more factor was key to Augustus's success and to the persuasiveness of his message: the degree of ***selflessness*** and commitment to the good of Rome that he displayed as the first man in Rome, a commitment that earned him the trust of his followers and was communicated through many of his actions. Clearly, he was not purely selfless. His establishment of a hereditary monarchy and tireless promotion of his family's interests, as well as his accumulation of extraordinary wealth, would appear to be persuasive evidence of that. Yet when he was gravely ill in 23 BCE and thought to be on his deathbed, he gave his signet ring to Agrippa, the best man at the time to become his successor, not to Marcellus, his nephew and presumed heir. Similarly, years later, when his beloved daughter Julia violated the adultery laws, he exiled her for the rest of her life. We interpret his patient grooming of potential successors solely from within his family as being driven by his reasonable belief that a hereditary succession was the best and perhaps only way to avoid a relapse into the civil wars of his youth. Reinforcing this reading, Suetonius tells us that Augustus "never nominated his adopted sons for offices of state without adding: 'If they deserve this honour,'" and once, at the theatre, "while they [his sons] were still boys and the entire theatre audience stood to cheer them, he expressed his annoyance in no uncertain terms."[63] Augustus's reluctance to accept additional powers and honors may not have been wholly calculation. He had devoted his life to Rome, which must have been exhausting, especially given the mask he wore to hide his emotions and intentions. When he asked his family and friends gathered around his deathbed in 14 CE whether they had enjoyed his performance, we see his question as an indication of the degree to which, over a long lifetime, he had sublimated his natural emotions to his duty to Rome. He was a complex man with many, sometimes conflicting, motives. But his actions suggest to us that he evolved into an exceptional leader who was devoted to Rome's interests. "Seeming" really had become "being" during his long tenure as the first man in Rome.

★ ★ ★

In conclusion, while a multitude of variables contribute to the life spans of empires, in our view the differences between the leadership of Augustus and that of Napoleon are critical to an understanding of why the Roman Empire survived its infancy and the French Empire did not. Where Augustus "made haste slowly" and waited until the people were aligned behind him and the direction in which he wished to move, Napoleon impatiently charged ahead. Where Augustus consistently honored the form, if not the substance, of republican government, Napoleon dropped all pretense of doing so by the time of the Empire. Where Augustus slowly accumulated the functions of power, but accepted the positions of power only temporarily, Napoleon actively sought and acquired the positions as well. Where Augustus, as his deathbed comment indicated, successfully sublimated his ego over the course of a long lifetime, Napoleon's ego ultimately corrupted the persuasiveness of his vision and the effectiveness of his supporting military and civil organizations. Finally, where Augustus consistently communicated his vision of a Rome grounded in its traditions and past—and his own role as nothing but a humble facilitator—Napoleon's message evolved into one where he was the embodiment of the new France, not the people's France of the Revolution, but an empire cast in his own militaristic, autocratic image. Augustus learned from the mistakes of his adoptive father, Julius Caesar. Napoleon, who was a great admirer of Caesar, simply repeated them.

PART IV

Transforming Visions

At the heart of leadership is a vision that attracts followers and inspires them to work together toward the goal that the leader has articulated in one fashion or another. If that goal or the strategy for achieving it is ill-conceived, we would judge it to be a case of failed leadership. If, however, there is a well-conceived vision, persuasive communication, and a capable supporting organization, the ingredients for effective or even exceptional leadership are in place. At that point, the only condition beyond exogenous factors that can derail a leader's success is a perception by his followers that the leader's motivations for promoting the vision are essentially selfish and inconsistent with their collective interests.

The last two sets of case studies feature leaders with potentially transforming visions, who ultimately succeeded or failed based upon each leader's selflessness or selfishness. We first compare the effectiveness of John Humphrey Noyes, the founder of a fascinating but short-lived experiment in communal living—the Oneida Community—and George Fox, the founder of another contrarian but long-lasting religious community—the Quakers. Then we contrast the impact of two African political leaders whose careers and opportunities to build a new postcolonial nation mirrored each other, but whose legacies were radically different—Robert Mugabe and Nelson Mandela.

CHAPTER NINE

John Humphrey Noyes and George Fox: Religious Visionaries

George Fox and John Humphrey Noyes were visionaries who founded Christian movements in seventeenth-century England and nineteenth-century America, respectively. Yet while the Quaker movement founded by Fox in 1647 had an estimated 50,000 members by 1660 and remains a vital denomination today, the Oneida Community founded by Noyes in 1848 never had more than 300 members and disbanded in 1881, eight years before Noyes's death. Why was Fox's achievement so much more enduring than Noyes's? Certainly part of the answer lies in the highly radical nature of Noyes's vision. But another reason was their effectiveness as leaders. And while the difference in their effectiveness involved all of the elements in our framework, it was rooted in the relative selflessness or selfishness of their visions.

John Humphrey Noyes

> I would never go on board any ship again unless I could have the helm, meaning that I would never connect myself with any individual or association in religion unless I was the acknowledged leader.[1]
> —John Humphrey Noyes, 1837

The Oneida Community was a social experiment that continues to fascinate students of religion, sociology, and psychology. Founded in the conservative social environment of the mid-nineteenth-century American Northeast, it was a communal society where everything was shared, even spouses and child rearing. That it endured for more than 30 years is testimony to the charismatic leadership qualities of John Humphrey Noyes.

Born the first of seven children in 1811 to a prominent family in Brattleboro, Vermont, Noyes had a strict religious upbringing overseen by his deeply pious mother. At the age of 15, Noyes entered Dartmouth College, where he won Phi Beta Kappa honors. After graduating he prepared for the bar at his brother-in-law's law office. A year later, to please his mother, Noyes attended a four-day revival meeting and afterward announced that he had experienced a conversion, was abandoning law, and would henceforth devote his life to serving God, saying he "found more, infinitely more, enjoyment in the exercises of religion than I ever took in the most fascinating pleasures of the world."[2]

Noyes entered Andover Theological Seminary to study for the ministry but found the curriculum too conservative and confining. In 1832, he transferred to Yale and studied under Nathaniel Taylor, a liberal theologian. To some, Taylor was a dangerous heretic; Noyes decided that Taylor was not radical enough. After close examination of the New Testament, Noyes concluded that anyone who failed to live a perfect life could not be counted as a true Christian. But he struggled with the question of how perfection was to be achieved. In his *Confessions*, Noyes recalls the experience in 1834 that changed him: "Three times in quick succession a stream of eternal love gushed through my heart...'Joy unspeakable and full of glory' filled my soul...I knew that my heart was clean and that the Father and the Son had come and made it their abode."[3] Noyes began to preach that he was morally perfect, a claim that shocked his fellow students and professors. His Congregational minister's license was revoked, a rebuke that cast him into despair. But Noyes persevered, proclaiming that man should not allow his inner convictions to be overruled by any church.

Although Perfectionism was not a new Christian theme, Noyes proclaimed an extreme version. Older strands taught the best ways to strive for perfection, but rarely claimed its actual achievement. In contrast, Noyes believed that Christ had returned to earth in 70 CE and that redemption from sin already had been accomplished; therefore, when a person accepted Christ, he or she became inwardly perfect, the will "quickened and actuated by Christ's will."[4] Noyes's role was to share this truth with mankind. After his revelation, he traveled around the Northeast studying and spreading Perfectionism, a missionary among a people, who, he said, "(though professedly Christian) needed to be converted quite as much as the heathen."[5] Often rebuffed, Noyes eventually won small groups of believers in New Jersey, Vermont, New York, and Massachusetts. But his campaign suffered from the scandal caused by the exposure in August 1837 of a private letter Noyes had written eight months earlier detailing his ideas about sex in the kingdom of heaven. Although Christ's statement that "in the resurrection [the saved] neither marry nor are given in marriage"[6] was usually taken to mean that there is no sex in heaven, Noyes was convinced that it meant that there was sex without monogamy—free love.

One motive for this doctrine was intensely personal. Soon after he started his ministry, Noyes had fallen in love with a convert, Abigail Merwin, but she refused his attentions. Even when she became engaged to another man in 1835, the infatuated Noyes clung to the hope that he had not lost her forever. His call for free love was a result of this thwarted passion. Monogamous marriage, as sociologist Maren Carden writes, now appeared to him as "a tyrannical institution."[7]

During his travels, Noyes also came to believe that the best way to prepare for the coming of the kingdom of heaven was for true Christians, those "who have obtained eternal life, the root of heart-righteousness," to "separate themselves more or less from the world, and form a Community for the purpose of establishing good society as the nurse of external character."[8] Thus, in 1838 he started his own community, what became known as the "Bible School," in Putney, Vermont. He began with a small nucleus of family members that included his new wife, Harriet Holton, whom he married in June of that year. By 1844, the group had evolved into a society of some two dozen members practicing communism—sharing work, food, housing, resources, and schooling.

Though married, Noyes soon became strongly attracted to another community member, Mary Cragin. Drawing on his beliefs about sex in heaven, Noyes decreed that perfected Christians should, with his guidance, partake of what he called "complex marriage." Thus, after convincing Mary's husband George, in 1846 Harriet and John together with Mary and George adopted the practice of rotating spouses. A year later, Noyes's two sisters and their husbands also began to experiment with complex marriage. This loose sexual system created the problem of potential offspring who would be branded as illegitimate. Additionally, Harriet had undergone five difficult pregnancies in six years, four of which had ended in stillbirths. Noyes was determined to spare her further pain. His solution was male continence, as he called it—or intercourse without ejaculation—a practice that allowed Noyes's followers to enjoy the freedom of complex marriage without fear of unwanted pregnancies.

Noyes's early leadership at Putney was a portent of the future. The Community was no democracy. Noyes, as sociologists William Kephart and William Zellner write, was "both the leader and the binding force" and "there was no doubt in anyone's mind—including his own—about who made the rules."[9] Followers took a vow of obedience acknowledging his divine authority: "John H. Noyes is the father and overseer whom the Holy Ghost has set over [us]. To John H. Noyes as such we submit ourselves in all things spiritual and temporal."[10] Noyes's domination reached into all aspects of his followers' lives. In one instance, a couple that fell in love was expelled from the Community because he had not sanctioned the relationship.

Not surprisingly, the institution of complex marriage outraged the townspeople of Putney, and in 1847, Noyes was arrested on a charge of adultery. Released on bail and amid rumors of mob action, he fled to New York City. He wrote a Putney follower that "I thought that my presence with you would only increase the fury of the storm, and that it would do you no good to see me imprisoned or assassinated."[11] Though the fury in Putney abated, Noyes began to search for a new, safer home for his community.

Jonathan Burt was an early Perfectionist convert who had recently bought some land in Oneida, New York, and suggested it as a place to form a "heavenly association."[12] Noyes accepted the offer. It was the new home the Putneyites needed, as well as an opportunity to bring New York Perfectionists under his direct authority.[13] Noyes quickly seized control of the tiny community that Burt, his wife, and three other Perfectionist families had started. Within months he was joined by his Putney followers, as well as new members. By the end of 1848, the group totaled 87. The aim at Oneida was individual perfection and communal good, with Noyes arguing, as Carden puts it, that "individual perfection could be fully achieved only in the context of a community to which each person subjugated all of his selfish interests."[14]

In 1849, Noyes left Oneida for New York City to work at the branch community in Brooklyn, believing that God wished him to spread "Bible Communism" and turn the whole world into an earthly kingdom of heaven.[15] In the early 1850s branches were also established in Connecticut, New Jersey, and Vermont. Five years later, though, Noyes returned to Oneida to cope with a financial crisis. Since its inception, the Community had lived primarily off capital contributed by those who joined, as well as meager profits from agriculture. Against this was the cost of maintaining the branches, particularly in New York City, and the Perfectionists' printing enterprises. Noyes had long believed that the best way to win converts was with a newspaper explaining the Community's beliefs, but production of the *Circular*, as it was called, was quite expensive. Thus in 1854, upon returning to Oneida Noyes shut down all the branch communities with the exception of the one in Wallingford, Connecticut. Sewell Newhouse, a blacksmith and experienced hunter who had joined the Community in 1848, solved the financial problems with the invention of a steel trap. Noyes persuaded Newhouse to share his design and soon the production of traps became a Community project that eventually produced more than 100,000 highly profitable traps a year. Over time the enterprise was expanded to include other manufactured items as well, including silverware. In general, Oneidans were efficient and dedicated workers, who were taught that improvements in work paralleled increases in spiritual perfection. It was a winning formula, and it ensured the Community's financial prosperity.

From its inception, the Community received a multitude of applicants. Naturally, Noyes led the process of carefully screening them, choosing those who were committed to his teachings and also possessed practical skills. In addition, as Carden observes, "they also brought their savings...one suspects that Noyes shrewdly selected at least some of them for their wealth."[16] The Community grew steadily, exceeding 200 members by the early 1850s. Eventually, a decision was made to curtail growth, and as a consequence, there were never more than 300 members. Noyes believed that for his communal experiment to succeed, members needed to live together under one roof, thus limiting the potential size. That limit also enabled Noyes to maintain control.

Noyes insisted that divine inspiration authorized his absolute power over the Community. Accepting his "theocracy" and confessing one's "union with Christ and Mr. Noyes" were prerequisites for membership.[17] But he did not lead completely unaided; a members' committee helped with decisions ranging from economic policy to sexual matters to Perfectionist doctrine. Numerous other committees had a say in day-to-day management. The aim on controversial measures, according to the Community *Handbook*, was consensus: "The majority never go ahead leaving a grumbling minority behind."[18] Still, the fact that the community members were carefully screened and intensely indoctrinated predisposed them to agree with whatever Noyes desired. As historian Spencer Klaw notes, all this "did not mean that Oneidans were free to think and feel in ways that Noyes would not approve... The only way to be sure of doing what God wanted was to do what Noyes wanted."[19]

As absolute leader, Noyes commanded the fierce loyalty of all his followers necessary for the Community's total communism to work, and especially for the successful implementation of complex marriage, which in turn enhanced members' devotion to Noyes. In order to ensure that the sharing of partners did indeed contribute to group solidarity and did not degenerate into monogamy, Noyes required that each time a member wanted to have sex with another member, he or she had to send him a proposal. This meant Noyes controlled who was sleeping with whom, thereby preventing regular partnerships from forming. He also limited unwanted conceptions and ensured partners for older members by instructing the Community to adhere to the principle of "ascending fellowship." Noyes believed that Perfectionists ranged from least to most nearly perfect, with older members at the latter end of the scale. Even before the advent of complex marriage, Noyes had encouraged members to associate with spiritual superiors. Now, he dictated that each sexual union must be between partners at different levels of ascension. Older women, who might otherwise have lacked partners, were paired with younger, inexperienced men who may not have mastered the practice of male continence. Thus, complex marriage's two major pitfalls were avoided. The young girls of the community, meanwhile, were paired with older men—after their introduction to sex by Noyes himself. In this mentorship role, Noyes inspired extreme loyalty among these women, enabling him to use sex as both reward and punishment for the rest of his followers. Klaw in fact suggests that it was Noyes's control of sexual access to the Community's young and attractive women that, "more than anything else, enabled him to govern at Oneida so long and so effectively."[20]

One last issue accompanied complex marriage: procreation. Noyes believed that from a spiritual viewpoint, some members were more qualified than others to produce offspring. Like most other matters at Oneida, the stirpiculture process, as it was called, was heavily controlled by Noyes himself, as the declaration of 53 women attested: "[W]e do not belong to ourselves in any respect, but... belong first to *God*, and

second to Mr. Noyes as God's true representative."[21] There was defi-
nite bias within this process. As George Bernard Shaw, himself a propo-
nent of eugenics, later noted, "[T]he question of what sort of men they
should strive to breed [was] settled at once by the obvious desirability of
breeding another Noyes." Noyes himself bred 9 of the 58 stirpicultural
babies.[22] Children at Oneida were brought up by the entire membership
to avoid conflict between family loyalty and loyalty to the Community.
"There was room for only one family at Oneida," writes Klaw, "the one
at which Noyes was the father and the head."[23]

Mutual criticism was another novel Oneida practice. Its goal was to
bring self-improvement to individual members through public criticism
by groups ranging in size from small committees to the entire community.
One Oneidan described the process as a washing: "I would call the truth
the soap; the critics the scrubbers; Christ's spirit the water."[24] Everyone
periodically underwent mutual criticism except Noyes himself. But he
promised that when Christ or St. Paul or even some lowlier member of
the Primitive Church returned to earth, he would drop his "officiality"
and submit to criticism.[25]

For over 20 years, the Oneida Community was a great success. Evening
meetings contributed to group unity, combining religious services with
entertainment, community news and business, and mutual criticism. After
its move into commerce, the Community prospered, eventually hiring
outside workers for help in the factories and at the main house. Noyes's
ingenious system of complex marriage and ascending fellowship succeeded
with few complaints. Finally, just as he wanted, the Community revolved
around Noyes himself as the ultimate authority. The result was a remarkably stable community with high individual morale and group solidarity.

In the 1870s, however, a convergence of forces led to Oneida's dissolution. For one, internal forces caused dissension. Members not chosen to
bear children were becoming discontented. Younger members returning from college rebelled against Noyes's authority. Older members were
concerned that the original Perfectionist ideals were being compromised
as the Community's focus became more secular. In general, Perfectionists
no longer felt unquestioning confidence in Noyes. One member at
Wallingford expressed an increasingly common view when she wrote that
one of her close friends "goes to God for herself—doesn't need to go to
Mr. Noyes."[26] By this period, the aging Noyes, deaf and with a speech
difficulty, also had lost much of his sexual appeal. His influence with the
younger generations faded, particularly the young females, thus weaken-
ing his control of the Community.

More dissension arose when Noyes arbitrarily appointed his agnostic son,
Theodore, to succeed him in 1877. He was convinced that Theodore had
inherited superior qualities and thus could assume much of the daily management of the Community and bring unity. But Theodore's secular and
autocratic managerial tendencies only worsened division. By 1878, even
Noyes had to declare the experiment a failure and resume his position.

But the challenge to Noyes only mounted as James Towner emerged as the leader of the dissenters. A longtime member of a secular free love society in Ohio, he and his family had joined the Oneida Community in 1874. Towner, a skilled lawyer and former judge, had quickly become one of Noyes's chief deputies in business affairs. But he was soon in rebellion against Noyes's theocratic power, calling for an elected government to replace it. The Community split between Townerites and the Noyes loyalists who fought back against this challenge to the founder's divine authority. As Noyes himself told one member, "I have not been put in my present position by the members of this Community. The real stockholders in our institution are the men and women of the invisible world...and it is to them that I am accountable. I am resolved not to relinquish one iota of the authority they have given me."[27]

During this period, aggressive external opposition also arose, led by Hamilton College professor and Presbyterian minister John Mears. He and a number of other clergymen became obsessed with destroying what they viewed as a "Utopia of obscenity."[28] By late June 1879, their public campaign led Noyes to fear that he might be charged with statutory rape. Soon thereafter, he stole away in the night and fled two hundred miles to Canada. Even though charges against him did not materialize, Noyes never returned to Oneida, unwilling to face the possible loss of his leadership to those who no longer believed in him. From Canada he issued recommendations designed to placate both external critics and dissident members, including the abandonment of complex marriage, the option of monogamous marriage, and the encouragement of celibacy. But the adoption of these recommendations did not end disagreements over the Community's ends and means. Monogamous marriage was far more popular than celibacy, but the communal arrangements at Oneida were ill-suited for it. Consequently, on January 1, 1881, the Community was dissolved and became a successful joint stock company—Oneida Ltd.—that continues to manufacture silverware. Noyes lived in Canada with a few followers until his death in 1889.

★   ★   ★

From the vantage point of the early twenty-first century, it may seem surprising that Noyes's communitarian venture and its theological rationale would have been tolerated and successful for as long as it was. But in the context of nineteenth-century frontier revivalism, with its emphasis on perfectionist sanctification and its attraction to the secular doctrine of progress that emanated from the Enlightenment, doctrinally the Oneida Perfectionists can be seen as close to the mainstream of American Protestant Christianity. Such figures as John Wesley, the founder of Methodism, and the great Congregational evangelist and Oberlin president Charles G. Finney were among the many who proclaimed the message of Christian perfection. And North America, with its vast openness, was ready-made for social and religious experimentation and inventiveness.[29] As Ralph Waldo Emerson wrote to Englishman Thomas Carlyle in 1840: "We are all a little wild here with numberless projects of social reform. Not a reading man but has a draft of a new community in his waist coat pocket...One man renounces the use of animal food; and another of coin; and another of domestic hired service; and another of the State..."[30]

Nonetheless, Noyes's combination of perfectionism and communitarianism with the institution of complex marriage made his *vision* radical, even for its time. Moreover, Noyes unquestionably was the catalytic force without which the Oneida community would not have come into being. How was he so successful for so long?

Because of his magnetic presence and his sincere belief in his spiritual superiority and God-given mission to establish the kingdom of heaven on earth, Noyes inspired the utmost faith and devotion in others. Indeed, he appears to be a textbook example of Max Weber's charismatic leader. His followers believed his gifts to be "supernatural," and their "duty" was "to recognize him as their...leader."[31] He won their loyalty through *persuasion*, not psychological coercion. He never "threatened his followers with hell-fire," Klaw writes. "His method was, rather, to persuade those who wished to be true Christians that to do what God wanted them to do was the most natural and reasonable thing in the world."[32] His followers, moreover, were not an unsophisticated audience; Oneidans were skilled artisans and professionals drawn to the idea that they were part of a crusade to transform not just themselves but the world. And though Noyes had massive power within the community, for many years his followers did not perceive him as abusing it. As one Oneidan summarized Noyes's charismatic hold over his followers in 1867, "The world cried despot to Mr. Noyes, but those...who are honest and true call him father and liberator."[33]

Noyes's charisma was institutionalized at Oneida through an *organization* brilliantly constructed to promote group cohesion while reinforcing his own authority. For example, his strategy of keeping the Community small in numbers facilitated easier and more personal control over the group. By carefully screening applicants, Noyes was also able to gain the skills (and money) needed by the Community, as well as to ensure both the "fit" of new members with the rest of the group and their willingness to obey Noyes. The formation of over 21 committees and 48 departments allowed everyone to have a voice in the day-to-day life and management of the Community, while all major decisions were reserved for Noyes. This complex and ingeniously designed organization, including the regular routines and rituals, all encouraged members' devotion and contentment even as individual interests were consistently subordinated to communal imperatives. Indeed, as Carden notes, Noyes's interpretation of self-perfection included the sacrifice of self for the Community.[34] That same complexity proved to be a fundamental limitation on the scale of Perfectionism. The movement's long-term growth depended entirely on the proliferation of small communities.

But that spread of Perfectionist communities was undermined by Noyes's essential *selfishness* of the messianic variety. While he appeared to believe sincerely in his spiritual mission, it offered powerful sexual and secular benefits to him personally. He was unable to deny his libidinal impulses or his desire for control of the Community. As a result, he eventually ceased to embody his vision and lost credibility with at least a significant fraction of the group, thereby contributing to its ultimate dissolution. Noyes's initial vision of spreading Oneida-like communities around the world suffered from this need to maintain supreme leadership. "He could not bear the idea," Klaws writes, "of having rival dukedoms in the kingdom of heaven" with "a realistic apprehension that they would inevitably have their own ideas about communism."[35] This in turn could have threatened his authority at Oneida. Throughout, Noyes maintained a conviction in his infallibility and was never slow to point out that to reject his divine authority was also to rebel against God and the entire basis of the Community.

Although the Oneida Community did not last, it was highly successful given the unconventional nature of Noyes's vision and the general public's attitudes during that time, particularly regarding marriage and sex. At a time when many Utopian communities were being born and quickly died, that Oneida was one of the few to flourish and endure was a testament to Noyes's leadership skills. However, as Max Weber predicted about charismatic leaders, Noyes's authority lasted only as long as he could "prove" to the other Community members that he was truly God's messenger on earth. When he failed to institutionalize the communal movement because of his desire to retain personal control and power, the Oneida Community and the Perfectionist movement died as his followers became disillusioned with him.

George Fox

> [The Lord] sent...unto us a man of God, one of ten thousand, to instruct us in the ways of God more perfectly, who laid down the sure foundation...whose testimony reached unto all our consciences and entered into the innermost part of our hearts, which drove us...to a diligent inquisition concerning our state, which we did come to see through the Light of Christ Jesus.[36]
>
> —Francis Howgill, early convert to Quakerism, on George Fox

By 1643, 19-year-old George Fox was already having doubts about his Puritan upbringing, disturbed by the competing claims of the Protestant sects jostling for position in England during the tumultuous reign of Charles I. It took only a chance meeting to catalyze in him a determination to seek the truth himself. One day he ran into his cousin, a fellow dissenter, and his cousin's friend while in a village near his home in Leicestershire. When they invited him to have a drink with them, he politely accepted. To his dismay, after sitting down his companions proposed a drinking contest with the loser footing the bill. Shocked at their frivolity, George immediately laid his money on the table and left. From the experience, he concluded that his dissolute generation would not bring about the change in the religious environment he felt was needed: "[T]hou must forsake all…and keep out of all, and be as a stranger unto all."[37]

Born to a Puritan weaving family in July 1624, George Fox grew up a solitary youth, exhibiting, as he wrote in his memoirs, "a gravity and stayedness of mind and spirit, not usual in children."[38] From early on, Fox showed an unwillingness to submit to authority unless it was God's. As he was reaching adulthood, the English Civil War began, and Fox felt deep concern for those oppressed by the ensuing turmoil. Yet he found hope too in the new sense of individual freedom from the church and other established institutions that was emerging from the revolution. But he was troubled by the competing claims of Presbyterians, Baptists, and other Protestant sects, and shortly after the experience with his cousin he embarked on a long pilgrimage throughout England visiting clergy and laypeople in search of answers. Not liking what he found, he concluded that most Christians were insincere and "did not possess what they professed."[39]

In 1647, after four years in search of truth, Fox found himself wandering the northern moors in great spiritual confusion. There he experienced a revelation, one of what he termed his "openings," claiming that God spoke to him: "When all my hopes…were gone, so that I had nothing outwardly to help me, nor could I tell what to do; then, oh! then I heard a voice which said, 'There is one, even Christ Jesus, that can speak to thy condition': and when I heard it, my heart did leap for joy."[40] Based on this and other "openings" and his years of wandering, Fox became convinced that truth was not to be found in churches, or at Oxford or Cambridge where churchmen were trained.[41] Instead, he believed that all Christians were spiritually equal, God was present within them as the "Light of Christ," and thus no mediator was needed between them and God. Fox believed that if they acknowledged this "Inner Light," it was possible for them to become free of all sin, to "come up into that state in which Adam was before he fell."[42] But if they ignored the light, they would be lost and ultimately damned.

Fox felt himself called to be a religious reformer and in that year began his mission. Though characterized as "fanatical, extravagant in language, [and] denunciatory," Fox's "transparent spiritual sincerity, his earnestness, his courage, and the impression that he conveyed of being the bearer of a message not his own, won many converts."[43] In other words, he had a powerful message, which he embodied and through which he was able to persuade many to join his movement. Those who became Quakers were said to have been "convinced." Initially referred to as "Children of the

Light" and later officially the "Religious Society of Friends," these converts became, in turn, messengers of Fox's vision.

As he continued preaching, Fox developed an approach that tapped into such popular issues as the tithe and combined them with his own religious message. When, for instance, he attacked a clergyman "for 'choking' himself on the parish's tithes," biographer H. Larry Ingle notes, "he placed himself firmly on the side of the tax resisters."[44] At the same time that he stressed equality, justice, and poor relief, he also taught that God "did not dwell in temples made with hands...but in people's hearts,"[45] transferring control over religion from churches and the warring sects to the individual. By uniting his social concerns with this personalization of religion, Fox created a compelling vision that resonated with the needs, grievances, and hopes of a large population. Nevertheless, he and the Quakers remained primarily concerned with "the autonomy of the soul," its freedom from "outside compulsion in religious matters."[46]

Though Fox believed he was simply reviving the faith of primitive Christianity, the nature of his revelation led him into constant conflict. Fellow spiritual leaders were threatened by his insistence that true Christians did not need ministers for guidance, that "the Lord would teach His people Himself."[47] He would often interrupt church services to speak and, adding insult to injury, won converts on the spot. His belief that men and women were spiritually equal was a radical idea, and his insistence that women qualified as preachers and evangelists was blasphemy to many. Because of their spiritual egalitarianism, Fox and his Friends did not doff their hats to authorities. Furthermore, Fox never took an oath, claiming that outward sacraments were unnecessary because all religion occurred within. When one judge asked him to swear allegiance to the king, he replied, "Christ commands me not to swear...and whether I am to obey God or man, do thou judge."[48]

With such revolutionary principles, the movement, and Fox himself, faced much persecution. Quakers often were attacked and driven out of towns, and accused of crimes from witchcraft to treason. In 1650, charged with blasphemy and sent to Derby Jail, Fox made of prison a host of opportunities. Allowed visitors, he used every chance to pass on his message. Invited to the high sheriff of Nottingham's house, he proceeded to win over the host and all of the staff. At one point, his captors offered Fox the freedom to roam within a mile radius of the prison, hoping that he would escape, but he did not. A year after his arrival, he was released.

In June 1652, Fox went to visit a family by the name of Fell who welcomed evangelists of all persuasions to their home, Swarthmoor Hall in Ulverston. Little did Fox know the pivotal role Judge Fell and his wife Margaret would play in his movement. Within a few days, Margaret and the entire household, with the exception of the judge, had been convinced. Although Judge Fell would never become a Quaker, he was a benevolent neutral who allowed the Friends free use of his home, giving Fox a base from which to consolidate his movement. Margaret Fell became vital as a skilled administrator and close confidant of Fox. Indeed, in 1669, over a decade after Judge Fell's death, she and Fox were married.

The Quaker movement saw early success under Fox's leadership, increasing in number during the 1650s to between thirty and sixty thousand out of a total English population of five million.[49] Fox was blessed by the leadership exercised by many of his followers, who played key roles in expanding the movement. Some of his strongest leaders were early converts, including Francis Howgill, Edward Burrough, and Richard Hubberthorne. Burrough served as the movement's chief political pamphleteer for a time, and together with Howgill developed the regional Quaker organization around London. Hubberthorne was a gifted speaker and writer who also contributed much during these early stages.

Starting around the time of Oliver Cromwell's installation as the Lord Protector in 1653, many of the Quaker movement's more extreme manifestations subsided. In earlier years, Fox had condemned those who drank too much, merchants who cheated, and what he called frivolous events, such as plays and shows, pastimes that had made life bearable for country-folk for centuries.[50] Eventually, he realized the damage such criticisms did to his appeal. His interruptions of church services and attacks on priests became less frequent, eventually disappearing altogether. The Quakers also found a protector in Cromwell, who met with Fox numerous times. Fox promised him that Quakers would not violently revolt against the government, and persecution diminished. In turn, Fox and the Friends gained respectability from Cromwell's courtesy.

In 1656, the first true challenge to Fox's authority broke out in the person of the movement's chief theologian, James Nayler. A gifted speaker and writer, Nayler was a Quaker preacher in London whose large and admiring following included an early convert, Martha Simmonds. She persuaded him that God could directly inspire him, even going so far as to imply that he could be the next Jesus Christ. When Fox learned of Nayler's messianic pretensions, he resisted them aggressively, fearing that they would split the Quaker community and bring new persecutions to Friends, as well as threaten his own role as the sole leader of the movement. In truth, according to biographer Harry Emerson Wildes, Fox had "not the faintest sympathy for any idea different from his own" and saw in Nayler "an enemy as black as any hireling priest."[51] The threat relented only when Nayler was arrested for blasphemy, publicly whipped, pilloried, and then jailed at hard labor for three years. Fox stood away from Nayler's persecution. His concern was not for his fallen disciple but for the movement, which he identified with his own leadership. In the aftermath, Fox acted to ensure that his leadership was not challenged again. He worked to reestablish his doctrinal authority, putting out 18 publications in 1656 and 22 more in 1657, as well as strengthening what Wildes calls "one of the first well disciplined, nation-wide propaganda agencies" under central control and censorship.[52] With Fox in charge, the public face of the Friends was to be harmonious and filled with "convincement."

In 1661, however, dissension again rose within Quaker ranks, this time from an ambitious and energetic Irishman named John Perrot who claimed greater spiritual powers than George Fox. Perrot declared that while imprisoned in Rome, God had ordered him to tell Quakers to wear their hats while praying. To Fox, this was blasphemy. Wearing a hat among other humans indicated equality, but wearing one while praying denied the Lord's superiority. At stake once again was not only Fox's authority but Quaker unity. "If continued revelations were accepted uncritically," as Wildes writes, "the uniformity of doctrine and the common practices that united and strengthened Quakerism throughout Britain...would be destroyed."[53] Although he lacked Nayler's solid base of supporters, Perrot was a reminder of that previous rebelliousness, and Fox fought hard to halt him. The furor subsided when Perrot emigrated to Barbados, and Fox once more emerged as sole leader of the movement.

Throughout the Civil War, Fox had resisted resort to violence, and insisted that his followers also refrain. When Cromwell's Protectorate collapsed and Charles II took the throne in 1660, the new royal government labeled Quakers along with other dissenting sects as dangerous. But early in 1661, Fox sent the king a "Peace Testimony," which vowed that Quakers would never resist authorities or use force "for any end, or under any pretence whatsoever."[54] This submission impressed Charles and brought the release of all Quakers imprisoned for religious reasons.

Yet not long after, the government resumed its persecution of Quakers and other dissenters. Passed by Parliament in 1662, the Conventicle Act, which became known as the Quaker Act, barred more than five people from assembling for worship unless they were with the Established Church. It led to new arrests of thousands of Quakers. Three years later, the Five Mile Act banned dissenting ministers from living within five miles of a town from which they had been expelled for preaching outside of the Established Church unless they swore a loyalty oath. Fox used his voice and pen to try to check the onslaught. On the Quaker Act, he appealed to Parliament that large gatherings were less likely to result in conspiracies because of the numerous viewpoints that would inevitably exist. Fox also resisted the execution of such laws, often finding flaws in writs that made them invalid, like incorrect dates of arrest.

But Fox could not forestall his own arrest in January 1664 for once more refusing to swear an oath of allegiance. Weakened by imprisonment in cells that provided little protection from harsh weather, Fox initially made no headway with guards and fellow prisoners as he had done in the past. He did, however, enjoy constant argument as the prison's Catholic governor, hoping to convert Fox, sent a stream of theologians to debate with him. And by the time Fox went free in September 1666, he had won the guards' respect with his steadfast adherence to his religious principles, receiving the testimonial: "He is as stiff as a tree and as pure as a bell."[55]

In August 1671, Fox set off for the American colonies to visit Quaker groups, but also to scout for a place for English Quakers to settle if they were forced out of the home country. He worked to unify the many scattered Friends communities in America and to increase their organizational efficiency. Upon his return to England, after a last imprisonment—again for refusing to swear an oath—Fox settled into semiretirement at Swarthmoor, his control over the movement already dwindling as leadership shifted to the next generation. Nevertheless, until his death in 1691, Fox continued to write widely circulated letters and remained a welcomed presence at meetings.

A new era of toleration began to unfold in March 1686, when upward of 1600 Quakers were freed from prison by a royal pardon from James II, Charles's brother and successor. In May 1689, Parliament passed the Toleration Act, which granted dissenters the right to worship freely and released Quakers from the necessity of swearing most oaths. By then, the Society of Friends was present not only in England and North America, but also in Scotland and Ireland, and across Europe to Turkey and Palestine. After Fox's death in 1691, the movement continued to flourish, most particularly in North America. In less than half a century, Fox and his followers had developed the Quaker movement into an international force that remained surprisingly unified. "Many sons have done virtuously in this day," William Penn offered as Fox's epitaph, "but dear George, thou excellest them all."[56]

★   ★   ★

Fox's success as a leader began with his compelling *vision* and his persuasive communication of it. His message of a personal relationship with God was broadly appealing when, as Ingle phrases it, people were "seeking inward assurance in such an unsettled age."[57] The idea that one needed only the law of God and not that of any established institution was immensely attractive. Although his primary concern was always religious, Fox also ministered to the worldly needs of those hurt by the chaos of the period. Even those who disliked Quaker religion praised the Friends' quest for social justice. By challenging the basic institutions and assumptions of his times, Fox created a legacy that continued to pervade Quaker life, one that combined religion with social concerns.

Though perhaps not notably eloquent, Fox was a highly versatile speaker and effective *communicator,* in part because of his charismatic embodiment of his message. Having grown up among people regarded as lowly, Fox could speak their language, utilizing traditional words and symbols and molding them to his message. His spiritual sincerity and earnestness went a long way toward winning converts. Whenever he spoke in the open, as was his preference, he commanded attention.

Although Penn reported that Fox's oratory "fell abruptly and brokenly" and that his sermons "had nothing of man's wit and wisdom to recommend them," yet he confessed to being "overcome in myself" by Fox's "sensible and practical truths."[58] As biographer Harry Emerson Wildes puts it, "[K]nowing but two types of man, the good and the depraved, he owned but little subtlety...if listeners were ready to receive his message, he won them by love, but if they resisted, he would warn and wait until the terror worked within their hearts to soften them."[59] Fox also authored numerous epistles and other publications, which, though lacking the passion evoked when he spoke, could reach a wider audience. They worked to unify the movement as a whole, and like Fox's ministering, used a common English speech readily received by all.

Through a combination of his compelling vision and persuasive communication of it, Fox developed a large group of followers and the Quaker movement thrived despite hostility from the government and the Church of England. He excelled at winning converts among the discontented, those looking for something new to which they could attach themselves. He also persuaded his followers to defy authority aggressively, interrupting services of other denominations, refusing to take oaths in court or pay taxes to support the Church of England, and holding public worship services even when they were banned. Though beaten, jailed, and exiled, most Friends viewed their persecution as an opportunity to suffer for the truth and expose the wrongs inflicted on them. Moreover, they saw Fox as truly embodying his message and leading by example, as over his lifetime he was brought to courts and magistrates on sixty occasions and imprisoned eight times.[60]

At first glance, Fox's success seems to have little to do with his ability to create an effective *organization*. Because of his rejection of traditional church hierarchy and the focus of the Quaker movement on inward life and direct conversation with God, the Society of Friends had little formal structure. There were no ministers to stand apart from the laity and no fixed order of worship service. Indeed, opponents saw Quakerism as religious anarchy. But a movement based almost wholly on the individual never became chaotic or splintered off into countless factions. The key organizational unit was the local society, through which, Quakers believed, divine grace acted on worshippers. These societies formed regional and then national networks held together by correspondence, by visits from leaders like Fox, and by a hierarchy of monthly, quarterly, and annual meetings. Thus, over time, Fox shaped the Society into a reasonably effective organization, capable of supporting the explosive growth of the Quaker movement in the face of persecution, even if his actions were largely ad hoc and probably not informed by any master plan.

While the fundamental vision and goal of the Society never changed, as the movement aged the fanatical and extravagant conduct of its early days gave way to a culture of sobriety and good order, which became hallmark characteristics of Quakers and helped them resist persecution. Fox led the way in abandoning the radical style. He also found ways to streamline Quaker doctrine. Early on, he appointed a group of spiritually advanced elders to ensure that only truth was spread. In 1652, Fox also asked that all Quaker writings be sent to him before publication to ensure the uniformity of doctrine, eventually creating a clearinghouse for both internal and public presentations of Quakerism and its faithful.

Willing to share the burdens of organization and decision-making, Fox was fortunate that the mostly working-class members of the early movement were supplemented over time by a cadre of well-educated, affluent, and very capable people. Early converts like Hubberthorne, Howgill, and Burrough not only became key leaders in their own right, but they knew others who would welcome Fox's message, including many he would not have found on his own. Later converts such as Isaac Penington, Robert Barclay, and William Penn provided another influx of leadership and brought additional talents, knowledge, and contacts with outsiders. Penn in particular was important to the future of the movement. Under his leadership, the first Quaker colony was established in Pennsylvania, where the sect would flourish. Margaret Fell provided critical administrative skills as well as a large fortune. These individuals proved as willing as Fox to brave arrest. Indeed, virtually every major leader would be jailed at least once. To his credit, the unlettered Fox was wise enough in turn to recognize their skills, and he encouraged them to take responsibility for promoting the Quaker message and attracting more followers themselves. As Ingle notes, a lesser man than Fox would have "insisted on his prerogative. That he understood the necessity of keeping a lowered profile underscored his essential genius."[61]

Underlying all of Fox's success was his relative *selflessness* compared to Noyes. Although in his later writings Fox alluded to the idea that he was Christ himself returned to earth, he never wavered from his antipathy to hierarchies. And while less admirable impulses might have been on display in the struggles against dissidents such as Nayler and Perrot, even then he acted primarily for the good of the movement rather than from a desire to preserve his personal power. In contrast to Noyes, there are many examples of his selfless behavior. Encouraging Quakers to keep up public worship even if it meant certain arrest, Fox himself served as an example with his many court appearances and jailings. He declined opportunities to escape prison and refused privileges such as early release not offered to all Quakers. Additionally, Fox minimized his personal contributions, giving all credit and glory to God. As persecution in England worsened over the years, many Quakers yearned to establish a community abroad. Fox, though, preferred to spread the truth on home ground, despite all the hardships. Perhaps most importantly, at his death he left the Society in the hands of an exceptionally capable and devoted leadership group. As William Penn summarized the nature of Fox's appeal: "And truly, I must say, that though God had visibly clothed him with a divine preference and authority, and indeed his very presence expressed a religious majesty, yet he never abused it; but held his place in the Church of God with great meekness, and a most engaging humility and moderation."[62]

★   ★   ★

As intimated earlier, Fox's vision appealed to a much larger population than that of Noyes. But the greatest difference between the leadership of Fox and of Noyes was in the relative selflessness of their visions and actions. Although both men sincerely believed in their divine mission to spread God's true word, Fox's vision of each individual having a personal relationship with God did not bring him significant worldly benefits. In contrast, Noyes's vision of a perfectionist Community with him at its center gave him many personal benefits, not the least of which were a number of devoted and adoring sexual partners. While Fox consistently confronted civil authority in pursuing his vision, suffering persecution and imprisonment as a result, Noyes abandoned his followers to avoid arrest in both Putney and Oneida. Fox eschewed any position of formal power and encouraged his followers to become leaders in turn, but Noyes took great care to preserve and protect his personal authority, groomed no successors, and briefly anointed his incompetent son, who lacked credibility with the Community. In short, Fox passed the litmus test of placing the Quaker movement's interests over his own, and consequently Quakerism continues to be a vital movement today. Noyes failed his test, and the Oneida Community disappeared.

CHAPTER TEN

Robert Mugabe and Nelson Mandela: Revolutionary Leaders

Robert Mugabe of Zimbabwe and South Africa's Nelson Mandela were political leaders and contemporaries whose backgrounds, stories, and ascents to power initially mirrored each other. Close in age, both were educated in Christian missionary schools, earned law degrees at the University College of Fort Hare in South Africa, became political activists, rose to prominence in their respective national liberation movements, and were sent to prison for their roles, Mugabe for 11 years and Mandela for 27. Upon emerging from prison, however, their paths diverged. Both were elected the first modern black leaders of their countries based on similar visions of freedom, reconciliation, and a "rainbow nation," but while Mandela led South Africa out of the apartheid era into an effectively functioning multiracial democracy, Mugabe devolved into a despot who divided Zimbabwe by race and by tribe and led the country to ruin. For the purposes of our study, two questions are particularly pertinent. What were the keys to Mandela's exceptional leadership? Correspondingly, why did Mugabe, after a similarly promising start, become an ineffective leader and eventually a despot?

Robert Mugabe

I have drawn a line through the past. From now on, we must trust each other if we are to work together for the benefit of the majority. I want people to believe in my policy of reconciliation and to respond accordingly.[1]

—Robert Mugabe, 1980

When you show mercy to your former enemy...you think you are being noble. But, if you ask me now how I feel about it, I think we made a mistake.[2]

—Robert Mugabe, 2000

Robert Mugabe was a man of two faces. The first was the heroic liberator of his country from the grips of the dominant white minority. In 1980, a decade before Mandela's release from prison, Mugabe was elected the first black African prime minister of Zimbabwe, the former Rhodesia. Despite strong reasons for bitterness toward his former jailers, initially he appeared devoted to ending the divisions between black and white Zimbabweans, and reconciling with his political rivals. Indeed, Mugabe seemed intent on harnessing the best efforts of every race, party, and tribe to build a prosperous nation that would serve the interests of all its citizens.

Mugabe's second face, however, was that of a ruthless tyrant who would go to any lengths to preserve his own power and position, regardless of the consequences for his people and his country. It was this face that Mugabe increasingly displayed as Zimbabwe slid from being one of Africa's most prosperous nations—albeit with its wealth concentrated overwhelmingly in the hands of its tiny white population—to one of the poorest and most corrupt.

Wearing his first face, Mugabe was an indisputably effective leader, as indicated by the growth in Zimbabwe's economy and its provision of health and education services during his early years as prime minister. Even then, however, there were signs that his first face masked another, sinister one. That face was evident to everyone as he entered the second decade of his rule. We will trace the evolution of his leadership to understand what made it so effective at the beginning and disastrously ineffective as his mask slipped.

★ ★ ★

Robert Mugabe was born on February 21, 1924, in a village in Southern Rhodesia. His mother was a pious Bible teacher, his father a carpenter who disappeared when Mugabe was ten years old. As a boy, he spent much of his time alone. After attending a Jesuit mission school, in 1949 he received a scholarship to Fort Hare University College in South Africa, where his studies in education, law, and economics exposed him to Marxist thought. He completed his university degree and then spent several years teaching. His teaching career eventually took him to Ghana, where the influence of its Marxist prime minister, Kwame Nkrumah, shaped his political and economic views. While in Ghana, Mugabe also met Sally Hayfron, a fellow teacher whom he later married and who was viewed as a steadying influence in his political life. Their courtship had more to do with politics than romance.[3]

When Mugabe returned home in 1960, Southern Rhodesia was still a self-governing colony of Great Britain dominated by a white minority and ruled by its white prime minister, Ian Smith. Mugabe was plunged immediately into politics through an event later known as the March of 7,000. On July 19, three prominent officials of the National Democratic Party (NDP), the main vehicle for black dissent against white rule, were arrested. That night 7,000 black Africans, Mugabe among them, marched in protest. By the following day the crowd had grown to more than 40,000 and a makeshift platform was assembled for speakers. Having been invited by friends in the nationalist movement, Mugabe gave his first political speech, where he described his vision for the future of "Zimbabwe," the nationalist movement's name for the country. The excited audience received the speech with resounding applause and from this moment, Mugabe was irrevocably committed to the nationalist cause and became a full-time activist. In April 1961 he and Sally were married in Salisbury.

There was much for the nationalist cause to protest and for the dominant white minority to protect. In 1888, the South African magnate Cecil Rhodes had signed a treaty with the king of the Ndebele in Matabeleland and established the British South Africa Company (BSAC) to mine gold in his territory. An invading white population systematically appropriated the power and resources of what became the British colony of Southern Rhodesia. After the military defeat of the Ndebele and their Shona allies in the 1890s, Africans were herded into arid Native Reserves, which even colonial officials acknowledged were unfit for settlement. Through a series of legislative acts, Africans were banned from owning the most fertile land and were channeled into serving as poorly paid laborers in white-owned agricultural, mining, and industrial enterprises. At the time of independence in 1980, 70 percent of the black population, or 4.5 million people, was living on Native Reserves that occupied half of the country's arable land, the poorest, least fertile portion. Meanwhile, 6,000 white farmers owned roughly 46 percent of the arable land—and all of the country's most fertile land—while 8,500 black farmers owned the remaining 4 percent, land mainly in drier regions. Rhodesia's minority white population, only 3 percent of the total, controlled the country's wealth and the levers of power. No wonder the nationalist movement arose—and was feared by whites.

A powerful orator, Mugabe soon rose within the NDP leadership. After failed negotiations with the white government led to the party's banning, Mugabe became secretary-general of its successor, the Zimbabwe African People's Union (ZAPU). In April 1963 he and his wife, with other ZAPU activists, fled to Tanzania at the urging of the party's leader, Joshua Nkomo, who hoped to continue the nationalist fight through a government-in-exile. But soon internal disagreements led to the formation of a rival party, the Zimbabwe African National Union (ZANU). Ndabaningi Sithole was elected leader and Mugabe secretary-general.

Returning to Southern Rhodesia in December 1963, Mugabe was arrested under the draconian Law and Order Act on charges of subversion, and given a 21-month sentence. He remained in prison for the next 11 years, an experience that steeled his resolve to pursue revolution. His hatred for the white government intensified when Smith personally blocked him from attending the funeral of his three-year-old son. Meanwhile, Mugabe continued to advance politically while still in prison. In 1974, after deposing Sithole, he was elected head of the ZANU party.

Later in 1974, Ian Smith released Mugabe under pressure from South Africa's apartheid government. Mugabe fled to Mozambique and became head of the Zimbabwe African National Liberation Army (ZANLA), ZANU's military arm, which infiltrated Rhodesia from its Mozambican bases. Success in forcing the white government to the negotiating table came after five years of fighting. Nkomo's ZAPU also joined the struggle with its own guerilla forces, but he was never fully committed to the war. It was Mugabe's ZANLA that did most of the fighting, though Mugabe himself remained aloof from day-to-day operations and instead ran an effective propaganda war. His time as a guerilla leader, biographer David Blair notes, revealed elements of his future leadership style: "Few people were close to him and almost all of ZANLA's top commanders fell under his suspicion at some stage. Many paid a bitter price for defiance, real or imagined."[4] One of these was his second-in-command, Wilfred Mhanda, imprisoned in 1977 with dozens of other fighters who questioned Mugabe's leadership.

The Liberation War ended in 1979 when Mugabe, Nkomo, and Smith met in London for what were termed the Lancaster House negotiations. The focus was on two seemingly intractable issues, land redistribution and a transition to majority rule. Mugabe and Nkomo concluded that their central goal must be political control over Zimbabwe, even at the cost of falling short of full resolution of the two core issues. Specifically, they agreed to a ten-year period in which white-owned land would be purchased only on a "willing seller, willing buyer" basis at market rates, backed by vague understandings that the United Kingdom, the United States, and others would create an international fund for land purchases. To smooth the transition of government control from the defeated whites to the victorious African majority, the Lancaster House constitution also guaranteed whites 20 percent of the seats in Parliament while constitutional amendments were forbidden before 1987. Defending his actions to supporters, Mugabe said: "We had...to compromise on certain fundamental principles, but only because there was a chance, in the future, to amend the position. We had got the main concession of the creation of democracy."[5] Understanding the vital importance of the negotiations' success, Mugabe emerged from them as "the liberation hero of an era."[6] A ceasefire agreement was extended until February 1980, when the first free election would be held. Pitted against his former ZAPU colleague, Nkomo, Mugabe won everywhere but in Nkomo's Matabeleland stronghold. He was elected the first prime minister of independent Zimbabwe on a platform of racial equality, nondiscrimination, and reconciliation.

In organizing his new government, Mugabe appeared to show genuine magnanimity and moral courage.[7] In a speech shortly after the election, he proclaimed: "We will ensure that there is a place for everyone in this country," and he invited blacks and whites "to join me in a new pledge to forget our grim past, forgive others and forget, join hands in a new amity and together, as Zimbabweans, trample upon racism."[8] Ken Flowers, the former head of Rhodesia's intelligence service who had once tried to organize his assassination, said that Mugabe seemed to have "a greater capacity and determination to shape the country's destiny for the benefit of all its people" than his white predecessors.[9] Africans and Europeans alike saw in Mugabe a leader who might overcome the problems that had plagued the new governments of many former colonies over the preceding 20 years.

Mugabe reached out to the white population, urging them to stay and help rebuild the country. Recalling a meeting with him soon after the 1980 election, Ian Smith said that he "couldn't get over this bloke's reasonableness, the breadth of his vision and particularly his desire for reconciliation and keeping the white people, accepting the need for them."[10] Mugabe's cabinet included white ministers—most notably, Denis Norman as agricultural minister, which greatly eased the fears of white farmers—as well as his political rival Joshua Nkomo. With his talk of "our country, all of us, together,"[11] Mugabe seemed to be building the rainbow nation that Mandela would promote in South Africa a decade later.

In short, up to this point Mugabe appeared to have a compelling vision, which he embodied and articulated persuasively, initially to black Zimbabweans and then, after the Lancaster House agreement, to whites and other groups as well. His story was of a free and democratic Zimbabwe in which there would be no racial discrimination, with land redistributed equitably and fair compensation paid to its owners, and with illiteracy, disease, and poverty attacked aggressively. Did he mean it, or was it a sham? Certainly in light of the many political threats he faced in his first years as prime minister, it was an effective stance to take. Three armies had to be consolidated into one, and its loyalty assured. He needed the support of the urban working class and unions. He had to meet the heightened expectations of ZANU's peasant supporters and 45,000 ex-guerillas for improved education and health care, land redistribution, and job opportunities. He also hoped to attract potential international investors and encourage the United Kingdom and the United States to follow through on funding land purchases. For all of these reasons, maintaining economic stability and political unity was critical. Despite ZANU's 1977 declaration that it aimed for a one-party state, perhaps Mugabe now viewed a multiparty democracy as the best way to govern and prosper, and even as the means to become a great man.

During his first decade or so in office, some real progress was made toward the promised reforms. Mugabe immediately set about trying to rectify the inequities in land ownership, and by the end of the 1980s, 52,000 families (or 416,000 people) had been resettled on 6.5 million acres of land. This was a significant accomplishment, even though the land was often inferior and the resettlement fell far short of Mugabe's initial three-year plan to move 162,000 families onto 20 million acres, largely because of the "willing buyer, willing seller" clause and inadequate funds.[12] Furthermore,

Mugabe oversaw the expansion of health services and guaranteed educational opportunities for Zimbabwe's blacks who previously had little access to secondary schools and universities. The high-school enrollment rate soared from 2 percent at the time of independence to 70 percent by 1990, while literacy jumped from 45 percent to 80 percent.[13] During the same period, child immunization rates grew from 25 percent to 92 percent. With these results, Mugabe was widely praised as one of the postcolonial era's most effective and progressive leaders.

For those watching closely, however, telltale inconsistencies appeared in his story very early in his first term. Most vividly, in 1982 he launched Operation Gukurahundi (loosely translated as both storm and purification), a mission with the professed purpose of wiping out dissidents in Matabelelands who threatened to overturn the government. In reality, these dissidents never numbered more than 400 and had no aim except random sabotage.[14] Mugabe's real goal was to eliminate his rival Joshua Nkomo by targeting ZAPU's primary supporters, the Ndebele people, in their Matabelelands stronghold. The scale of the ensuing violence was far worse than anything that had occurred during the Liberation War. It was, a village headman said, "fearful, unforgettable and unacknowledged."[15] Over four years, as many as 25,000 civilians were killed, and countless more were beaten or tortured.[16] Nkomo finally surrendered in December of 1987, signing the Unity Accord that in essence dissolved ZAPU by merging it with ZANU to become ZANU-PF.[17]

Mugabe's Matabelelands campaign served as the first evidence of his contempt for law and his willingness to exercise persistent and extreme violence in order to consolidate his power. In a telling speech to Parliament in 1982, he had warned that "an eye for an eye and an ear for an ear may not be adequate... [W]e might very well demand two ears for one ear and two eyes for one eye."[18]

Mugabe's talk of racial reconciliation also was discredited by his reaction to events surrounding the 1985 election. That election became a turning point when 15 of the 20 seats in Parliament designated for whites were won by Smith's antigovernment party rather than by whites favoring cooperation with Mugabe. In a speech after the elections, Mugabe let slip the mask as he threatened that "whites who have not accepted the reality of a political order in which the Africans set the pace will have to leave the country... [added in native chiShona:] We will kill those snakes among us, we will smash them completely."[19]

Perhaps Mugabe had been sincere about his newfound vision of a multiparty, nondiscriminatory democracy, but felt betrayed by white farmers who took advantage of the "willing buyer, willing seller" clause to demand high prices and sell their poorer land, or none at all, and by other whites who transferred their wealth outside the country. Perhaps he was frustrated by the United Kingdom and United States who had not contributed or raised funds sufficient to fund needed land purchases, and by the political parties, white and black, who opposed him and thwarted his plans. More likely, while his resentment toward those obstructing him was real, his true vision had always been for one-party rule. In any event, he amassed power as quickly as he could. As soon as the freeze on revising the Constitution expired in 1987, he abolished the position of prime minister and replaced it with an executive presidency of sweeping authority. On December 31, he was duly sworn in as the first president. He also eliminated the guarantee that 20 of the 100 seats in Parliament would be reserved to whites, which effectively removed all parliamentary opposition as they were the only seats not held by Mugabe's ZANU-PF. Then, immediately prior to the 1990 elections, the number of members of Parliament was increased to 150, 30 of whom would be presidential appointees.

After those elections, ZANU-PF ended up in control of 147 of the total of 150 seats. Not only was there no significant opposition party, but in the elections Mugabe aggressively used his primary political weapons, land and race, to divide and conquer, saying, "It makes absolute nonsense of our history as an African country that most of our arable and ranching land is still in the hands of our erstwhile colonizers, while the majority of our peasant community still live like squatters in their own God-given land."[20] While it is true that the continuing inequity in land ownership was due in large measure to factors beyond Mugabe's control, it was exacerbated by the ineffectiveness and corruption of his government. By the early 1990s, the government had incurred massive deficits, which caused it to turn to the IMF as a lender of last resort. The IMF, of course, required significant structural adjustments as conditions of lending, including major cutbacks in the civil service and in programs that had propped up economic performance. Under the austerity regime, growth dropped to below zero, while both inflation and unemployment reached 30 percent.[21] Political pressures on Mugabe and ZANU-PF escalated, and rather than acknowledge any failures in policy, the president sought scapegoats. He would eventually condemn the IMF as a tool of western imperialism. Closer to home, he made white farmers targets of his demagoguery and punitive legislation. After the expiration of the ten-year term for the "willing buyer, willing seller" clause, he sent an act to Parliament that empowered the government to simply confiscate land, fix the price it paid, and deny the right to appeal to courts for fair compensation. "It flies in the face of all accepted norms of modern society, and the rule of law," Enoch Dumbutshena, Zimbabwe's first black chief justice, said at the time.[22] Ultimately, Mugabe removed the clause that barred courts from overturning a government land value assessment, but the basic provisions of the 1992 Land Acquisition Act remained. Later, when a group challenged its legality, Mugabe retorted that he would "not brook any decision by any court."[23]

A few years later, the war veterans, a group that had traditionally remained loyal to Mugabe, were furious with him over the corruption that had emptied the War Victims Compensation Fund.[24] On the defensive,

Mugabe once again used the weapon of land, creating a vast new list of white-owned farms to be expropriated. The list included about 45 percent of the land held by Zimbabwe's 4,500 commercial farmers, and the move exacerbated Zimbabwe's economic problems, as well as racial tensions.

A startling example of Mugabe's fixation on his own power needs rather than on the needs of his people was his 1998 invasion of the Congo. He justified this adventure as a defense of the Congo government's sovereignty in the face of rebel uprisings. In truth, Mugabe's poor relations with the IMF, which led to the withholding of loans, left him with few options to turn around the economy's collapse, worsened by a series of droughts. The Congo invasion offered an opportunity to distract the country and retain the loyalty of his cronies by enabling them to pillage the Congo for diamonds, cobalt, and timber. But Zimbabweans at home could not be distracted from their daily struggle to find food, buy fuel, pay their debts, and fight the ravages of inflation, which at that time reached 57 percent. They were victimized again in 1999, when Mugabe instated an "AIDS levy," a 3 percent tax on every Zimbabwean's salary to be used to fight the rampant AIDS epidemic that had infected more than 25 percent of the adult population.[25] Most of this money, not surprisingly, simply disappeared.

As biographer Martin Meredith concludes, Mugabe had become "an irascible and petulant dictator" who had "failed to satisfy popular expectations in education, health, land reform, and employment" and had "alienated the entire white community." Even so, Meredith writes, "Mugabe continued to believe in his own greatness."[26] And clearly he was determined to remain in power. In 2000, he introduced a referendum on a new constitution that would enable him to serve two more terms, give immunity from prosecution to senior leaders accused of crimes while in office, and allow the seizure of lands without compensation. He was confident the people would support this constitution, but instead it spurred his diverse opponents—now including trade unions, displaced civil service workers, white farmers, and others—to coalesce and form the Movement for Democratic Change (MDC). As his leading rival and new head of the MDC, Morgan Tsvangirai, pointed out, "That draft constitution is not representative of what the people want. It represents what those in power want."[27] With the opposition campaigning hard, Zimbabweans dealt Mugabe a sharp rebuff, sending the president's constitution down to a decisive defeat. Characteristically, Mugabe looked for someone to blame and punish. Journalist Peter Godwin notes that he announced afterward that he would respect the will of the people, but "his face was tight with anger...And you could see that this was a man fueled by thoughts of revenge...It couldn't be his own people who had done this...it must have been other people, white people, leading them astray. He would show us."[28]

He did, scapegoating white farmers again with another incendiary round of land reforms, inciting a third *chimurenga*, or "liberation war."[29] When Zimbabwe's Supreme Court ruled that the government had seized land illegally, Mugabe responded, "No judicial decision will stand in our way."[30] "If white settlers just took the land from us without paying for it," he said at the time, "we can in a similar way just take it from them, without paying for it."[31] Although many Zimbabweans, including white farmers, continued to believe that land reform was necessary, Mugabe's approach was disastrous for almost all. Too often farmlands were handed to the president's cronies and loyalists who "lacked the agricultural expertise to manage their holdings, and once-profitable farms turned into wastelands."[32] The costs to Zimbabwe included disastrous declines in food production exacerbated by drought, mass unemployment of black farm workers, and the collapse of any semblance of the rule of law.[33]

As land grabs intensified, Mugabe called for parliamentary elections only a few months after the referendum defeat, and more than ever he relied on brutality, murder, and threats to have his way. Biographer Stephen Chan points out that the land war "ran both in tandem with and parallel to the election campaign." It was a promise of "redistribution to come" and had the additional purpose of distracting attention "from too close a scrutiny of electoral tactics of violence."[34] Even so, the MDC won 57 seats in Parliament, nearly matching ZANU-PF's 62.

Mugabe struck back against his foes. In 2005, he launched Operation Murambatsvina, or "Drive Out Rubbish," a campaign to bulldoze shanty-towns in Harare and other cities, targeting the slums where the MDC had its most loyal support, including small traders who constituted the back-bone of the prodemocracy movement. The main result of the operation was 700,000 homeless Zimbabweans. Mugabe's follow-up—Operation Garikai, or "Stay Well"—was designed to build 31,000 houses, small factories, and shops, but it quickly fell apart amid allegations of favoritism and corruption. Fewer than 500 houses were completed.[35]

During the 2008 presidential campaign, more than 150 opposition supporters were murdered and thousands were beaten, tortured, or raped. Despite the terror tactics, in March, opposition leader Tsvangirai won 48 percent of the votes and Mugabe 43 percent. With no majority, a run-off was required. In the weeks preceding the June vote, Mugabe's party forced thousands of opponents into "reeducation camps." Many others were intimidated, beaten, tortured, or murdered. The president was bent on reminding the Zimbabwean people what they owed to the party that had given them liberation—and what it would cost them if they forgot. He used state-controlled media to portray himself as the beloved leader of the nation and to blame the MDC as the cause of all the election violence. Five days before the election, Tsvangirai pulled out, saying that he could no longer ask Zimbabweans to cast their vote for him "when that vote could cost them their lives."[36] One reporter wrote that a Mugabe victory would "represent the last, desperate gambit of a regime that long ago lost any shred of legitimacy."[37]

After a storm of international protest, Mugabe agreed to a power-sharing deal with Tsvangirai wherein he remained president while

Tsvangirai became prime minister. However, the effectiveness of the deal was questionable, especially as Mugabe kept control over the most important ministries, including Defense, Home Affairs, and Justice.

Mugabe's use of violence and terror in the 2008 election continued a long trend of single-minded, relentless pursuit of total control. As he had said in 2000, "I do not want to be overthrown and I will try to overthrow those who want to overthrow me."[38] The result of his decades of despotism was the destruction of Zimbabwe. In 2008 the country experienced 11 million percent inflation, widespread food shortages, international sanctions, and the mass exodus of whites and educated blacks.[39] The unemployment rate was 80 percent, and 80 percent of the population was impoverished. Mugabe's few achievements—most particularly improvements in education and healthcare—were undermined by his mismanagement of the economy and the chaos of his rule. Thousands of teachers fled or were evicted, and dozens of schools closed.[40] As Samantha Power writes, "How could the breadbasket of Africa have deteriorated so quickly into the continent's basket case? The answer is Robert Mugabe...who by his actions has compiled something of a 'how-to' manual for national destruction."[41]

★   ★   ★

Looking over the total sweep of Mugabe's long career, the most plausible explanation of his leadership effectiveness in the early years and its dramatic deterioration as time passed is the growing (or emerging) selfishness that drove him ultimately to become a tyrant.

Clearly, Mugabe's *vision* upon becoming prime minister was compelling. During the initial stages of opposition and throughout the period of guerilla warfare, liberation was a genuinely popular vision shared by virtually all black Zimbabweans. After being elected prime minister of the newly free Zimbabwe, Mugabe's ambitious and progressive goals for racial reconciliation, economic growth, and improvements in health and education were ones that blacks and whites, Zimbabweans and foreigners alike, praised and worked to support. They brought Mugabe enormous popularity among his constituents and captured their loyalty, which the people were slow to abandon. Consequently, despite the trauma of the Matebelelands and growing racial tensions, he had widespread popular support through 1990 and even beyond. Many believed that he was delivering blacks from colonial injustices and thereby empowering them.

His powerful skills as a *communicator* were an important element of his success. His 1960 speech following the March of 7,000 vaulted him almost immediately into the upper ranks of the liberation movement. With his 11 years in prison and leadership of the guerilla movement, he embodied his message. And his success in propaganda warfare as much as in guerilla fighting persuaded other African and European leaders that he was a key player who needed to be at the negotiating table in creating the new Zimbabwe. Afterward, he ran successfully for the premiership in 1980, persuaded many whites to stay, and had the support of numerous world powers for his vision to rebuild Zimbabwe.

In conveying his vision, Mugabe initially seemed to act selflessly and in the best interests of his country. He put aside bitterness toward whites and reached out to them with conciliatory words and by including them in his cabinet.

Finally, though we know less about the inner workings of ZANU in its early years, it is clear that Mugabe had sufficient *organizational skills* to shape it (together with ZANLA) into an effective platform both for forcing his inclusion at the Lancaster House negotiations and for winning the subsequent 1980 election. His organization was not, however, capable of fulfilling his promises of land reform, health and education improvements, and economic prosperity.

With the government's continuing inability to deliver on those promises in the 1990s, Mugabe's commitment to one-party rule and his determination to hold onto personal power at any cost—his innate *selfishness*—became clear. Despite his avowed vision of a racially diverse, multiparty democracy, when challenged he quickly reverted to the original ZANU vision of a one-party state and ruthlessly used the land issue, racial dissension, repression, and violence to maintain and enhance his power. Perhaps he believed only he could successfully lead postcolonial Zimbabwe, and that the end justified his means. Perhaps his appetite for power and reputation—to be the liberation hero, the Big Man—overwhelmed any selfless impulses he may have felt at one time or another. Perhaps his wife's untimely death in 1992 removed any moderating influence on his basest impulses. As time passed, maybe he felt, too, that his survival depended upon retaining power. Whatever the combination of motivations, it is clear that his personal interests eventually trampled the interests of the people of Zimbabwe, once one of the richest and now one of the poorest countries in Africa.

Mugabe's ability to maintain power since the end of the "honeymoon period" was also based on his communication and organizational skills, although they were now used as coercive means to immoral ends. With censorship, government control of virtually all media, and the skills he first learned in the liberation war, he used propaganda for many years to persuade Zimbabweans and foreigners of what he wanted them to believe. In addition, by surrounding himself with sycophants, rewarding his closest followers with large grants of land and other gifts, and tolerating their corruption and incompetence, he also maintained control of ZANU-PF, which after the forced merger of ZAPU and the destruction of the white opposition, enjoyed monopolistic control of the government. With these means, Mugabe bound his followers to him through greed and fear.

Yet after the failure of the 2000 constitutional referendum, cracks in the monolithic façade of his party became evident. Already existing rifts widened, factions hardened as party "big men" wrestled over the spoils of corruption and the succession, and Mugabe's isolation increased. Instead of reconciling the factions, Mugabe's response was to lash out at them, accusing them of vying for power.[42] He even alienated a key member of his staff, Jonathan Moyo, who had once served as his mouthpiece. "Their relationship degenerated into name-calling games," according to an opposition activist.[43] In 2002, when Mugabe sent three bills to Parliament that increased the government's power, a ZANU-PF baron, Edison Zvogbo, led his faction to block a bill that would impose government controls on the press. The bill became law eventually but not before Zvogbo denounced it as a calculated assault on civil liberties.[44] And in the 2007 party congress elections to nominate a presidential candidate, a top official of ZANU-PF ran against Mugabe in an unprecedented display of disaffection. Some senior officials even called Mugabe's nomination "a fraudulent process" marred by "blatant intrigue and manipulation."[45] Thus, even though Mugabe clung to power as the leader of ZANU-PF and of Zimbabwe, his loyal bastion began to split and drift away. Dissidents doubtless understood that he would never put anyone else's interests before his own, and they understood too the implications of the Zimbabwe people's dissatisfaction with the ZANU-PF government for their own futures.

In summary, the champion of human rights and democracy, as he was hailed at the outset of his reign, two decades later was condemned as "a deranged despot" by Morgan Tsvangirai[46] and "a fraud" by Wilfred Mhanda, Mugabe's old colleague from the guerilla movement.[47] Once an admired leader able to persuade blacks, whites, and the world of the promise of an independent and democratic Zimbabwe, Robert Mugabe revealed himself over time to be an egregiously selfish and immoral despot willing to resort to any form of coercion to maintain his power, even at the cost of ruining his entire country. "It's a mystery he is not trying to do something about his legacy," said a Zimbabwean journalist. "He must know that there's nobody left who can write him a good obituary."[48]

Nelson Mandela

During my lifetime...I have fought against White domination, and I have fought against Black domination. I have cherished the ideal of a democratic and free society in which all persons live together in harmony and with equal opportunities. It is an ideal which I hope to live for and to achieve. But if needs be, it is an ideal for which I am prepared to die.[49]

—Nelson Mandela at the Rivonia trial, 1964

The time for the healing of the wounds has come...We enter into a covenant that we shall build the society in which all South Africans, both black and white, will be able to walk tall, without any fear in their hearts, assured of their inalienable right to human dignity—a rainbow nation at peace with itself and the world.[50]

—Nelson Mandela in his presidential
inauguration speech, 1994

Unlike Robert Mugabe, Nelson Mandela was consistent in his vision and in his actions over the three decades between his 1964 trial and 1994 inauguration and throughout his five-year term as the first black president of South Africa. Though he had as many reasons as Mugabe for bitterness toward the dominant white minority and an equally difficult apartheid legacy to overcome, Mandela said and meant that he harbored no anger toward white people. Instead, he "hated the system that turned us against one another,"[51] and promoted racial reconciliation in word and deed. He lived by his beliefs in the rule of law and democracy, and, having set South Africa on the right course, he retired from the presidency after one term, just as he said he would. Unlike Mugabe, in Mandela's case, "[t]he man and the mask were one."[52] As a result of Mandela's leadership, South Africa today, though beset with challenges, is a prosperous and effectively functioning nonracial democracy that offers hope for the rest of Africa. What made his leadership not just effective, but exceptional?

★   ★   ★

Rolihlahla Mandela—his given name meaning, roughly, "troublemaker"—was born on July 18, 1918, into the royal family of the proud Tembu people. He was descended from a famous Tembu king, and when his father died, nine-year-old Nelson was adopted by the Regent, Jongintaba. While the royal family was quite poor by European standards, they still held an honored place among their people, and thus Mandela grew up seeing himself as a member of a privileged elite. Richard Stengel, who collaborated with Mandela on his memoirs, thought that his political confidence originated from "the security and simplicity of his rural upbringing."[53]

Mandela was also raised with the values of *ubuntu*, an all-encompassing, humanistic Xhosa term that incorporates the concepts of human brotherhood, caring, and kindness. *Ubuntu* inclined him to see the best in others and would prove to be a key principle of his leadership. "You encourage people by seeing good in them," he said.[54]

Another fundamental aspect of his political education as a boy came through his observations of Jongintaba presiding over the tribal courts. He greatly admired his adopted father's ability to listen carefully and unemotionally to all sides of a dispute and achieve consensus among the various parties involved.[55] As Mandela reflected years later when he was in prison: "One of the marks of a great chief is the ability to keep together all sections of his people, the traditionalists and the reformers, conservatives and liberals, and on major questions there are sometimes sharp differences of opinion...the Regent was able to carry the whole community because the court was representative of all shades of opinion."[56] It was a skill Mandela developed as well.

Having grown up as a proud member of the ruling family of a proud people, it came as a shock to Mandela when, at his coming-of-age circumcision ceremony in 1934, Chief Meligqili, a brother of Jongintaba, "told the boys that they would never really be men because they were conquered people who were slaves in their own country."[57] It was only after completing his boyhood education at mission school and entering the University College of Fort Hare in 1939 to study law that Mandela began to understand more clearly Chief Meligqili's message. At Fort Hare he was exposed to the increasing segregation and inequities in South African society and came to know other black students impatient with the older generation's strategy of gradual social change through education.[58] Mandela would come to favor a more activist approach based on passive resistance,[59] and upon joining the ANC in 1943, he promoted this strategy. When its leadership was unsupportive, he, along with others from his generation including Oliver Tambo and Walter Sisulu, branched off to form the ANC Youth League in 1944. In 1949 and 1950, the Youth League made its first determined efforts to use boycotts, strikes, and other forms of civil disobedience. A national work stoppage day in June 1950 was particularly successful. In late 1950 Mandela became president of the Youth League. He also joined the ANC's executive committee that year and was elected its deputy president in 1952.

In 1952, Mandela passed his qualifying exam to become an attorney as well, and soon thereafter he and Tambo started their own law practice. They quickly were inundated with clients, mostly blacks charged with violations of apartheid laws such as using whites–only public restrooms. Mandela seized on these court cases to challenge white authority, an experience that would be extremely valuable in the future when it would be Mandela himself, or his colleagues, on trial.

Initially, Mandela had favored an exclusively Africans-only approach toward change in South Africa. But after he collaborated with Indian and Colored activists in organizing the Defiance Campaign of 1952, which resulted in the imprisonment of eight thousand activists and attracted many new members to the ANC, he began to shift to a more encompassing multiracialism as both means and end, including a steadfast belief in creating a nonracial democracy. Moreover, Mandela's increasing contacts with white communists during this period led him to broaden his critique of apartheid to include "monopoly capitalism" as an oppressive force. He also relinquished African "exclusivism," to the dismay of racial separatists who saw this as a "watering down of his affiliation" to his own people in favor of seeking common interests with communists.[60]

Mandela decided that the benefits of cooperating with other political parties that were fighting the wave of apartheid legislation outweighed any differences. When he was criticized for joining hands with the Communist Party, he replied that: "Theoretical differences amongst those fighting against oppression is a luxury we cannot afford... They were the only political group which was prepared to work with the Africans for the attainment of political rights and a stake in society."[61]

In 1955, the ANC took another big step when it united with other opposition groups, including the Indian Congress and the Colored People's Organization, to form the Congress of the People. The coalition drafted a sweeping "Freedom Charter" that affirmed the right of all citizens to vote, to hold office, and to be equal before the law. Mandela called it "a revolutionary document precisely because the changes it envisages cannot be won without breaking up the economic and political set-up of present South Africa."[62] For years to come, the Freedom Charter would serve as the guiding statement of principles for the entire liberation movement.

Mandela became increasingly frustrated with the ineffectiveness of passive resistance, reflecting that "fifty years of non-violence had brought the African people nothing but more and more repressive legislation."[63] Yet it took events like the Sharpeville massacre[64] and the banning of the ANC, both in 1960, to persuade him finally that the government had indeed barred "all channels of peaceful progress."[65] At an ANC meeting in June 1961, Mandela argued that the party's followers were losing confidence in the nonviolence policy and would resort to violent protest on their own if the leadership did not respond. Mandela was authorized to establish a military wing, *Umkhonto we Sizwe*, meaning Spear of the Nation, abbreviated as MK. Within months, Mandela and the MK launched an underground sabotage campaign that targeted government buildings and installations, railways, power plants, and telecommunications. While they also made contingent preparations for guerilla warfare, the focus on sabotage underscored Mandela's commitment to a nonracial postapartheid South Africa. As he said later, "Sabotage did not involve loss of life, and it offered the best hope for race relations. Bitterness would be kept to a minimum."[66]

In 1962, when Mandela returned to South Africa from a world tour to garner support, he was arrested for his role in organizing a strike the prior year. During his trial, he attempted to turn the tables on the government and prosecute the system of justice, commenting: "I detest most violently the set-up that surrounds me here. It makes me feel that I am a black man in a white man's court. This should not be."[67] He also seized the moral high ground, vowing that when he had completed his sentence, "I will still be moved by my dislike of the race discrimination against my people" and would "take up again, as best I can, the struggle for the removal of those injustices until they are finally abolished once and for all."[68] During the three-year term in jail that followed, Mandela won much respect from fellow prisoners with challenges to the prison regime, as when he refused to run as commanded and instead walked slowly. That meant, as one prisoner said, "We are going to set the terms."[69]

In 1964, a police raid of an ANC hideout in Rivonia near Johannesburg uncovered documents that included plans for guerilla warfare and implicated the main leaders of the ANC. Mandela and his colleagues, including Walter Sisulu and Govan Mbeki, were brought back to court for plotting to overthrow the government. Once again, Mandela sought to "turn the trial into a showcase against the government."[70] Though they assumed that a death sentence was likely, the three ANC leaders decided that they would not appeal the verdict, believing that, as Mandela said, "[o]ur message [to our supporters] was that no sacrifice was too great in the struggle for freedom."[71] Most profoundly, he emphasized the morality of their cause in his closing statement, expressing his "ideal of a democratic and free society in which all persons live together in harmony and with equal opportunities."[72]

Mandela was sentenced to life in prison, not death, and with his ANC colleagues, he was sent to Robben Island Prison, where he would spend most of the next 27 years. In stark contrast to Mugabe, Mandela was not embittered by his experience in prison. Instead, he became ennobled, earning the respect and admiration of his fellow prisoners, of his warders, and eventually of the world. He did so through four means. First, as the leader of what grew to be an army of some 1,000 ANC prisoners, he engaged in an active political dialogue with the other political parties represented in the prison population. Showing the qualities he had admired in Jongintaba, Mandela deepened his understanding of the various approaches to the liberation struggle and was able to find at least some common ground with many of them.

Second, Mandela immediately launched a series of protests to the prison authorities about living conditions at Robben Island, starting with a successful challenge to the rule that complaints could be made only in individual cases, not on behalf of all prisoners. Always professional and polite, he was nonetheless determined, and honing skills he would later use on a much grander stage, he won many concessions for fellow inmates.

Third, he never wavered in his belief in democracy. While a few of his colleagues in prison saw a large degree of hereditary chieftaincy in his leadership style, those close to him did not. As Sisulu said, "He tried to be a builder, to take a position which he thinks is more suitable for a leader of the ANC. He avoided expressing emotion: he would rather want a balanced picture."[73] As another colleague, "Mac" Maharaj, added, "In his political life in the early years he gave vent to the anger he felt. In prison he got his anger almost totally under control. That control has come about through a deliberate effort by Mandela."[74] Mandela always thought of himself as a member of a team, not a chief, saying later: "I find it difficult to personalize the collective experience of prison."[75] Indeed, he said later, "I didn't see myself as a leader until I was elected" Tambo's successor as president of the ANC in 1985.[76]

Finally, throughout his prison years Mandela continued to insist on the critical importance of racial reconciliation to achieving the goal of a nonracial democracy. The only bitterness he expressed was toward the system of apartheid, not toward whites. In 1985, after over 20 years in prison, he said: "Unlike white people anywhere else in Africa, whites in South Africa belong here—this is their home. We want them to live here with us and to share power with us."[77]

Mandela's moral authority was further enhanced in 1985 when he turned down an offer from the government to release him, conditional upon his renunciation of violence by the ANC. He responded that violence was the ANC's only means of countering the government's own violence and its unwillingness to respond to any other form of protest. Moreover, he refused to bargain with the apartheid regime that imprisoned him. "Only free men can negotiate," he said.[78]

The government's offer of release reflected the enormous pressure from antiapartheid forces within South Africa and throughout the world by the mid-1980s. At the same time, there was fear among white South Africans about the implications of black majority rule. Yet even within the hard-line apartheid government, some officials recognized that their system was doomed and that a peaceful means of transition was needed. In the late 1980s, the government finally agreed to begin the talks that Mandela had been requesting for years. Initially, the government insisted that they be held in secret, and Mandela courageously agreed, despite the risk of appearing to sell out the ANC for his own advantage. The first discussions proceeded without the knowledge even of his ANC colleagues in prison. Then the talks became more intense. Other ANC leaders developed their own government contacts, while Mandela met regularly with a committee of officials. But after two years, dozens of sessions, even a conversation with South African president P. W. Botha, they were still merely "talking about talks." The government refused to negotiate with the ANC until it renounced violence and the Communist Party and gave up its goal of majority rule.[79]

Real progress did not come until Frederik Willem de Klerk succeeded Botha as president. In fact, Botha, who regarded the ANC as a menace to white civilization, hoped to use the contacts with Mandela to detach him from his colleagues and split the ANC, and to make a separate deal with Chief Buthelezi, the head of the Inkatha Freedom Party whom the government was building up publicly as a rival to Mandela.[80] But in early 1989 Botha suffered a stroke, and while he remained president, he resigned as head of the National Party and was succeeded by de Klerk. Later that year, de Klerk forced him out as president as well. De Klerk recognized the urgency for change. Over the following year, he unbanned the ANC and other organizations, authorized the release of hundreds of political prisoners, and began dismantling apartheid legislation. Most importantly, de Klerk served as a key negotiating partner with Mandela, helping to lead the fearful white community through the momentous process of transition to black rule. Mandela once said, "My worst nightmare is that I wake up and de Klerk isn't there. I need him. Whether I like him or not is irrelevant. I need him."[81]

Mandela was the last ANC leader freed, in early 1990, thereby removing any remaining doubts about his "selling out." Soon thereafter he became the operational as well as the titular president of the ANC. Over the following three years, he led the negotiations to dismantle apartheid and hold elections open to all races. These achievements required that he unite the ANC, find common ground with Inkatha and other political parties, and reassure both the white community and the world. Through it all, Mandela applied the lessons he learned from observing

Jongintaba; he would seek common ground without wavering in the commitment to national reconciliation and nonracial democracy.

Still, large obstacles remained. Perhaps the most significant was the wave of political violence that had begun in the late 1980s. Though much of it was small in scale, its persistence was destructive. No party, white or black, had clean hands, but Buthelezi's Inkatha Party was the most desta-bilizing force, since the chief's primary means of guaranteeing himself a seat at the negotiating table was to resort to ambushes and indiscrimi-nate killings. Moreover, Inkatha's heavy recruitment of Zulus and Xhosas heightened ethnic tensions among blacks. Inkatha's actions also created conflicts between Mandela and de Klerk.

The rift between the latter two deepened at the opening day of the Convention for a Democratic South Africa (CODESA) in 1991. The pur-pose of CODESA was to negotiate a new constitution banning apartheid and facilitating a peaceful transition to an inclusive democracy. While the 19 parties attending agreed in the opening session on a Declaration of Intent "to bring about an undivided South Africa,"[82] de Klerk, in the final speech of the day, accused the ANC of refusing to abandon armed struggle or dismantle its military wing while professing to seek peacefully negotiated solutions, prompting a furious response from Mandela.[83] The exchange harmed the reputations of both men and created more problems for Mandela in controlling his increasingly fractious organization even as the two men shook hands the following day and the talks proceeded.

After two years of negotiation, all conducted under the shadow of con-tinued protests, strikes, and violence, a climactic act of bloodshed rocked the nation as CODESA was struggling to reach a final accord. On April 10, 1993, Chris Hani, the former head of ANC military operations, was killed in his home in a predominantly white neighborhood. Confronting a volatile mixture of black anger and white fear, Mandela provided a calming presence, insisting, "Now is the time for all South Africans to stand together against those who, from any quarter, wish to destroy what Chris Hani gave his life for—the freedom of all of us."[84] His response to the crisis gave him new prominence as a truly national leader and shielded the negotiations from the turbulence outside the conference room. When CODESA adjourned, the participants had set the date for the first national elections—April 27, 1994.

On that day, Nelson Mandela was elected the first black president of South Africa. He was perhaps the only person with a reasonable chance to create the rainbow nation that he so eloquently described in a speech after the vote: "The time has come for men and women, Africans, Coloureds, Indians, whites, Afrikaners and English-speaking, to say: we are one coun-try; we are one people."[85] For pursuing so consistently and so long the goal of national reconciliation, he was the one person trusted by all parties in the complicated new nonracial democracy of South Africa. Blacks consid-ered him the hero of liberation and a man who had devoted his life to their freedom, while whites respected him and believed in his sincerity.

Mandela and his government justified that trust with their pursuit of national reconciliation, the most critical challenge facing the country. The president established the Truth and Reconciliation Commission in May 1995, chaired by Archbishop Desmond Tutu, to bear witness to the crimes committed under the apartheid system, to grant amnesty under certain conditions to those who committed them, and to provide reparations to the victims. As Mandela explained to reporters: "Only by knowing the truth can we hope to heal the terrible open wounds that are the legacy of apartheid...Only the truth can put the past to rest."[86] Archbishop Tutu ensured that the Commission focused on the crimes of both the apartheid regime and the liberation movement, which proved to be a crucial component of achieving national reconciliation.

Mandela took many other steps instrumental to healing the country. For example, he met with Percy Yutar, his prosecutor at the 1964 trial, who said, "I wonder in what other country in the world you would have had the head of the government inviting someone to lunch who prosecuted him thirty years ago. It shows the great humility of this saintly man."[87] In another instance, he hosted a luncheon for women, both black and white, who had stood by their husbands during the apartheid era, calling them "heroes of both sides."[88] Adelaide Tambo, remarking on the event and echoing a phrase often used by Mandela, said that he had set an example of the spirit of reconciliation: "We cannot forget the past, but we can endeavour to forgive."[89] Perhaps the landmark moment for racial reconciliation came during the 1995 Rugby World Cup tournament held in South Africa. Although white enthusiasm for the tournament already was overwhelming, Mandela turned it into a national event, embracing the South African team, which had only one black member, and wearing its cap. The team itself adopted a Xhosa song as its own, one that Mandela and his fellow prisoners had sung on Robben Island while working in the lime quarries. When the South Africans won the World Cup after a close final game, the streets of Johannesburg became one giant party, whites and blacks equally excited, the game bringing the races together in a way that was more effective than philosophical treatises, government policies, and new laws could ever be.

Mandela would never become as effective an administrative leader as he was a moral and inspirational leader of South Africa, although he did have a realistic understanding of what needed to be done and the hardships that lay ahead. He told one crowd that "[i]n a period of transition...we are bound to make mistakes and experience failure. We must make sure we recognize these quickly, assess them, criticize ourselves when necessary...and emerge from these stronger and better able to carry out our historic mission."[90] With the ANC learning to govern, he was right to forewarn constituents who might have hoped for fast progress on practical problems like housing, unemployment, corruption, and crime. But Mandela's own impact on such issues was mixed at best. He did not like paperwork or working through a bureaucracy, and his independence sometimes brought him into conflict with the ANC and his own cabinet. He often behaved more like a constitutional monarch than a president.[91]

Nonetheless, Mandela's leadership was exceptional in moving South Africa toward national reconciliation and thus making his goal of a truly multiracial democracy possible. To the very end of his presidency, Mandela worked persistently and tirelessly to make his vision a reality, warning in his last annual speech to Parliament that reconciliation required the continued "dismantling of what remains of apartheid practices and attitudes."[92] He concluded with the words: "The long walk continues."[93]

★   ★   ★

Why was Mandela a successful, indeed an exceptional, leader? First, he had a compelling *vision* that he communicated consistently over decades and that he truly embodied. From early in his years as an activist, throughout his years in prison and his presidency, he aspired not only to free the black and other nonwhite racial groups subjugated by apartheid, but also to build a prosperous, nonracial democracy where blacks and whites could live harmoniously in a rainbow nation. As his followers were well aware, he gave his life to this goal and even after spending 27 years in prison, he recalled, "When I walked out of prison, that was my mission, to liberate the oppressed and the oppressor both."[94] Moreover, he understood that for this goal to be achieved, the oppressed must forgive their oppressors and put their former enmity behind them. As he said in 1995, "In putting aside quarrels of the past we have a country which has the opportunity to acquire education, skills and expertise in many fields. We want this. Let's forget the past. Let's put down our weapons; let's turn them into plough-shares. Let's build our country."[95]

Although far from a charismatic speaker, Mandela was nonetheless a very effective *communicator*. Early in his career, he took advantage of the opportunities given to him by his trials to proclaim his vision and expose the apartheid government's contradictions and injustices. Later he used the platforms provided by his leadership of the ANC, his status as the most famous political prisoner in the world, and eventually his presidency, to eloquently articulate his vision.

A man of great intelligence and dignity, he was equipped to deal with those in authority as equals, from his warders in prison to the Afrikaner presidents Botha and de Klerk. At the same time, he had a common touch, "an exceptional ability," de Klerk observed, "to make everyone with whom he came into contact feel special,"[96] from children, servants, and dishwashers to the upper levels of society. On a state visit to Britain in 1995, he established a warm relationship with Queen Elizabeth II, whose former prime minister had once branded him a terrorist.[97]

His moral authority and his inherent dignity derived principally from his embodiment of his vision as manifested by his willingness to forgive his oppressors and sacrifice his personal life for his oppressed people.

Like Pericles, Mandela was always honest and willing to disagree with his followers, especially on the imperatives of national reconciliation and tolerance. At one protest in 1993 Mandela chastised an ANC crowd for its willingness to use violence, saying that "as long as I am your leader, I will tell you, always, when you are wrong."[98] Similarly, when necessary, he acted in ways that could be misconstrued, as when he initiated secret meetings with the apartheid government while in prison. As Mandela explained, "There are times when a leader must move out ahead of his flock, go off in a new direction, confident that he is leading his people the right way."[99]

In summary, by using the moral stature gained through his actions, his rhetorical eloquence, and the ability he learned from Jongintaba to listen to all views and find common ground, over the years Mandela persuaded blacks and whites, ANC and Inkatha, educated and illiterate, of the practicability of his preeminently moral vision.[100]

The third element of Mandela's success was his ability to create and shape *effective organizations* that leveraged his personal impact, kept his followers working cooperatively toward each organization's goal, and ultimately institutionalized his vision of a nonracial democracy. Early in his activist career, he founded the ANC Youth League as a vehicle for implementing the strategy of nonviolent civil disobedience developed in the late 1940s. It also propelled Mandela into the top tier of leadership of the ANC. He shaped the ANC into a highly disciplined organization that carefully developed its goals and strategies and aligned its systems and people to achieve them. When the ANC was banned in 1960, after a decade of civil disobedience that appeared to have accomplished nothing, Mandela led the planning for a new campaign of underground violence and reorganized the ANC's structure into a series of clandestine cells.[101]

In prison as well, Mandela quickly built an effective organization, with an elaborate set of committees, to unite the prisoner population around his campaign to improve conditions, maintain morale and discipline, inculcate his vision, and eventually negotiate with the government. He and the other ANC leaders also developed an ingenious message system for communications among prisoners and with their colleagues outside.[102]

Another key to Mandela's effectiveness as a leader was to surround himself with followers who were also exceptionally able leaders in their own right. Walter Sisulu and Oliver Tambo, for example, were his close partners from the beginning. For virtually all of the years that Mandela was in prison, Tambo on the outside led the fractious ANC through very difficult times, while Sisulu sat with Mandela on the key prison governing committee, the High Organ. Younger colleagues like Thabo Mbeki also played critical roles in support of their elders, and Mbeki eventually succeeded Mandela as president of South Africa.

Perhaps most importantly, Mandela was willing to delegate to these other leaders as he worked to create a culture of democracy. He left most of the management of his presidential administration to Mbeki, and he regularly deflected any praise for his role, saying: "Many of my colleagues are head and shoulders above me in almost every respect. Rather than being an asset, I'm more of a decoration."[103] Nonetheless, like any good manager, Mandela was also careful to retain the power to hold colleagues accountable for their performance through his ability to hire and fire them. Accountability, however, did not mean agreeing with him. While some still saw signs of the tribal chief in Mandela's style, he prided himself on being a loyal ANC member and fostering a democratic culture within the party. During the difficult transition period between prison and the presidency when he had trouble maintaining control of the party's executive group, he explained, "Sometimes I feel they are very wrong, but I have to pay respect to the majority. I have to go to them one by one to try to persuade them."[104] As he later stated, a leader "must keep forces together: but you can't do that unless you allow dissent... People should be able to criticize the leader without fear or favor."[105]

Underpinning every aspect of Mandela's leadership was his *selflessness*. By the testimony of many close to him, he truly lived by the Xhosa dictum, "I am human through other humans." On many occasions, he transcended his personal interests for the good of his followers, his party, and his country. When civil disobedience earned only further repression during the 1950s and the ANC turned to sabotage, he left his family and went underground in South Africa, rather than flee to a safe haven. When put on trial for his life at Rivonia, he courageously stated his case against apartheid and sought to put the government on trial instead. After his conviction, Mandela continued the struggle from within the prison walls, rather than succumb to despair. Even when Botha's government offered in 1985 to release him after more than 20 years on the condition that he reject violence, he refused. He recognized that his imprisonment was a symbol for his people, to whom he said: "I cherish my own freedom dearly, but I care even more for your freedom... Your freedom and mine cannot be separated."[106] He refused an offer of 500,000 rand (about $180,000) just to have his picture taken in 1988 because he feared it would upset his secret discussions with government officials.[107] Mandela would not jeopardize his vision for personal reward—whether freedom, money, or anything else.

In a speech shortly after his release in 1990, Mandela again focused upon his commitment to the people, telling them: "I stand here before you not as a prophet but as a humble servant of you, the people... Your tireless and heroic sacrifices have made it possible for me to be here today. I therefore place the remaining years of my life in your hands."[108]

Finally, unlike Mugabe, once Mandela achieved the power of the presidency, he began to plan a democratic transition to his successor, even though retaining the office would have been easy. Biographer Martin Meredith notes that "there was deep apprehension about the prospect of his departure. He was seen as not only the founding father of democracy but also the guarantor of its stability."[109] Yet quite early in his term,

Mandela made it clear that he would not run for a second term and that there were many capable of taking his place. According to biographer Anthony Sampson, Mandela was "very aware of the dangers of the personality cult, which had misled other African countries. He talked less about 'I' and more about 'we.'"[110] By doing so, he accomplished one of the most difficult leadership tasks, the institutionalization of his vision. While his successors, Thabo Mbeki and Jacob Zuma, were perhaps inevitably much less effective, South Africa remains marked by Mandela's leadership, his vision and commitment. It is "the continent's most successful country,"[111] and the best hope for all who aspire to democratic, egalitarian societies in Africa.

★   ★   ★

In summary, the key distinction in the relative effectiveness of Mandela and Mugabe as leaders would appear to be the difference in their respective degrees of selflessness. Both rose to the leadership of their parties and eventually their countries as they related compelling visions about establishing free, egalitarian, and democratic societies. Each man appeared to embody his story, had the ability to communicate it to a diverse group of followers in the face of competing narratives, and built or shaped organizations that effectively supported and leveraged his impact. Their visions persuaded blacks and whites of all classes ultimately to elect each man the head of his country's government. The crucial difference between the two was Mandela's selflessness in contrast with Mugabe's selfishness. Mandela meant what he said. Whether or not Mugabe ever truly believed the assurances he provided after coming to power, he soon retreated to a self-centered vision of one-party, one-person rule, in which he was the indispensable man. The result was the successful transition of South Africa into a racially diverse democracy with the chance to evolve into the prosperous, "colorblind" society Mandela envisioned. In contrast, Mugabe devolved into a despot, not a leader, ruining Zimbabwe in the process.

EPILOGUE

Implications for Leaders and Followers

In the first chapter, "The Leadership Conundrum," we proposed three criteria for testing the usefulness and comprehensiveness of our framework. First, does it satisfactorily explain the key principles underlying effective and ineffective leadership in all domains? Second, does it also do so across cultures and in different eras? Finally, does it have *prescriptive* power as well as *explanatory* power? In other words, can it provide insights to followers in choosing their leaders, to those responsible for shaping and developing prospective leaders, and to leaders themselves in responding to the major challenges that they face?

We believe that the case studies provide evidence for affirmative answers to all these questions. Consequently, the purpose of this chapter is to outline the key principles emerging from the case studies, the potential implications for followers, the critical questions for leaders themselves, and the primary lessons for the development of leaders. While we further believe that the findings in this chapter are well supported by both the case studies and our experience, we understand that sixteen cases comprise a limited sample. Thus we present our findings as strong hypotheses, and in some cases as open questions, that we invite other students of leadership to test and explore.

Key Principles of Effective Leadership

The foregoing chapters demonstrate that the effectiveness of the leaders in our sixteen case studies varied widely. To summarize, we rate nine of these leaders as *exceptional*, which we define as having a "socially useful" and often transforming impact on the leader's domain or institution. These nine include the team of Elizabeth Cady Stanton and Susan B. Anthony, George Fox, John Gardner, William Rainey Harper, Soichiro Honda, Nelson Mandela, Sir William Osler, and most controversially, Caesar Augustus. Two other leaders, Margaret Sanger and Edward Teller, contributed to transforming impacts in their respective domains, but were *less effective* than they might have been because of deficiencies in their leadership profile. In addition, whether Teller's impact was "socially useful" remains a contentious question.

Three of the leaders studied—Napoleon Bonaparte, Henry Ford, and John Humphrey Noyes—were initially effective and perhaps even exceptional, but ultimately their flaws led them to become *ineffective* or failed leaders. It is worth noting, however, that in the cases of Napoleon and Ford, some of the transforming impact of their earlier leadership survived them, including Napoleon's "blocks of granite" and Ford's assembly line. Another case subject, Robert Mugabe, had the potential to be an exceptional leader, but instead became a despot who relied on coercion and ruined his country. Finally, Robert McNamara and G. Stanley Hall simply were *ineffective* leaders whose initial promise was unfulfilled.

In all the cases, which cover an array of domains, cultural settings, and time periods, our comprehensive framework appears to explain well why these leaders were ineffective, effective, or exceptional. To varying degrees, they were either more or less capable with respect to the three core skills of leadership: developing a compelling and well-conceived vision, persuasively communicating that vision, and building a strong supporting organization. Similarly, when their personal interests were in conflict with their followers' interests, acting in a selfless manner enhanced their effectiveness, and selfish actions harmed or destroyed their effectiveness.

In contrast, the other individual traits and behaviors of the leaders studied have no broader explanatory power. While Mandela was the personification of nobility in his appearance and personal manner, Augustus was small, sickly, and unprepossessing. While Osler was always a model of rectitude and calm in his dealings with others, Fox could be "fanatical and extravagant" early in his career. Harper and Gardner had kind and caring personalities that inspired great loyalty, while Honda had a temper that his employees feared. Although the team of Stanton and Anthony was highly principled, Augustus had a much weaker moral character (or a ruthless streak of pragmatism), judging by the bloody proscriptions in which he was complicit. In short, though the effective leaders' personal traits and behaviors needed to be broadly suitable for the distinctive situations in which they were leading, only their degree of selflessness and the strength of will they exhibited in acting selflessly were common determinants of success or failure. While Fox willingly was jailed for his beliefs and never wavered, Noyes ultimately fled to Canada and abandoned key tenets of his vision.

Analysis of the case studies strikingly reveals how distinctive each leader's profile is on the four core elements of the framework. Like a genome, the combination of the strengths and weaknesses on those four elements appears unique to each individual, even when two leaders might both be assessed as exceptional, effective, or ineffective. For example, Fox was exceptional because of the power of his vision and his selfless embodiment of his message, even though his organizational skills were less strong. Augustus made brilliant use of the symbol systems of his time. When combined with his organizational and managerial skills, his genius for communication enabled him to promulgate his vision across the Roman

Empire's vast geographic territory and multiplicity of languages and cultures.

Despite the distinctive characteristics of each leader's profile, however, several key principles appear to be affirmed by or emerge from the case studies.

1. *Effective leadership requires both a well-conceived, compelling vision and good-to-outstanding communication skills.* Neither alone will result in enduring positive impact. For example, despite his initial influence as a close advisor to both Kennedy and Johnson, McNamara was entirely unsuccessful as a leader during the Vietnam War because he had a narrow, ill-conceived managerial vision for the purpose and conduct of the war. Worse yet, his strong, even intimidating, communication skills arguably caused the country great harm by dampening dissent within the Johnson administration and encouraging the escalation of the war. It was only after the flaws in the vision he was promoting became evident, even to him, that his influence evaporated.

By contrast, Hall's vision of a stand-alone graduate research institute was not outlandish, as illustrated by the establishment of The Rockefeller University in 1901 and the Institute for Advanced Study at Princeton several decades later. But he made little effort to convince Jonas Clark and other potential donors of the virtues of his vision, either because he thought he could not or simply because of his habitual duplicity. The result was his inability to realize his vision. Meanwhile, his contemporary, Harper, led the University of Chicago into the ranks of the leading US research universities.

2. *Exceptional leadership requires that the vision be even more powerful and the leader's communication skills even stronger, given the change and commitment often required of the followers in order to achieve a transforming impact within a given domain.* Mandela's success in healing the rifts between races and leading a peaceful transition from apartheid to democratic rule required both a compelling vision of the promise offered to all of South Africa's citizens by an egalitarian, multiracial society and the exceptionally persuasive communication of that promise to whites, blacks, and other citizens of color. Similarly, though more modestly, for Gardner to deliver on Johnson's promise (and Gardner's shared personal vision) of a Great Society, he had to persuade tens of thousands of civil servants in the hodgepodge of 14 disparate agencies he inherited at HEW that they were the "department of people" with a common and noble mission. Moreover, it is not necessary for a leader to have a transforming impact on an entire field or society to be exceptional. Arguably, the impacts of Harper and Honda were primarily on their own institutions. In our view, there are exceptional leaders of schools, teams, local nonprofits, and small businesses, as well as of nation-states, armies, religions, and broad social movements.

3. *A leader's effectiveness can be substantially enhanced or diminished by the quality of his or her organizational and managerial skills. However, these skills are only a necessary, not a sufficient, condition for success.* Stanton and Anthony, Augustus,

Gardner, and Harper are all good examples of how the ability to build and manage capable supporting organizations can be critical to the effectiveness of a leader. Without this ability, it is doubtful they could have succeeded. Noyes would not have been as successful for as long as he was without his strong organizational skills. The same is true of the early Napoleon, when he appeared to be an effective and perhaps exceptional leader. Honda and Osler possessed much less organizational capability, but they understood the importance of an effective organization and knew enough to surround themselves with capable managers. At the other extreme, the archetypal professional manager McNamara sometimes seemed to mistake a managerial approach for a well-conceived vision. Finally, Sanger and Ford illustrate how weak organizational skills can diminish a leader's effectiveness. While Sanger had a transforming vision and was very persuasive, her need for control and difficulty working with others caused the birth control movement to splinter, with the result that success may have taken longer to achieve. Ford's contempt for organization and purging of his most capable managers, together with his rigidity, almost cost him his company.

4. *As the placement of selflessness in the foundation of our Greek temple suggests, if a leader acts selfishly or is even suspected of selfish motives by his followers, his effectiveness will be reduced dramatically, regardless of how strong he may be on the other three variables.* When Noyes fled to Canada, his influence was already waning due to health problems and a number of poor decisions. Thereafter it largely disappeared. In contrast, when Fox demonstrated his selflessness through numerous imprisonments and his willingness to delegate to new leaders within the Quaker movement, the effectiveness of his leadership was greatly enhanced. Despite his "religious majesty," as William Penn put it, Fox "held his place in the church of God with great meekness, and a most engaging humility and moderation."[1]

Indeed, as we discussed in the second chapter, "The Temple and the Genome," when a leader's selfishness becomes evident, his vision typically is revealed as narrow and self-interested as well, his ability to persuade is usually impaired, and many followers desert him. As a result, too often such leaders turn to coercion to maintain their grip on power. Among our case studies Mugabe is the most egregious example, but Napoleon and Ford illustrate the tendency as well. Despite some very worthy achievements in the first half of his career, Napoleon succumbed to his own ambition in the latter half, confusing his own interests with those of the people, crowning himself emperor, trusting fewer and fewer men, and ruling ever more despotically. Ford, too, after an early period when he became an American folk hero for being both innovative and a champion of the working man, began to believe his press clippings. Convinced he could do no wrong, he undertook his naive peace mission to Europe during World War I and an unsuccessful Senate race shortly thereafter. He also fired his gifted business partner, James Couzens, and almost ran his enormously successful company into bankruptcy during the 1920s and 1930s. His coercive and thuggish tactics left Ford Motor with some of the worst labor relations in American industry. Whether we classify Napoleon and Ford as failed leaders or as tyrants is a matter of debate.

5. *When a leader's selfishness is driven by personal insecurities or a narcissistic personality, rather than explicit desires for material wealth or power, it can be far more difficult for followers to detect, especially if the leader's vision appears to be worthy. This subtler form of self-centeredness often displays itself in controlling behavior, rigid thinking, an inability to listen, and poor organizational skills. Even worse, the leader's need for recognition or glory can impact the shape of the vision itself.* Sometimes these characteristics become evident to a group of followers, as in the case of Hall, whose duplicity eventually poisoned his relationships with Jonas Clark and many faculty members. The result then is simply failed leadership as followers withdraw their support. In other cases, however, the behavior is not evident to the great majority of followers, even if it is far clearer to those working more closely with a leader. Sanger's narcissism certainly led to conflicts in every organization with which she was affiliated. Happily, her vision was sound, and the result of her self-centered behavior was at worst the delay of its realization. More ominously, Teller's deep-seated insecurities not only contributed to his conflicts within Los Alamos and the physics community at large, but some of his detractors would argue that his need for recognition along with his paranoia about the Soviets clouded his vision as well. The result, they believed, was a proliferation of nuclear weaponry that could have led to catastrophe and that remains a crisis-in-waiting.

6. *Effective leaders, and especially exceptional leaders, recognize, respond, and adapt their strategies and styles to the different challenges before them, just as genes are activated or suppressed in response to their environment.* Mandela began his long fight against apartheid favoring an Africans-only strategy. However, after the successful collaboration with Indian and Colored activists during the Defiance Campaign of 1952, he changed his views. Over the next few years, Mandela welcomed all who wished change in South Africa, including whites, and his vision of a rainbow nation was born. Stanton and Anthony changed tactics many times in their half-century battle for women's suffrage, allying with temperance reformers and abolitionists at various points and seeking to change the law through legislation, the courts, and the court of public opinion. Fox recognized that his and his followers' early extravagance of faith was attracting more persecution than converts, so he created the sober character for which the Quakers have remained known.

In contrast, Ford was never able to adapt as his company grew larger and more complex and as the automobile market changed. Consequently, he dismantled, rather than built an effective organization. He also focused obsessively on lowering costs, rather than investing in new technology and building cars that appealed to an increasingly sophisticated consumer. Hall, too, remained stuck in his original vision of a research-focused graduate institution. Despite the need for greater financial stability and the role that an undergraduate college could play in providing that stability, he stubbornly refused to change his ways. McNamara not only did not adapt to different situations, he saw no reason to do so, proclaiming: "Running the Department of Defense is not different from running Ford Motor Company, or the Catholic Church, for that matter. Once you get to a certain scale, it's all the same."[2]

Implications for Followers in Choosing Leaders

In any circumstance requiring leadership, followers, of course, play a critical role, one coequal with the leader's. It is the followers' needs, wants, goals, and values, in James MacGregor Burns's description, to which the leader responds.[3] Followers decide whether to adopt the vision promoted by the leader and take the actions necessary to pursue it successfully. From the ranks of followers will emerge the senior and junior leaders needed to supplement the original visionary leader and sometimes even to supplant him if success is to be achieved. Perhaps most importantly, it is the followers who choose their leaders, and the best followers make the best choices.

Sometimes followers have the opportunity to vote formally upon their choice of leader, especially in a democratic society or institution. In other cases, a small representative body such as a board of directors or trustees decides who will lead an organization. Even more often, a superior appoints or promotes someone into a lower level position of authority, whether as the head of a business department, an officer in a military unit, or the coach of a team. The superior may do so in the belief that the appointee will be a leader, but it is those serving under the appointee who will make an implicit or explicit choice about whether they will become her followers or simply remain subordinates. Yet too often those making these decisions rely simply on their observations of the potential leader's traits and behaviors, or on superficial impressions of her vision, organizational capabilities, and motivations. Such approaches to choosing leaders are fraught with risks and uncertainties.

We argue instead that the elements in our comprehensive framework suggest a series of questions that prospective followers should ask themselves and a set of fact-based analyses they might undertake in answering these questions.

1. *Does the prospective leader have the experience, knowledge, and temperament to develop a viable vision for the group or organization he would head? Does he have a track record of success or failure in doing so? Can he recognize when the best course of action is to facilitate a process through which his followers themselves develop such a vision, a process, in Ronald Heifetz's term, of "adaptive" problem-solving?*

For example, McNamara had virtually no relevant experience or knowledge that would qualify him to develop a successful strategic vision for undertaking and winning the Vietnam War with its complex military, geopolitical, and domestic implications. Nor was he temperamentally suited to facilitating a genuinely open problem-solving process that might compensate for his lack of knowledge and experience. Indeed, it will be recalled that his instinctive reaction to giving Kennedy bad advice in the Bay of Pigs fiasco was to become the de facto desk officer for Vietnam instead of seeking the involvement of those who might have had the experience to raise and answer the far more sophisticated questions McNamara discussed in his memoirs three decades later. Moreover, this lack of relevant experience combined with his misplaced self-confidence that a professional manager could lead any large-scale organization regardless of domain should have been evident to those vetting McNamara and advising Kennedy on his appointment. Perhaps a different secretary of defense would have had no impact given the political pressures and personal beliefs driving Johnson's decisions to escalate the war. Still, maybe a wiser secretary could have made a convincing case for abiding with Kennedy's professed intention to withdraw. Perhaps he even could have facilitated a process through which Johnson and his key advisors reached this conclusion themselves. In any event, such questions and considerations argue persuasively for a thoughtful examination of a prospective leader's track record and his problem-solving approach before choosing him.

2. If the leader being considered already has a vision, is it realistic and wise, as well as appealing? Are the key assumptions and the inherent risk/reward tradeoffs reasonable? Have alternative options been considered and thoroughly explored? Does the leader's past track record indicate that her judgment is sound and selfless?

For example, Hall's core vision of a graduate research institute dedicated to the pursuit of scientific knowledge attracted many of the best scientific minds to Clark University, where they could focus primarily on their research with minimal teaching requirements or other distractions. However, the financial aspect of Hall's vision was hopelessly unrealistic. He proudly refused to raise funds, asserting that a university is not a business, and resisted opening an undergraduate college, whose tuition would have been another source of money. Hall seemed to assume that the founder would provide all the needed funds, even though an undergraduate college was central to Jonas Clark's vision. Finally, had Clark thoroughly analyzed Hall's track record and his core beliefs and values, he might have discovered the pattern of thought and self-serving behavior that would undermine the new university. With a different choice (perhaps even Harper), the future of Clark University might have been very different.

3. Can the prospective leader persuasively communicate his vision to all of the core constituencies necessary to its successful realization? Can he inspire those constituencies when that is a critical need? Is he able to use a wide array of communication media skillfully—speaking, writing, and other symbol systems—or is he dependent on just one? If the latter, might it limit his future effectiveness in any important way? Finally, does he embody his message, both in perception and in reality?

John Humphrey Noyes is an interesting example of a leader with a mixed ability to communicate. Clearly, he was very successful with the small number of Perfectionists he was able to attract to the radical lifestyle of the Oneida Community. With them, his personal charisma and speaking abilities were inspiring. Moreover, Noyes understood the importance of public relations, and he and the Community produced periodicals and other publications to attract converts and convince society at large that the Community's idealistic lifestyle deserved tolerance and peaceful coexistence.

At the same time, however, Noyes did not consistently embody his message within the Community itself. There was a fundamental contradiction between his communal message and his actions, which centered all authority in his hands. While his ostensible position as God's representative on earth made this disconnect understandable to his followers initially, over time it led to dissension and contributed to the Community's dissolution.

Noyes's case illustrates why discerning followers should always attempt to understand whether, like Harper, Mandela, and Osler, a prospective leader embodies his message and thus communicates it through his own actions. In addition, followers should try to determine whether the potential leader has the range of communication skills needed to persuade not just a small group, but all the constituencies needed for success, as Gardner, Stanton, and Anthony could with their mastery of speaking, writing, and the mass communications media of their times.

4. Does the potential leader recognize the importance of a strong, capable supporting organization to the successful implementation and institutionalization of her vision? Does she further understand that a capable organization requires the mutually consistent alignment of all the elements necessary to make it operate effectively? Those elements include its people, their incentives, the various information and other systems that support decision-making. Does the leader have the ability to build and manage such an organization? If not, does she have the self-awareness to recognize her own shortcomings, choose good people with complementary strengths, and delegate to them accordingly?

Honda and Ford offer fascinating contrasts on this dimension of leadership. Both had enough self-awareness to know that their strengths and interests were in engineering—and in Ford's case, the manufacturing process itself—rather than marketing, sales, finance, and the other functions of an industrial company. Consequently, both men hired talented administrators in their firms' fledgling years to whom they entrusted the tasks of overall management. James Couzens at Ford and Takeo Fujisawa at Honda helped guide their respective companies to great success. The key difference, of course, is that only Honda understood the need for a well-functioning organization. As a result, Henry Ford eventually fired Couzens and every other capable senior manager, eschewed formal organization, and listened to no one, with disastrous results.

Once more, it is important to underscore that a prospective leader's track record can provide fact-based insight into whether she has the requisite understanding and skills. Even where there is no background of experience with a similar organization, one can gain insights from whether those organizations she has led have run smoothly and effectively. For example, a presidential candidate whose campaign organization is run poorly and has regular turnover among his senior aides should not give a voter confidence that he can choose good people for his administration and effectively manage organizations as large as the federal government and the military.

5. *Are a prospective leader's motivations essentially selfless, or are they largely self-interested? Does his track record indicate that he has the values and willpower to forgo his personal interests and resist selfish impulses when responsible for the interests of followers? Is the ambition that drove him to this point in his career shaped by a healthy and well-integrated ego? Or is he motivated by personal insecurities, an unhealthy narcissism, or a desire for personal wealth, power, or fame? Might his judgment ultimately become clouded about what is in the group's best interests?*

A prospective leader's internal motivations can be among the most difficult leadership elements to assess, especially from a distance. For example, long before Napoleon had achieved any form of power, his written statements suggested his appetite for glory and ambition to dominate others. Had they been widely known, they might have given pause to those who promoted him to successive positions of power. Similarly, Teller's obsession with the Super and the change in his formerly collegial behavior when he encountered opposition were recognized by Hans Bethe and other close friends as stemming from his deep-seated insecurities. However, those in power either did not notice or chose to ignore these signs that Teller's judgment on vital policy decisions should be questioned. Early in Mugabe's first presidential term, while he was still regarded by many as the great African hope, his words began to belie his campaign rhetoric when he threatened to kill the white "snakes among us, we will smash them completely."[4] Would Zimbabwe be the ruined country it has become had the United Nations, its African neighbors, and the Zimbabwean people acted then to withhold their support for Mugabe?

Obviously, there are limits to what can be determined about a prospective leader's skills and character prior to voting for, promoting, or appointing him. Nonetheless, there are clues available to the discerning follower. For example, does the prospective leader's track record suggest that he is able to listen to and be influenced by other perspectives in shaping vision and strategy? Does he know his own management strengths and weaknesses, and is he willing to delegate to others accordingly? Is he able to manage his time effectively and encourage and support the emergence of new leaders who can enhance the organization's effectiveness in achieving collective goals? Does he truly embody his message, or is there a disparity between his actions and his words? Last, do his decisions in highly stressful situations indicate strong willpower and a focus on the best interests of his followers? Or conversely, do they suggest a lack of self-control and a tendency to make rash and impulsive decisions?

Of course, past performance and behavior cannot always reliably predict the future. The early track records of Ford and Napoleon belied their eventual leadership failures. Lyndon Johnson's career before the presidency did not suggest that he would become a transforming leader in terms of domestic legislation. Still, it is imperative to make the most informed judgments one can rather than trust to luck in choosing leaders.

Critical Questions for Leaders

Followers can improve their ability to choose leaders by asking a series of questions concerning a prospective leader's visionary abilities, communication skills, organizational capabilities, degree of selflessness, and the strength of his will. Leaders can ask a parallel series of prescriptive questions aimed at determining how to respond to a specific challenge or assess the effectiveness of their leadership in general. These questions in turn will often suggest fact-based analyses or other steps that might enhance the effectiveness of their response to that challenge or improve their leadership more broadly. We frame the following questions around a challenge that a leader might be facing.

1. *Do I have a well-conceived vision for how to respond to the opportunity or problem that my followers or my organization face? If so, have I carefully considered all of the options, been clear about my key assumptions, gathered the pertinent facts, thoroughly understood the risks and benefits, and made as objective a judgment as possible about what is in the best interests of my followers? If I lack such a vision, is it, in Heifetz's terminology, a "technical" problem, whose solution should be straightforward if I thoughtfully draw on the experts in the field? If so, who are the experts I need and what is the process I will use to test the soundness of their recommendations and to resolve any conflicts that may arise between them? Or is this what Heifetz would define as an "adaptive" problem for which neither I nor the experts currently have a satisfactory solution?[5] If so, what is the best design for a problem-solving process aimed at developing an appropriate solution—for instance, who should be involved, how should it be run, what role should I and others play in facilitating the process?*

As the foregoing questions indicate, the challenge of testing or developing a vision (along with a strategy for achieving it) has a large, objectively analytical component. That component is not a substitute for creativity and judgment, but is rather the foundation on which such creativity and judgment must be built for a sound vision to emerge. As such, one prescription for all those with leadership aspirations is to develop the required analytical, problem-solving skills.

2. *Am I conveying my vision persuasively to all of my key constituencies? If not, what is the full range of communication vehicles available, and how should I develop a communications strategy that uses them optimally? Am I crafting my message in an inspirational way both in writing and orally? How can I improve it, through coaching, practice, or other means? Am I delivering the message via the best mix of personal appearances and various forms of mass media, including television, the Internet, widely circulated publications? Does the communications strategy fully utilize the capabilities of other leaders within my organization to deliver and reinforce the message as well? Are there still other means of indirectly and symbolically communicating the message—by celebrating successes, for example, or sponsoring worthy and symbolically consistent causes? Finally, are my personal actions, those of my followers individually, and those of my organization consistent with the message? Do we collectively embody the vision being promulgated? If not, what changes in our actions are required?*

As with developing a sound vision, there is a similar, objectively analytical component to developing an inspiring message and delivering it through an optimal communications strategy. Moreover, communications skills can be enhanced. There may be no substitute for personal charisma or creativity, but any leader can improve his communications skills substantially beyond his natural endowments.

3. *Is my organization as effective as it might be and needs to be? Are all of the key organizational elements mutually consistent, and is each well designed and reinforcing? Am I spending my time optimally given my strengths, my weaknesses, and the critical success factors in implementing the vision? Are the other key leaders in the organization highly capable and able to compensate for my weaknesses? Have I given them sufficient freedom to realize their full leadership potential and to maximize the effectiveness of the organization? At the same time, have I retained close control over the few factors—and only those few factors—that are critical to the organization's success?*

Enhancing the effectiveness of the supporting organization is, in our view, the challenge most amenable to objective, fact-based analysis among the three process elements in our comprehensive framework. While there are still very important subjective tasks required—for example, choosing the best people and understanding the interplay of people's motivations—many of the tasks necessary to ensure that all organizational elements are optimally designed and mutually reinforcing are subject to thoughtful, fact-based analysis.

4. *If I am completely honest with myself, how important to me is achieving personal success, as opposed to achieving the best outcome for my followers? Is there a risk I will not recognize when my interests are in conflict with the group's interests? For example, am I truly open to dissenting views and criticism either from my followers*

or from others? Do I assess such views objectively and make adjustments to my own perspectives based on the validity of the arguments and the facts? If I do not, is it because of an unfounded assumption on my part that I am far better informed than my critics, or is it because I am at some deep level insecure and fearful that they may be right? As one litmus test, am I surrounding myself with the best possible people, including some who think differently than I do and perhaps even those with more potential capability than I have? Am I listening to them and helping them develop into future leaders? As another test, under what conditions would I be willing to step aside for another leader who is better positioned to achieve success?

The question of one's selflessness is, of course, the most difficult one for any human being to be objective about, and it is the least susceptible to analysis. Nevertheless, simply asking the foregoing questions may raise a leader's awareness of the issue and spur corrective actions when warranted. Moreover, a leader needs to be cognizant of the setting within which he is making key decisions. Is it a stressful one, where the sheer number and difficulty of the decisions I need to make could result in mental fatigue? If it is, what can I do to reenergize my self-control and willpower in order to make well-reasoned, objective decisions, and avoid impulsive or rash choices? For example, can I mitigate the effects of ego depletion through reframing the decision-making context or even by simply replenishing my blood glucose levels?[6]

Implications for Developing Leaders

Are leaders born or made? It is an intriguing and age-old question whose persistence is easy to understand. It reflects our fascination with "great" men and women over time, and our speculations about the traits required to achieve greatness. It also mirrors the more contemporary debate over the roles of nature and nurture in shaping our personalities. There have always been strong views on either side. For every Carlyle with his belief in the uniqueness of the heroic leader, there is an Eisenhower who argued that "[t]he one quality that can be developed by studious reflection and practice is the leadership of men."[7] For every Weber with his postulation of a charismatic leader who possesses a gift of grace, there has been a Plato aspiring (with scant success) to turn statesmen into philosophers in his famous Academy.

A corollary question is whether leadership is an art or a science. If an art, the argument would go, then leadership cannot be taught. It is a gift of creative genius with which one must be born. If leadership is a science, however, then it can be broken down into systematic principles and laws, which a good student can learn.

In our view leadership contains elements of both art and science, and each can be learned to a differing degree through a combination of conventional and unconventional education. Just as a genetic inheritance represents a potential, not a fixed actuality, so within limits inherent leadership strengths can be enhanced and weaknesses overcome. In other words, leaders can to some extent be "made."

Can anyone be taught to be a "great" or exceptional leader in this manner? No, innate talent is required to become an exceptional leader, along with circumstances enabling that talent to emerge. However, anyone can develop into a more effective leader, presuming he possesses a threshold level of social and intellectual skills, a threshold that in turn will be driven by the requirements of the domain and situation within which he will be leading. For example, to be a credible leader in an academic or scientific setting will typically require a different mix and threshold of social and intellectual skills than to be a credible political or military leader.

Our hypothesis is that by focusing on the four variables in our comprehensive framework, delineating the elements of art and science in each, and utilizing a combination of traditional and nontraditional forms of pedagogy, the effectiveness of leadership development could be greatly improved. To do so most effectively would require a multiyear course of study and apprenticeship, not a few days, weeks, or even months.

For example, the variable of *vision*—together with the development of a strategy to pursue that vision—contains elements of science, which can be studied conventionally, and art, which can be enhanced through practice and the guidance of a mentor. The science is in the skill of analyzing a given situation, developing options, and assessing risk and reward. These skills can be taught, as they are today in the best military, business, and government schools. What such institutions cannot teach is the art of developing a wholly creative option or of choosing wisely among options with uncertain outcomes. These abilities come in part, of course, from natural talent, but they can be enhanced through practice, ideally under a mentor, as Augustus benefited from his apprenticeship with his great-uncle, Julius Caesar. Similarly, Mandela was shaped by his observations of the Regent of his Tembu tribe, Jongintaba,[8] and Eisenhower by his service under General Fox Conner in the 1920s.[9] The best consulting firms, investment banks, and law firms structure the career paths of entering associates to give them such opportunities for mentorship, as do many of the highest performing business, military, and other organizations.

The aspects of science and art in the variable of *organizational capability* are similar to those of vision. Once again, there is an element of analytical problem-solving that is highly amenable to a relatively conventional form of teaching. For example, the case study pedagogy used by a number of business schools can convey the analytical, "scientific" methodology required to assess the effectiveness or ineffectiveness of an organization, diagnose the reasons why (a misalignment of one or more organizational elements with its goals, for example), and identify changes that may need to be made. There is even a greater amount of science in the technical disciplines of management such as accounting, budgetary and control systems, and the statistical foundations of market research. The art, however, of choosing the right people for the right positions and determining what responsibilities to delegate and which to control closely are typical of the skills that can be learned only through apprenticeship and mentorship.

Communication skills also contain healthy proportions of science and art. Rhetoric, for example, has elements of each. Indeed, *Webster's New Collegiate Dictionary* defines rhetoric as both "the art of speaking or writing effectively" and "the study of principles and rules of composition formulated by critics of ancient times."[10] Rhetoric was once a required subject in virtually all liberal arts programs, but it is studied formally by relatively few undergraduate students today. Yet as both science and art, it is quite amenable to a conventional mode of teaching. Extracurricular activities such as debating also make an undergraduate setting a good one for honing this variable of effective leadership. Similarly, the science and art of broad-based communication strategies that combine the use of multiple forms of mass media and message formats also can be taught effectively through conventional case and classroom teaching methodologies. Although the extraordinary rhetorical gifts of Lincoln, Franklin Roosevelt, Reagan, or Obama cannot be taught, almost everyone can enhance the skills he or she does possess. Anthony grew dramatically on this dimension through her mentoring by Stanton, exposure to great orators such as Frederick Douglass, and much practice. Osler, too, greatly improved his speaking and writing skills through self-disciplined practice. A more formal, well-designed program would doubtless have made both even more effective.

As we argued in "The Temple and the Genome," *selflessness*, unlike the other three variables in the comprehensive framework, is not a skill. Selflessness may be a core element of character that emerges naturally from a leader's personality, values, and perhaps even biological heritage. More often it is a hard-won element of character achieved only through struggling to balance the instinctive impulse to take selfish actions with the higher motivations to act selflessly. Conversely, many who have deep-seated personal insecurities, are narcissistic, or lack meaningful exposure to a religious or ethical tradition lose that battle and are more likely to act in a self-interested manner in the same circumstances. Given that the opportunity to reshape fundamentally an adult's values or psychological profile is limited, can anything be done to strengthen a prospective leader's character or at least the willpower he brings to bear in the battle between warring impulses?

There are some reasons to be optimistic about the possibility of helping a leader strengthen his willpower and, thus, his ability to make good decisions in stressful circumstances. Current research indicates that willpower, like a muscle, becomes fatigued under the stress of making numerous, complex decisions. The same research also suggests, however, that self-control can be strengthened by regularly exercising one's willpower in a variety of ways, structuring one's life to conserve it for the most important decisions, reframing a decision situation to temporarily reenergize it when possible, and recognizing the need to raise one's blood glucose levels when "decision fatigue" cannot be overcome.[11] As Roy Baumeister, one of the leaders of the recent research on self-control, has said, "The best decision makers are the ones who know when *not* to trust themselves."[12] All of the foregoing lessons and practices can be learned, and arguably any leader would benefit from them. They could help those leaders whose values and psychological profiles are strong to make sound, selfless decisions consistently rather than succumb to impulse or self-interest when their will is tired and under stress. And these practices might help those whose values and psychological profiles are generally weak to rise above their normal characters and self-orientation to make more disinterested and selfless decisions.

We are less optimistic about what meaningfully can be done to strengthen a prospective or aspiring leader's character as an adult. Nonetheless, we believe that military, professional, and other schools that aim to develop leaders in their respective domains would profit by requiring courses on ethics and perhaps even training in meditative techniques as means of inculcating a broad set of humanistic values. Such measures might help leaders control impulses toward making decisions on the basis of conscious or unconscious self-interest by placing the leader's actions in a larger context that provides perspective. While our expectations for what such steps might accomplish are quite limited, we believe them worthwhile to pursue.

★   ★   ★

This book began with the observation that the topic of leadership has fascinated both mankind's greatest thinkers and ordinary individuals through the ages. Given the impact that our leaders have on us, for good and ill, this interest is not surprising. Moreover, many have tried to understand why some leaders are effective, many are ineffective, and only a few are exceptional. Identifying the causes for the differences in leadership outcomes is an important enterprise because of the promise it holds for humanity to improve the development of its leaders, choose leaders more wisely, and make them more effective in their work.

We hope that we have contributed to the collective understanding of what is essential to effective leadership and most importantly, how leaders can be better developed, chosen, and made more effective. We recognize, however, that the realization of this hope will require much additional building on the framework we have developed, a framework that was in turn constructed on the foundations created by many before us. For example, will the analysis of numerous other case studies from various domains, cultures, and eras confirm the four elements pictured in the Greek temple and the multitude of unique, dynamic patterns among them, as expressed by the genome? Will the key principles that we have identified be reinforced or modified? How can followers be better educated to play their roles proactively and well, especially their role in choosing leaders? Are there more concrete tools that could be developed for leaders to use in applying our comprehensive framework prescriptively to the challenges they are facing and in enhancing the effectiveness of their leadership more broadly? Perhaps most importantly, what pragmatic steps can our schools, businesses, nonprofits, governmental organizations, and other institutions take to develop more effective leaders on all four elements of the framework?

We accept these challenges for ourselves and entertain the hope that we will be part of a large company of students of leadership who are similarly motivated.

NOTES

Introduction

1. Howard Gardner, *Leading Minds: An Anatomy of Leadership* (New York: BasicBooks, 1996), 6.

1 The Leadership Conundrum

1. Most notably by James MacGregor Burns, *Leadership* (New York: Harper & Row, 1978), 12–23; but by many others as well, e.g., Ronald A. Heifetz, *Leadership Without Easy Answers* (Cambridge, MA: Belknap Press, 1994), 23–24, 57–61; and Joseph C. Rost, *Leadership for the Twenty-First Century* (Westport, CT: Praeger, 1991), 105–107, 156–160.
2. Social psychologists John French and Bertram Raven defined five categories of power in their often-cited 1959 book, *The Bases of Social Power*: coercive (based on force), reward, referent (based on admiration), expert, and legitimate (positional). See French and Raven, "Bases of Social Power," in Dorwin Cartwright, ed., *Studies in Social Power* (Ann Arbor: University of Michigan Research Center for Group Dynamics, 1959), 150–167. In our view, all five categories can be abused and exercised coercively in certain circumstances. Conversely, leaders can also use them more benignly as a complement to persuasion.
3. Francis Oakley, *Kingship* (Malden, MA: Blackwell Publishing, 2006), 7, 10–14.
4. Max Weber terms this "bureaucratic authority" in the context of public government in the modern world and "bureaucratic management" in the context of the private economy. See Weber, *From Max Weber: Essays in Sociology*, H. H. Gerth and C. Wright Mills, eds. and trans. (New York: Oxford University Press, 1946), 196–197. We, however, use the term "management" to describe a position of authority in any institution in any domain, even including a hereditary ruler or an elected head of state, church, or private enterprise.
5. Burns, *Leadership*, 40.
6. As the foregoing discussion of management suggests, we see a high degree of overlap between what Burns defines as "transactional leadership" and what we would define as "management."
7. Ibid., 4.
8. See, e.g., Howard Gardner, *Leading Minds: An Anatomy of Leadership* (New York: BasicBooks, 1996), 297–298; Barbara Kellerman, *Bad Leadership* (Boston: Harvard Business School Press, 2004), 8–9, 11–14; and Rost, *Leadership for the Twenty-First Century*, 124–126.
9. Heifetz formulates his criterion of "socially useful results" as a means of avoiding the problem of using a hierarchy of moral values as part of his definition of leadership. He worries that such "a hierarchy that would apply across cultures and organizational settings risks either being so general as to be impractical or so specific as to be culturally imperialistic is its application" (*Leadership Without Easy Answers*, 21). He does so, however, in support of his belief that leadership is not "value-neutral," unlike others such as Kellerman, Rost, and Gardner.
10. For the various approaches to leadership developed in the twentieth century, see Rost, *Leadership for the Twenty-First Century*, chapters 1–4; Georgia J. Sorenson and George R. Goethals,

"Leadership Theories: An Overview," in Goethals and Sorenson, eds., *Encyclopedia of Leadership* (Thousand Oaks, CA: Sage, 2004), vol. 2, 867–873; and Bernard M. Bass, *Bass & Stodgill's Handbook of Leadership: Theory, Research, and Managerial Applications*, 3rd ed. (New York: Free Press, 1990).

11. Steven J. Rubenzer and Thomas R. Faschingbauer, *Personality, Character, and Leadership in the White House: Psychologists Assess the Presidents* (Washington, D.C.: Potomac Books, 2004).

12. These nine personality "predictors" included seven positive indicators (intellectually brilliant and smart, assertiveness, achievement striving, competence, activity, positive emotions, and tender-mindedness) and two negative ones (straightforwardness and vulnerability) (ibid., 52).

13. Ibid., 54 (table 3.6).

14. Joyce Hogan and Robert Hogan, "Evidence for the Big-Five Personality Dimensions," in Goethals and Sorenson, *Encyclopedia of Leadership*, vol. 1, 97.

2 The Temple and the Genome

1. Robert D. Kaplan, "What Rumsfeld Got Right," *Atlantic Monthly*, vol. 302, no. 1 (July–August 2008), 64–74.

2. Howard Gardner, *Leading Minds: An Anatomy of Leadership* (New York: BasicBooks, 1996), ix–x, 287–288.

3. James MacGregor Burns, *Leadership* (New York: Harper & Row, 1978), 18–19, 40, and 443.

4. As quoted in Thucydides, "The Policy of Pericles," *History of the Peloponnesian War*, Rex Warner, trans. (New York: Penguin, 1972), p. 159 (Book 2, §60).

5. Ronald A. Heifetz, *Leadership Without Easy Answers* (Cambridge, MA: Belknap Press, 1994), 125–129.

6. One exception is Fred Greenstein, who explicitly addresses what he terms "organizational capacity" as one of his six proposed measures of effectiveness in his study of presidential performance since FDR (*The Presidential Difference: Leadership Style from FDR to George W. Bush*, 2nd ed. [Princeton: Princeton University Press, 2004], 5, 195–197). However, he focuses on a president's ability to build an effective team rather than to manage a much larger and more complex supporting organization. Howard Gardner also lists "The Organization" as one of his "Six Constants of Leadership," and he recognizes that "enduring leadership ultimately demands some kind of institutional or organizational basis" (*Leading Minds*, 292–293). However, he does not probe deeply into the topic.

7. One set of criteria for judging organizational effectiveness that we find particularly helpful and simple to apply is the "7S" framework developed in the late 1970s by an internal task force conducting research on organizational effectiveness at the international management consulting firm, McKinsey & Company. Phrased as a mnemonic device, the "7S" framework includes seven variables that must be properly aligned for a business organization to operate effectively: (1) *shared values*, or goals; (2) *strategy*, or the long-term plan for achieving those goals; (3) *style*, i.e., the senior executive's personal style together with the cultural norms of the organization; (4) *structure*, or the reporting relationships reflected in an organization chart; (5) reward, information, and other *systems* that support the key decision-making processes; (6) the institutional *skills* possessed by the institution as a whole; and (7) *staff*, or the people occupying the positions on the organization chart. While the 7S framework was designed to diagnose problems and design solutions for business organizations, it applies with minor adjustments to organizations in any domain. The leaders of the task force were Thomas J. Peters and Robert H. Waterman, Jr., who a few years later coauthored the best-selling book *In Search of Excellence: Lessons From America's Best-Run Companies* (New York: Warner Books, 1982), in which the 7Ss are presented graphically on page 10.

8. John P. Kotter, *A Force for Change: How Leadership Differs from Management* (New York: Free Press, 1990), 3–8.

9. Ibid., 7–8.

10. Henry Mintzberg, "Society Has Become Unmanageable as a Result of Management," in *Mintzberg on Management: Inside Our Strange World of Organizations* (New York: Free Press, 1989), 342–343, 348–349.

11. Kotter, *A Force for Change*, 8, 17.
12. Charles Darwin, *On the Origin of Species* (New York: New York University Press, 1988); Sigmund Freud, *Civilization and Its Discontents,* James Strachey, ed. and trans. (New York: W.W. Norton, 1961).
13. Charles Darwin, *The Descent of Man and Selection in Relation to Sex*, rev. ed. (New York: D. Appleton, 1897), 130.
14. Michael A. Wallach and Lise Wallach, *Psychology's Sanction for Selfishness: The Error of Egoism in Theory and Therapy* (San Francisco: W.H. Freeman, 1983), 272–273.
15. Shankar Vedantum, "If It Feels Good, It Might Only Be Natural," *Washington Post*, May 28, 2007, A1.
16. Christian de Duve, *Life Evolving: Molecules, Mind, and Meaning* (New York: Oxford University Press, 2002), 200–201.
17. Edward O. Wilson, *The Social Conquest of Earth* (New York: Liveright, 2012).
18. Robert K. Greenleaf, *Servant Leadership* (New York: Paulist Press, 1977), 27; emphases in the original.
19. Thucydides, *History of the Peloponnesian War*, 164 (Book 2, §65).
20. Steven J. Rubenzer and Thomas R. Faschingbauer, *Personality, Character, and Leadership in the White House: Psychologists Assess the Presidents* (Washington, D.C.: Potomac Books, 2004), 99.
21. As quoted in Robert Dallek, *Lone Star Rising* (New York: Oxford University Press, 1991), 6–7.
22. For example, David Halberstam, *The Coldest Winter: America and the Korean War* (New York: Hyperion, 2007), 132–137, 274–275, 422–424, 567–575, and 591–601.

3   Margaret Sanger and Susan B. Anthony/ Elizabeth Cady Stanton: Social Reformers

1. As quoted in Elyse Topalian, *Margaret Sanger* (New York: Franklin Watts, 1984), 40.
2. Sanger, as quoted in David M. Kennedy, *Birth Control in America: The Career of Margaret Sanger* (New Haven: Yale University Press, 1970), 4.
3. Ibid., 23.
4. Topalian, *Margaret Sanger*, 59.
5. *U.S.* v. *One Package of Japanese Pessaries*, 86 F.2d 737 (2nd Cir., 1936).
6. Kennedy, *Birth Control in America*, 81.
7. Deborah Bachrach, *The Importance of Margaret Sanger* (San Diego: Lucent Books, 1993), 9.
8. Kennedy, *Birth Control in America*, 108–135, 235–240; Ellen Chesler, *Woman of Valor* (New York: Simon and Schuster, 1992), 407–409.
9. Kennedy, *Birth Control in America*, 93.
10. Bachrach, *Importance of Margaret Sanger*, 77.
11. Ibid.
12. Kennedy, *Birth Control in America*, 211.
13. As quoted in ibid., 267.
14. Ibid., 270.
15. Chesler, *Woman of Valor*, 413.
16. Bachrach, *Importance of Margaret Sanger*, 8.
17. As quoted in Geoffrey C. Ward, *Not for Ourselves Alone: The Story of Elizabeth Cady Stanton and Susan B. Anthony* (New York: Alfred A. Knopf, 1999), 6.
18. Ibid., 11.
19. As quoted in ibid., 14.
20. Ibid., 20.
21. Michael P. Farrell, *Collaborative Circles: Friendship Dynamics and Creative Work* (Chicago: University of Chicago Press, 2001), 219–220.
22. Ibid., 221.
23. As quoted in Ward, *Not for Ourselves Alone*, 38.

24. Reprinted in Elizabeth Cady Stanton, Susan B. Anthony, and Matilda J. Gage, eds., *History of Woman Suffrage* (Rochester, NY: Susan B. Anthony, 1887), vol. 1, 70–71.
25. As quoted in Judith Wellman, *The Road to Seneca Falls: Elizabeth Cady Stanton and the First Women's Rights Convention* (Urbana: University of Illinois Press, 2004), 195.
26. As quoted in Ward, *Not for Ourselves Alone*, 40.
27. As quoted in ibid., 38.
28. As quoted in ibid., 47.
29. Ibid., 63.
30. As quoted in ibid., 65.
31. Judith Nies, *Seven Women: Portraits from the American Radical Tradition* (New York: Viking, 1977), 85.
32. As quoted in Ward, *Not for Ourselves Alone*, 120.
33. As quoted in Farrell, *Collaborative Circles*, 206.
34. By the time the Nineteenth Amendment was eventually ratified, Stanton, Anthony, and their many successors had mounted 56 campaigns for state referendums, 480 campaigns urging state legislatures to put women's suffrage on the ballot, 47 campaigns for state constitutional conventions, 30 campaigns urging the inclusion of women's suffrage planks in presidential election platforms, and lobbying efforts with 19 successive Congresses (Nies, *Seven Women*, 91).
35. As quoted in Ward, *Not for Ourselves Alone*, 205.
36. As quoted in ibid., 6.
37. As quoted in Kathleen Barry, *Susan B. Anthony: A Biography of a Singular Feminist* (New York: New York University Press, 1988), 312.

4 Robert S. McNamara and John W. Gardner: Lyndon Johnson's Cabinet Warriors

1. Robert S. McNamara, "A Life in Public Service," interview by Harry Kreisler, *Conversations with History*, Institute for International Studies, UC Berkeley, April 16, 1996; http://conversations .berkeley.edu/content/robert-s-mcnamara.
2. Robert S. McNamara, *In Retrospect: The Tragedies and Lessons of Vietnam* (New York: Times Books, 1995), 6.
3. As quoted in Errol Morris, director, *The Fog of War: Eleven Lessons from the Life of Robert S. McNamara*, Columbia Tristar, 2003. Documentary film; http://www.errolmorris.com/film /fow_transcript.html.
4. As quoted in ibid.
5. McNamara, *In Retrospect*, 24.
6. Morris, *The Fog of War*.
7. Deborah Shapley, *Promise and Power: The Life and Times of Robert McNamara* (Boston: Little, Brown, 1993), 65.
8. Ibid., 52.
9. David Halberstam, *The Best and the Brightest* (New York: Random House, 1972), 220–223.
10. McNamara, *In Retrospect*, 22.
11. Harold Brown, Joseph Califano, John Connally, Paul Nitze, and Cyrus Vance.
12. McNamara, *In Retrospect*, 22.
13. Ibid., 23.
14. "Robert S. McNamara," *SecDef Histories*, Department of Defense biographies; http://www .defense.gov/specials/secdef_histories/bios/mcnamara.htm.
15. As quoted in ibid.
16. William Burr and Hector L. Montford, eds., "The Making of the Limited Test Ban Treaty, 1958–1963," *The National Security Archive*, posted August 8, 2003, 6; http://www.gwu.edu /~nsarchiv/NSAEBB/NSAEBB94/index2.htm.
17. Halberstam, *The Best and the Brightest*, 243.
18. Ibid., 245.

19. McNamara, *In Retrospect*, 26.

20. Ibid., 32.

21. Ibid., 39–40.

22. Halberstam, *The Best and the Brightest*, 214.

23. Ibid., 213.

24. Ibid., 247–250.

25. As quoted in Shapley, *Promise and Power*, 260.

26. James G. Blight and Janet M. Lang, *The Fog of War: Lessons from the Life of Robert S. McNamara* (Lanham, MD: Rowman & Littlefield, 2005), 157–158.

27. As quoted in ibid., 158.

28. Halberstam, *The Best and the Brightest*, 176.

29. H. R. McMaster, *Dereliction of Duty: Lyndon Johnson, Robert McNamara, the Joint Chiefs of Staff, and the Lies that Led to Vietnam* (New York: Harper & Collins, 1997), 61.

30. As quoted in Shapley, *Promise and Power*, 357.

31. As quoted in ibid., 356.

32. As quoted in ibid., 602.

33. One of the items in the Pentagon Papers is a remarkable position paper—"A Compromise Solution in South Vietnam"—that Ball sent to President Johnson on July 1, 1965; *The Pentagon Papers,* Gravel Edition (Boston: Beacon Press, 1971), vol. 4, 615–619.

34. Halberstam, *The Best and the Brightest*, 516.

35. As quoted in Shapley, *Promise and Power*, 429.

36. As quoted in ibid., 436.

37. George Christian, as quoted in ibid.

38. Halberstam, *The Best and the Brightest*, 246.

39. As quoted in ibid., 305.

40. Ibid., 45, 224, and 241.

41. Doris Kearns Goodwin, *Team of Rivals: The Political Genius of Abraham Lincoln* (New York: Simon and Schuster, 2005), xv–xix.

42. Thomas L. Hughes, "Experiencing McNamara (review of *In Retrospect*)," *Foreign Policy*, no. 100 (Autumn 1995), 165.

43. Halberstam, *The Best and the Brightest*, 234–235.

44. Shapley, *Promise and Power*, 87.

45. Blight and Lang, *The Fog of War*, 139.

46. George C. Herring, "The Wrong Kind of Loyalty: McNamara's Apology for Vietnam (review of *In Retrospect*)," *Foreign Affairs*, vol. 74, no. 3 (May/June 1995), 158.

47. Morris, *The Fog of War*.

48. John W. Gardner, *Living, Leading, and the American Dream*, Francesca Gardner, ed. (San Francisco: Jossey-Bass, 2003), 116.

49. As quoted in "A Sense of What Should Be," *Time*, vol. 89, no. 3 (January 20, 1967), 16.

50. Gardner, *Living, Leading and the American Dream*, xxii.

51. Ibid.

52. John W. Gardner, *Excellence: Can We Be Equal and Excellent Too?* (New York: Harper, 1961), 161.

53. Lyndon Johnson, "The Great Society," *American Rhetoric*; http://www.americanrhetoric.com/speeches/lbjthegreatsociety.htm.

54. Hugh Davis Graham, "The Transformation of Federal Education Policy," in Robert A. Divine, ed., *Exploring the Johnson Years: Foreign Policy, the Great Society, and the White House* (Austin: University of Texas, 1987), 162–166.

55. *Southern Education Report*, vol. 2, no. 8 (April 1967), 34.

56. As quoted in "A Sense of What Should Be," 16.

57. Ibid., 17.

58. Gardner, *Living, Leading, and the American Dream*, 15.

59. Ibid., 24.

60. Ibid., 13.

61. As quoted in "A Sense of What Should Be," 20.

62. Gardner, *Living, Leading, and the American Dream*, 22.

63. "John W. Gardner," *American President: An Online Reference Resource*; http://millercenter.org/academic/americanpresident/lbjohnson/essays/cabinet/800.
64. "A Sense of What Should Be," 17.
65. Gardner, *Living, Leading, and the American Dream*, 14.
66. Ibid., 11.
67. As quoted in "A Sense of What Should Be," 21.
68. As quoted in ibid., 20.
69. Gardner, *Living, Leading, and the American Dream*, 113.
70. Ibid., 16.
71. John W. Gardner, *On Leadership* (New York: Free Press, 1990), 14.
72. Gardner, *Living, Leading, and the American Dream*, 16.
73. Ibid., 22.
74. Ibid., 28.
75. Ibid., 14.
76. "A Sense of What Should Be," 18.
77. Gardner, *Living, Leading, and the American Dream*, 124–125.
78. Ibid., xxii.

5 Henry Ford and Soichiro Honda:
Business Entrepreneurs

1. As quoted in Peter Collier and David Horowitz, *The Fords: An American Epic* (New York: Summit Books, 1987), 100.
2. As quoted in Richard Bak, *Henry and Edsel: The Creation of the Ford Empire* (Hoboken, NJ: John Wiley & Sons, 2003), 9.
3. Collier and Horowitz, *The Fords*, 21.
4. As quoted in Bak, *Henry and Edsel*, 9.
5. Collier and Horowitz, *The Fords*, 22.
6. Bak, *Henry and Edsel*, 7.
7. Ibid., 8; Allan Nevins, *Ford* (New York: Scribner, 1954–1963), vol. 1, 59–61.
8. Henry Ford, *My Life and Work* (Garden City, NY: Doubleday, Page, 1922), 23.
9. Nevins, *Ford*, vol. 1, 70.
10. As quoted in Collier and Horowitz, *The Fords*, 24.
11. Bak, 14.
12. Nevins, *Ford*, vol. 1, 116–117.
13. As quoted in Bak, *Henry and Edsel*, 23.
14. R.W. Hanington, as quoted in ibid., 29; Robert Lacey, *Ford: The Men and the Machine* (Boston: Little, Brown, 1986), 45.
15. Bak, *Henry and Edsel*, 30.
16. As quoted in Douglas Brinkley, *Wheels for the World: Henry Ford, His Company, and a Century of Progress, 1903–2003* (New York: Viking, 2003), 41.
17. Ford, *My Life and Work*, 36.
18. Ibid., 50.
19. As quoted in Steven Watts, *The People's Tycoon: Henry Ford and the American Century* (New York: Alfred A. Knopf, 2005), 101.
20. As quoted in Nevins, *Ford*, vol. 1, 276.
21. George Brown, company accountant, as quoted in Watts, *The People's Tycoon*, 117–118.
22. Bak, *Henry and Edsel*, 75.
23. Ford, *My Life and Work*, 71, 145 (table).
24. Collier and Horowitz, *The Fords*, 64.
25. Ford, *My Life and Work*, 71, 145 (table).
26. Bak, *Henry and Edsel*, 56; Brinkley, *Wheels for the World*, 348.
27. Nevins, *Ford*, vol. 2, 91.

28. Bak, *Henry and Edsel*, 71.
29. Ibid., 133.
30. George S. May, "Ford Motor Company," in May, ed., *The Automobile Industry* (New York: Facts on File, 1989), 161.
31. Bak, *Henry and Edsel*, 88.
32. Ibid., 84.
33. Collier and Horowitz, *The Fords*, 73.
34. "Ford is an Anarchist," *Chicago Tribune*, June 23, 1916, 6.
35. As quoted in Collier and Horowitz, *The Fords*, 89, 88, respectively.
36. Ibid., 90.
37. As quoted in ibid., 79.
38. As quoted in Bak, *Henry and Edsel*, 107.
39. As quoted in Brinkley, *Wheels for the World*, 336.
40. Collier and Horowitz, *The Fords*, 97.
41. Ford once said that "there is no bent of mind more dangerous than that which is sometimes described as the 'genius for organization'" (Ford, *My Life and Work*, 91).
42. Bak, *Henry and Edsel*, 111.
43. Ford, *My Life and Work*, 99; Bak, *Henry and Edsel*, 110.
44. Bak, *Henry and Edsel*, 194.
45. Ibid., 108.
46. Collier and Horowitz, *The Fords*, 166.
47. As quoted in Brinkley, *Wheels for the World*, 383.
48. As quoted in David L. Lewis, *The Public Image of Henry Ford: An American Folk Hero and His Company* (Detroit: Wayne State University Press, 1976), 233.
49. Bak, *Henry and Edsel*, 191.
50. Edsel Ford's brother-in-law Ernest Kanzler, whom Henry Ford purged a few months later, as quoted in Lacey, *Ford*, 296.
51. Ford, *My Life and Work*, 72.
52. Collier and Horowitz, *The Fords*, 124.
53. Brinkley, *Wheels for the World*, 252–253.
54. Bak, *Henry and Edsel*, 215.
55. The one small step Ford took in the direction of GM's strategy of developing a full line of brands at different price points was his purchase in a 1922 bankruptcy auction of Lincoln Motors, the luxury car manufacturer his old rival, Henry Leland, had created after he sold Cadillac to GM. But the acquisition was not part of a well-considered strategy. The brand did nothing to improve Ford's overall market position. The company produced 1.8 million Model Ts in 1922 and only 5,242 Lincolns. Predictably, Henry Leland, whom Ford asked to stay with the promise of full control of the line, was soon forced out of the company. Equally predictably, Ford sold the same Lincoln models until 1936 (Brinkley, *Wheels for the World*, 301–309; Bak, *Henry and Edsel*, 215).
56. Bak, *Henry and Edsel*, 212.
57. As quoted in Tetsuo Sakiya, *Honda Motor: The Men, the Management, the Machines* (Tokyo: Kodansha International, 1982), 73.
58. Ibid., 49.
59. As quoted in Sol Sanders, *Honda: The Man and His Machines* (Boston: Little, Brown, 1975), 18–19.
60. Sakiya, *Honda Motor*, 49–50.
61. Ibid., 51.
62. Sanders, *Honda*, 35.
63. Sakiya, *Honda Motor*, 54.
64. As quoted in Masaaki Sato, *The Honda Myth: The Genius and His Wake,* Hiroko Yoda and Matt Alt, trans. (New York: Vertical, 2006), 65.
65. Sakiya, *Honda Motor*, 56.
66. Sato, *The Honda Myth*, 66; Sakiya, *Honda Motor*, 62.
67. As quoted in Sakiya, *Honda Motor*, 66–67.

68. Ibid., 67.
69. Sato, *The Honda Myth*, 73; Sakiya, *Honda Motor*, 71.
70. Sakiya, *Honda Motor*, 83–87.
71. Ibid., 82.
72. Sato, *The Honda Myth*, 99.
73. Ibid., 104.
74. As quoted in Sanders, *Honda*, 96.
75. As quoted in ibid., 97.
76. Aaron Frank, *Honda Motorcycles* (St. Paul, MN: Motorbooks International, 2003), 66.
77. Sanders, *Honda*, 82.
78. Ibid., 79.
79. http://en.wikipedia.org/wiki/Honda_S360.
80. Sato, *The Honda Myth*, 128–130.
81. As quoted in ibid., 158.
82. Sakiya, *Honda Motor*, 162–163; Sato, *The Honda Myth*, 155–161.
83. As quoted in Sakiya, *Honda Motor*, 160.
84. Sato, *The Honda Myth*, 211, 231.
85. Joe Guy Collier, "How the Civic Got its Groove Back," *Detroit Free Press*, May 15, 2006, E1.
86. http://en.wikipedia.org/wiki/Honda_Civic.
87. Sato, *The Honda Myth*, 199.
88. http://en.wikipedia.org/wiki/Honda.
89. As quoted in Sanders, *Honda*, 172–173.
90. Sakiya, *Honda Motor*, 150.
91. John P. Kotter, *A Force for Change: How Leadership Differs from Management* (New York: Free Press, 1990), 6.
92. Ibid., 112–114.
93. Sato, *The Honda Myth*, 167.
94. As quoted in ibid., 160.
95. Gene N. Landrum, *Profiles of Genius* (Buffalo: Prometheus Books, 1993), 186.
96. As quoted in Sakiya, *Honda Motor*, 99.
97. As quoted in Satoru Otsuki, Tanaka Fumiya, Sakurai Yoko, Masaru Ibuka, and Nihon Hoso Kyokai, *Good Mileage: The High-Performance Business Philosophy of Soichiro Honda,* Yuki Tung, trans. (New York: NHK Publishing, 1996), 76–77.
98. As quoted in Sakiya, *Honda Motor*, 162.
99. As quoted in Otsuki et al., *Good Mileage*, 89.
100. "Honda Way Hinges on Three Joys," *Automotive News*, August 26, 1991, 33.
101. As quoted in Sato, *The Honda Myth*, 61.
102. As quoted in ibid., 83; and Sakiya, *Honda Motor*, 19.
103. As quoted in Sakiya, *Honda Motor*, 178.
104. As quoted in Otsuki et al., *Good Mileage*, 41.
105. As quoted in Sakiya, *Honda Motor*, 70.
106. Sanders, *Honda*, 112–113.
107. As quoted in Otsuki et al., *Good Mileage*, 39.
108. As quoted in Joel Kotkin, "Mr. Iacocca, Meet Mr. Honda," *Inc.,* vol. 8 (November 1986), 37.
109. As quoted in Richard Johnson, "Founder's Influence Felt at First U.S. Plant," *Automotive News*, vol. 79 (September 6, 2004), H8d.
110. As quoted in Sakiya, *Honda Motor*, 112.
111. As quoted in Sanders, *Honda*, 8.
112. Which he modeled in principle after the assembly line for the Model T of his childhood hero, Henry Ford (Sato, *The Honda Myth*, 100).
113. Otsuki et al., *Good Mileage*, 81.
114. Sato, *The Honda Myth*, 106.
115. Sanders, *Honda*, 77–78.
116. As quoted in Sakiya, *Honda Motor*, 169.
117. As quoted in ibid., 166.
118. George Gilder, as quoted in Landrum, *Profiles of Genius*, 182.

6   G. Stanley Hall and William Rainey Harper: University Presidents

1. Dorothy Ross, *G. Stanley Hall: The Psychologist as Prophet* (Chicago: University of Chicago Press, 1972), 21.
2. Edward Everett Hale, as quoted in ibid., 59.
3. As quoted in ibid.
4. Ibid., 135–145.
5. Ibid., 146.
6. Ibid., 145–146.
7. William A. Koelsch, *Clark University, 1887–1987: A Narrative History* (Worcester, MA: Clark University Press, 1987), 17.
8. As quoted in ibid., 33.
9. Ross, *G. Stanley Hall*, 198.
10. As quoted in ibid., 222.
11. Koelsch, *Clark University*, 34, 35.
12. Ibid., 47.
13. Ibid., 48.
14. Ibid., 43, 82–84.
15. Ibid., 85.
16. Ibid., 88.
17. Ibid.
18. As quoted in Ross, *G. Stanley Hall*, 228.
19. As quoted in Koelsch, *Clark University*, 38.
20. As quoted in Ross, *G. Stanley Hall*, 226.
21. Ibid., 220–227.
22. As quoted in ibid., 240.
23. Koelsch, *Clark University*, 43.
24. As quoted in Ross, *G. Stanley Hall*, 426.
25. As quoted in Richard J. Storr, *Harper's University: The Beginnings* (Chicago: University of Chicago Press, 1966), 81.
26. See Ross, *G. Stanley Hall*, xiii–xvi.
27. *Science*, n.s., vol. 2, no. 45 (November 8, 1895), 627–628.
28. As quoted in Storr, *Harper's University*, 363.
29. Thomas Wakefield Goodspeed, *William Rainey Harper: First President of the University of Chicago* (Chicago: University of Chicago Press, 1928), 17–19.
30. R.J. Miller, as quoted in ibid., 21.
31. Ibid., 42–55.
32. As quoted in Thomas Wakefield Goodspeed, *A History of the University of Chicago: The First Quarter Century* (Chicago: University of Chicago Press, 1972), 105.
33. Storr, *Harper's University*, 14–17.
34. Ibid., 46.
35. As quoted in ibid., 50.
36. See ibid., chapter 4; Goodspeed, *A History of the University of Chicago*, chapter 5.
37. Frederick Rudolph, *The American College and University: A History* (Atlanta: University of Georgia Press, 1990), 356.
38. Storr, *Harper's University*, 164.
39. See Goodspeed, *A History of the University of Chicago*, chapter 3.
40. Ibid., 194; Storr, *Harper's University*, 109.
41. See Storr, *Harper's University*, 72–74.
42. Goodspeed, *A History of the University of Chicago*, 293.
43. Ibid., 189.
44. As quoted in Storr, *Harper's University*, 357.
45. As quoted in ibid., 359.
46. Goodspeed, *William Rainey Harper*, 291–295.

47. Laurence R. Veysey, *The Emergence of the American University* (Chicago: University of Chicago Press, 1965), 368.
48. Goodspeed, *A History of the University of Chicago*, 398.
49. As quoted in Goodspeed, *William Rainey Harper*, 148.
50. Storr, *Harper's University*, 87–89.

7   Edward Teller and Sir William Osler: Scientific Leaders

1. Edith Gittings Reid, *The Great Physician: A Short Life of Sir William Osler* (London: Oxford University Press, 1931), 66.
2. As quoted in Peter Goodchild, *Edward Teller: The Real Dr. Strangelove* (Cambridge: Harvard University Press, 2004), 398.
3. Stanley A. Blumberg and Louis G. Panos, *Edward Teller: Giant of the Golden Age of Physics* (New York: Charles Scribner's Sons, 1990), 20.
4. Edward Teller, *Memoirs: A Twentieth-Century Journey in Science and Politics* (Cambridge, MA: Perseus, 2001), 16.
5. Goodchild, *Edward Teller*, 12.
6. Teller, *Memoirs*, 70.
7. Goodchild, *Edward Teller*, 37.
8. Teller, *Memoirs*, 107–108, 182.
9. Fermi resolved his concern about his wife's safety by escaping with her a year later to the United States from Stockholm where he had gone to receive his Nobel Prize.
10. As quoted in Goodchild, *Edward Teller*, 128.
11. Blumberg and Panos, *Edward Teller*, 60.
12. As quoted in ibid., 118.
13. As quoted in Goodchild, *Edward Teller*, 80.
14. As quoted in Blumberg and Panos, *Edward Teller*, 72.
15. Kai Bird and Martin J. Sherwin, *American Prometheus: The Triumph and Tragedy of J. Robert Oppenheimer* (New York: Alfred A. Knopf, 2006), 283.
16. Ibid., 325–327; Goodchild, *Edward Teller*, 110–111.
17. Goodchild, *Edward Teller*, 111.
18. Teller, *Memoirs*, 181–183, quoted at 182.
19. As quoted in Goodchild, *Edward Teller*, 127.
20. Ibid.
21. As quoted in ibid., 130–131.
22. George Cowan, as quoted in ibid., 159.
23. Teller, *Memoirs*, 314–315, 327–328.
24. Ibid., 310.
25. Goodchild, *Edward Teller*, 178–182.
26. Jay Wechsler, as quoted in ibid., 213.
27. Teller, *Memoirs*, 333 fn. 4.
28. Ibid., 341.
29. Gregg Herken, *Brotherhood of the Bomb: The Tangled Lives and Loyalties of Robert Oppenheimer, Ernest Lawrence, and Edward Teller* (New York: Henry Holt, 2002), 256.
30. Teller, *Memoirs*, 342.
31. Goodchild, *Edward Teller*, 201.
32. Herbert York, as quoted in ibid., 202.
33. As quoted in Blumberg and Panos, *Edward Teller*, 160, 161.
34. Priscilla J. McMillan, *The Ruin of J. Robert Oppenheimer and the Birth of the Modern Arms Race* (New York: Viking, 2005), 244–250.
35. As quoted in Goodchild, *Edward Teller*, 282.
36. Ibid., 269–272, 284–285.

37. Ibid., 283.
38. As Herbert York recounts, he and his generation were also excited by the opportunity to participate in the epochal scientific challenges involved in thermonuclear research and to work with legendary figures like Teller, Fermi, Bethe, and Von Neumann (Herbert F. York, *The Advisors: Oppenheimer, Teller, and the Superbomb* [San Francisco: W.H. Freeman, 1976], 126).
39. Blumberg and Panos, *Edward Teller*, 42.
40. As quoted in Goodchild, *Edward Teller*, 216.
41. As quoted in ibid., 121.
42. Ibid., 265–266.
43. Ibid., chapter 26; Blumberg and Panos, *Edward Teller*, chapters 22–23.
44. Hans A. Bethe, "Comments on the History of the H-Bomb," *Los Alamos Science*, vol. 3, no. 3 (Fall 1982), 47. Bethe's article was written in 1954, but declassified only in 1982.
45. As quoted in Bird and Sherwin, *American Prometheus*, 283.
46. As quoted in Goodchild, *Edward Teller*, 215.
47. Bethe, "Comments on the History of the H-Bomb," 49.
48. Teller, *Memoirs*, 445.
49. Ibid., 438.
50. Bethe, "Comments on the History of the H-Bomb," 51–53.
51. As quoted in Reid, *The Great Physician*, 71.
52. Michael Bliss, *William Osler: A Life in Medicine* (Oxford: Oxford University Press, 1999), 226–227.
53. Reid, *The Great Physician*, 3.
54. As quoted in ibid., 8.
55. As quoted in ibid., 14.
56. Bliss, *William Osler*, 53.
57. Ibid., 57.
58. Reid, *The Great Physician*, 17.
59. Bliss, *William Osler*, 59–60.
60. Ibid., 64, 69–70.
61. Reid, *The Great Physician*, 25–26.
62. As quoted in Bliss, *William Osler*, 64; emphasis in the original.
63. Ibid., 73.
64. As quoted in ibid., 77.
65. Ibid., 84–85.
66. Ibid., 86–87; Reid, *The Great Physician*, 47–48, 51.
67. Edward Rogers, a student at Montreal General Hospital who lived with Osler, as quoted in Reid, *The Great Physician*, 59.
68. As quoted in Bliss, *William Osler*, 94.
69. Rogers, as quoted in ibid.
70. As quoted in ibid., 133.
71. As quoted in Reid, *The Great Physician*, 91.
72. As Osler wrote during a medical sightseeing trip to Germany in 1890, "The characteristic which stands out in bold relief in German scientific life is the paramount importance of knowledge for its own sake...The presence in every medical center of a class of men devoted to scientific work gives a totally different aspect to professional aspirations. While with us—and in England—the young man may start with an ardent desire to devote his life to science, he is soon dragged into the mill of practice" (as quoted in Bliss, *William Osler*, 179).
73. As quoted in ibid., 238.
74. Ibid., 227.
75. Ibid., 177–178.
76. As quoted in ibid., 201.
77. Reid, *The Great Physician*, 113–114.
78. As quoted in Bliss, *William Osler*, 80.
79. Ibid.

80. Ibid., 186.
81. As quoted in ibid., 108.
82. As quoted in ibid., 91.
83. Henry Christian, as quoted in ibid., 224.
84. As quoted in ibid., 264.
85. As quoted in ibid.
86. Dr. Henry Hurd, as quoted in ibid., 315.
87. Ibid., 306.
88. Reid, *The Great Physician*, 184.
89. Bliss, *William Osler*, 369–370.
90. As quoted in ibid., 480.

8 Napoleon and Augustus: Empire Builders

1. As quoted in Steven Englund, *Napoleon: A Political Life* (New York: Scribner, 2004), 30.
2. As quoted in ibid., 298.
3. Ibid., 19.
4. Ibid., 65.
5. Ibid., 134.
6. Michael Rapport, "Napoleon's Rise to Power," *History Today*, vol. 48, no. 1 (January 1998), 16.
7. As quoted in Peter G. Tsouras, "Napoleon and His Words," in Philip J. Haythornthwaite et al., *Napoleon: The Final Verdict* (London: Arms and Armour Press, 1996), 288, 289.
8. Army of Italy proclamation, as quoted in Englund, 105.
9. Ibid., 99.
10. As quoted in Tsouras, "Napoleon and His Words," 290.
11. As quoted in Englund, *Napoleon: A Political Life*, 130.
12. As quoted in E.E.Y. Hales, *Napoleon and the Pope* (London: Eyre & Spottiswoode, 1961), 7–8.
13. As quoted in Geoffrey Ellis, *Napoleon* (London: Longman, 1997), 37.
14. Englund, *Napoleon: A Political Life*, 329.
15. As quoted in ibid., 147.
16. As quoted in ibid., 397.
17. Ibid., 303.
18. As quoted in ibid., 288.
19. As quoted in ibid., 195.
20. As quoted in ibid.
21. Ellis, *Napoleon*, 100.
22. Englund, *Napoleon: A Political Life*, 284.
23. As quoted in Tsouras, "Napoleon and His Words," 286.
24. As quoted in Englund, *Napoleon: A Political Life*, 274.
25. As quoted in ibid., 314.
26. As quoted in ibid., 199.
27. As quoted in ibid., 108.
28. As quoted in ibid., 52.
29. As quoted in ibid., 404.
30. As quoted in ibid., 429.
31. Pat Southern, *Augustus* (London: Routledge, 1998), 39.
32. Augustus, *Res Gestae Divi Augusti*, P.A. Brunt and J.M. Moore, eds. and trans. (London: Oxford University Press, 1967), 25 (§13).
33. As quoted in Suetonius, "The Life of Augustus," in *The Twelve Caesars*, Robert Graves and Michael Grant, trans. (London: Penguin, 1979), 105 (§99).
34. While he did not receive the title Augustus until 27 BCE, for simplicity we use this title throughout the case study.
35. Southern, *Augustus*, 5.

36. Ibid., 28.
37. Ibid., 55–56.
38. Augustus, *Res Gestae*, 19 (§1).
39. Zvi Yavetz, "The Personality of Augustus," in Kurt A. Raaflaub and Mark Toher, eds., *Between Republic and Empire: Interpretations of Augustus and His Principate* (Berkeley: University of California Press, 1990), 35.
40. Suetonius, "The Life of Augustus," 94 (§84).
41. Southern, *Augustus*, 79.
42. Fergus Millar, "State and Subject: The Impact of Monarchy," in Millar and Erich Segal, eds., *Caesar Augustus: Seven Aspects* (Oxford: Clarendon Press, 1984), 44.
43. See Southern, *Augustus*, plate 6.
44. Millar, "State and Subject," 44.
45. Zvi Yavetz, "The *Res Gestae* and Augustus' Public Image," in Millar and Segal, 7.
46. W. Eder, "Augustus and the Power of Tradition," in Raaflaub and Toher, 96–97.
47. Southern, *Augustus*, 71.
48. Ibid., 96.
49. Yavetz, "The Personality of Augustus," 33.
50. Eder, "Augustus and the Power of Tradition," 85.
51. Augustus, *Res Gestae*, 37 and 57–59. At the time, a professional soldier earned perhaps nine hundred sesterces per year. And during the period of the Republic, the largest known estate was Pompey's, which totaled 280 million sesterces.
52. Ibid., 37 (§34).
53. Eder, "Augustus and the Power of Tradition," 112.
54. Augustus, *Res Gestae*, 21 (§5).
55. David Shotter, *Augustus Caesar*, 2nd ed. (London: Routledge, 2005), 22 (plate 1).
56. Ibid., 85 (plate 9).
57. Virgil, *The Aeneid*, in Virgil, *Works*, John Dryden, trans. (London: Jacob Tonson, 1697), 394 (Book 6, lines 1080–1082, 1085, 1083, respectively); emphases in the original.
58. Southern, *Augustus*, 86–87, 136.
59. Suetonius, "The Life of Augustus," 78 (§56).
60. Augustus, *Res Gestae*, 25 (§13).
61. Southern, *Augustus*, 152.
62. Ibid., 94.
63. Suetonius, "The Life of Augustus," 78 (§56).

9 John Humphrey Noyes and George Fox: Religious Visionaries

1. As quoted in Robert David Thomas, *The Man Who Would Be Perfect: John Humphrey Noyes and the Utopian Impulse* (Philadelphia: University of Pennsylvania Press, 1977), 84.
2. As quoted in Spencer Klaw, *Without Sin: The Life and Death of the Oneida Community* (New York: Penguin, 1993), 22.
3. As quoted in ibid., 26.
4. As quoted in Maren Lockwood Carden, *Oneida: Utopian Community to Modern Corporation* (Baltimore: Johns Hopkins Press, 1969), 13–14.
5. As quoted in Klaw, *Without Sin*, 29.
6. Matthew 22:30.
7. Carden, *Oneida*, 8.
8. As quoted in ibid., 17.
9. William M. Kephart and William W. Zellner, *Extraordinary Groups: An Examination of Unconventional Life-Styles*, 4th ed. (New York: St. Martin's Press, 1991), 47.
10. As quoted in Klaw, *Without Sin*, 10.
11. As quoted in ibid., 69.

12. Ibid., 70.
13. Ibid.
14. Carden, *Oneida*, 25.
15. Klaw, *Without Sin*, 80, 191.
16. Carden, *Oneida*, 37.
17. Ibid., 85.
18. As quoted in Kephart and Zellner, *Extraordinary Groups*, 53.
19. Klaw, *Without Sin*, 115.
20. Ibid., 182.
21. As quoted in ibid., 204; emphasis in the original.
22. Ibid., 206.
23. Ibid., 144.
24. As quoted in Kephart and Zellner. *Extraordinary Groups*, 61.
25. Thomas, *The Man Who Would Be Perfect*, 164.
26. As quoted in Klaw, *Without Sin*, 235.
27. As quoted in ibid., 238.
28. Ibid., 243.
29. John W. Chandler, "The Communitarian Quest for Perfection," in Stuart C. Henry, ed., *A Miscellany of American Christianity: Essays in Honor of H. Shelton Smith* (Durham, NC: Duke University Press, 1963), 58–70.
30. As quoted in Mark Holloway, *Heavens on Earth: Utopian Communities in America, 1680–1880* (New York: Dover, 1951), 19–20.
31. Max Weber, *From Max Weber: Essays in Sociology*, H.H. Gerth and C. Wright Mills, eds. and trans. (New York: Oxford University Press, 1946), 245, 247.
32. Klaw, *Without Sin*, 13.
33. As quoted in Carden, *Oneida*, 85.
34. Ibid., 108.
35. Klaw, *Without Sin*, 192.
36. As quoted in Rosemary Moore, *The Light in Their Consciences: Early Quakers in Britain, 1646–1666* (University Park: Pennsylvania State University Press, 2000), 207–208.
37. George Fox, *Journal*, Norman Penney, ed. (London: J.M. Dent & Sons, 1948), 3.
38. Ibid., 1.
39. Ibid., 3.
40. Ibid., 8.
41. Ibid.
42. Ibid., 17.
43. Williston Walker, *Great Men of the Christian Church* (Chicago: University of Chicago Press, 1922), 294.
44. H. Larry Ingle, *First Among Friends: George Fox and the Creation of Quakerism* (New York: Oxford University Press, 1994), 57.
45. Fox, *Journal*, 6.
46. Rufus M. Jones, *The Faith and Practice of the Quakers* (Philadelphia: Book and Publications Committee of the Religious Society of Friends, 1958), 43.
47. Fox, *Journal*, 7.
48. Ibid., 224.
49. Moore, *Light in Their Consciences*, 34.
50. Ingle, *First Among Friends*, 62.
51. Harry Emerson Wildes, *Voice of the Lord: A Biography of George Fox* (Philadelphia: University of Pennsylvania Press, 1965), 214.
52. Ibid., 225.
53. Ibid., 285.
54. As quoted in Ingle, *First Among Friends*, 194.
55. As quoted in ibid., 304.
56. Penn, "A Character Sketch," in Fox, *Journal*, xxii.
57. Ingle, *First Among Friends*, 44.
58. Penn, "A Character Sketch," in Fox, *Journal*, xviii.

59. Wildes, *Voice of the Lord*, 185.

60. Jones, *The Faith and Practice of the Quakers*, 31.

61. Ingle, *First Among Friends*, 252.

62. Penn, "A Character Sketch," in Fox, *Journal*, xxi.

10 Robert Mugabe and Nelson Mandela: Revolutionary Leaders

1. As quoted in Martin Meredith, *Our Votes, Our Guns: Robert Mugabe and the Tragedy of Zimbabwe* (New York: Public Affairs, 2002), 42–43.

2. As quoted in Joshua Hammer, "Big Man," *New Yorker*, June 26, 2006, 29.

3. Meredith, *Our Votes, Our Guns*, 24.

4. David Blair, *Degrees in Violence: Robert Mugabe and the Struggle for Power in Zimbabwe* (New York: Continuum, 2002), 24.

5. As quoted in Martin Meredith, *Mugabe: Power, Plunder and the Struggle for Zimbabwe* (New York: Public Affairs, 2007), 119.

6. Peter Bouckaert, as quoted in Jon Lee Anderson, "The Destroyer," *New Yorker*, October 27, 2008, 56.

7. Blair, *Degrees in Violence*, 17.

8. As quoted in ibid., 14.

9. As quoted in Meredith, *Our Votes, Our Guns*, 43.

10. As quoted in Blair, *Degrees in Violence*, 13.

11. As quoted in ibid., 9.

12. Meredith, *Our Votes, Our Guns*, 120–121; Jay Ross, "Zimbabwe Pushing Ambitious—and Risky—Resettlement Plan," *Washington Post*, February 25, 1983, A17.

13. Hammer, "Big Man," 29.

14. Meredith, *Our Votes, Our Guns*, 66.

15. As quoted in ibid., 73.

16. Samantha Power, "How to Kill a Country," *Atlantic Monthly*, vol. 292, no. 5 (December 2003), 98.

17. PF stood for Patriotic Front, in recognition of the shaky coalition ZANU and ZAPU had formed during the Liberation War.

18. As quoted in Meredith, *Our Votes, Our Guns*, 65.

19. As quoted in ibid., 56–57.

20. As quoted in ibid., 121–122.

21. Lloyd Sachikonye, "Bearing the Brunt: Labour and Structural Adjustment in Zimbabwe," *Southern Africa Report*, vol. 8, no. 5 (May 1993); http://www.africafiles.org/article.asp?ID=4063.

22. As quoted in Meredith, *Our Votes, Our Guns*, 122.

23. As quoted in ibid., 126.

24. In the most notorious example, Mugabe's own brother-in-law, Reward Marafu, received US$70,000 for a scar on his knee and ulcers that added up to a 95 percent disability. Others claimed injuries such as aching feet, loss of appetite, backache, and blisters (ibid., 136–137).

25. National AIDS Council of Zimbabwe, *Global AIDS Response Progress Report, 2012: Zimbabwe Country Report* (Geneva: UNAIDS, 2012), p. 10 (figure 1). HIV caused life expectancy to drop from 56 in the early 1970s to 35 by 2008 (Power, "How to Kill a Country," 96).

26. Meredith, *Our Votes, Our Guns*, 131.

27. As quoted in Stephen Chan, *Robert Mugabe: A Life of Power and Violence* (Ann Arbor: University of Michigan Press, 2003), 143.

28. As quoted in Joshua Hammer, "In the Pit of Africa," *New York Review of Books*, vol. 54, no. 20 (December 20, 2007), 30.

29. The first *chimurenga* was the original war with the invading white settlers in the 1890s, and the second was the war against the white Rhodesian government in the 1970s.

30. As quoted in Meredith, *Our Votes, Our Guns*, 17–18.

31. As quoted in Meredith, *Mugabe*, 126.
32. Hammer, "In the Pit of Africa," 30.
33. See Mahmood Mandani, "Lessons of Zimbabwe," *London Review of Books*, vol. 30, no. 23 (December 4, 2008), 17–21.
34. Chan, *Robert Mugabe*, 157.
35. Hammer, "Big Man," 28–29; Anderson, "The Destroyer," 60.
36. As quoted in "An Election With Only One Candidate," *Economist*, vol. 387 (June 28, 2008), 50.
37. Joshua Hammer, "The Reign of Thuggery," *New York Review of Books*, vol. 55, no. 11 (June 26, 2008), 26.
38. As quoted in Meredith, *Our Votes, Our Guns*, 17.
39. Anderson, "The Destroyer," 56–57.
40. Hammer, "The Reign of Thuggery," 28.
41. Power, "How to Kill a Country," 88.
42. "The Face of Oppression," *Economist*, vol. 382 (March 17, 2007), 49.
43. John Makumbe, as quoted in Hammer, "Big Man," 32–33.
44. Chan, *Robert Mugabe*, 176–177.
45. As quoted in Hammer, "The Reign of Thuggery," 26.
46. As quoted in Meredith, *Our Votes, Our Guns*, 228.
47. As quoted in Danna Harman, "Mugabe's Slow Fall from Grace," *Christian Science Monitor*, March 8, 2002; http://www.csmonitor.com/2002/0308/p01s01-woaf.html.
48. Peta Thornycroft, as quoted in Hammer, "Big Man," 30.
49. As quoted in Tim J. Juckes, *Opposition in South Africa* (Westport, CT: Praeger, 1995), 107.
50. As quoted in Martin Meredith, *Nelson Mandela* (New York: St. Martin's Press, 1997), 521.
51. As quoted in Brian Frost, *Struggling to Forgive* (London: Harper Collins, 1998), 6.
52. Richard Stengel, as quoted in Anthony Sampson, *Mandela* (New York: Alfred A. Knopf, 1999), 490.
53. As quoted in Tom Lodge, *Mandela: A Critical Life* (New York: Oxford University Press, 2006), 2.
54. As quoted in Sampson, *Mandela*, 12.
55. Ibid., 11.
56. As quoted in ibid.
57. As quoted in ibid., 16.
58. Juckes, *Opposition in South Africa*, 55.
59. Ibid., 60–61.
60. As quoted in Lodge, *Mandela: A Critical Life*, 48.
61. As quoted in Meredith, *Nelson Mandela*, 133.
62. As quoted in ibid., 139.
63. As quoted in Juckes, *Opposition in South Africa*, 102.
64. On March 21, 1960, a campaign in Sharpeville to flood the prison system in an effort to make pass laws unworkable ended when police fired without warning into a peaceful crowd of 10,000, killing 66 Africans and wounding 186 more. The massacre served as "a permanent symbol of the brutality of the apartheid regime" (Meredith, *Nelson Mandela*, 171).
65. As quoted in Juckes, *Opposition in South Africa*, 102.
66. As quoted in Meredith, *Nelson Mandela*, 208.
67. As quoted in ibid., 224.
68. As quoted in ibid., 229.
69. Neville Alexander, as quoted in PBS, "The Long Walk of Nelson Mandela"; http://www.pbs.org/wgbh/pages/frontline/shows/mandela/prison/.
70. Joel Joffe, a young lawyer who watched the trial, as quoted in Meredith, *Nelson Mandela*, 254.
71. As quoted in ibid., 272.
72. As quoted in Juckes, *Opposition in South Africa*, 107.
73. As quoted in Sampson, *Mandela*, 210.
74. As quoted in Frost, *Struggling to Forgive*, 4.
75. As quoted in Meredith, *Nelson Mandela*, 408.
76. As quoted in Sampson, *Mandela*, 424.

77. As quoted in Meredith, *Nelson Mandela*, 359.
78. As quoted in ibid., 356.
79. Lodge, *Mandela: A Critical Life*, 156–162.
80. Sampson, *Mandela*, 379.
81. As quoted in Meredith, *Nelson Mandela*, 499.
82. As quoted in Sampson, *Mandela*, 451.
83. Lodge, *Mandela: A Critical Life*, 175.
84. As quoted in Meredith, *Nelson Mandela*, 483.
85. As quoted in ibid., 519.
86. As quoted in Frost, *Struggling to Forgive*, 140.
87. As quoted in Meredith, *Nelson Mandela*, 529.
88. As quoted in Frost, *Struggling to Forgive*, 11.
89. As quoted in ibid., 12.
90. As quoted in ibid., 15.
91. Sampson, *Mandela*, 498, 528.
92. As quoted in ibid., 560.
93. As quoted in ibid., 570.
94. As quoted in Frost, *Struggling to Forgive*, 6.
95. As quoted in ibid., 10.
96. As quoted in Sampson, *Mandela*, 489.
97. In 1987, at the Commonwealth Summit in Vancouver, Margaret Thatcher claimed that all ANC members were terrorists (ibid., 381).
98. As quoted in Meredith, *Nelson Mandela*, 495.
99. As quoted in André Brink, "Mandela: A Tiger for Our Time," *Mail and Guardian*, vol. 15, no. 22 (June 4, 1999).
100. In one of numerous examples, many members of the student Black Consciousness Movement, who were imprisoned along with Mandela at Robben Island in the 1970s, converted to the ANC and its nonracialism because of Mandela (David Ottaway, *Chained Together: Mandela, De Klerk, and the Struggle to Remake South Africa* [New York: Random House, 1993], 3).
101. Juckes, *Opposition in South Africa*, 85; Lodge, *Mandela: A Critical Life*, 57–59.
102. One of their means was through the common-law prisoners who delivered meals and were persuaded to convey messages written on toilet paper and concealed in matchboxes or food containers. Occasionally, Mandela and others would provide legal advice for them (Lodge, *Mandela: A Critical Life*, 123).
103. As quoted in Meredith, *Nelson Mandela*, 552.
104. As quoted in Sampson, *Mandela*, 427.
105. As quoted in ibid., 536.
106. Mandela, *The Struggle is My Life* (New York: Pathfinder Press, 1996), 196.
107. Ottaway, *Chained Together*, 47.
108. Sheridan Johns and R. Hunt Davis, Jr., eds., *Mandela, Tambo, and the African National Congress: The Struggle against Apartheid, 1948–1990* (New York: Oxford University Press, 1991), 225.
109. Meredith, *Nelson Mandela*, 551–552.
110. Sampson, *Mandela*, 573–574.
111. "Queasy about the future," *Economist*, vol. 388 (September 27, 2008), 20.

Epilogue Implications for Leaders and Followers

1. George Fox, *Journal* (London: W. & F.G. Cash, 1852), 34.
2. Robert S. McNamara, "A Life in Public Service," interview by Harry Kreisler, *Conversations with History*, Institute for International Studies, UC Berkeley, April 16, 1996; http://conversations.berkeley.edu/content/robert-s-mcnamara.
3. James MacGregor Burns, *Leadership* (New York: Harper & Row, 1978), 41.
4. Martin Meredith, *Our Votes, Our Guns: Robert Mugabe and the Tragedy of Zimbabwe* (New York: Public Affairs, 2002), 56.

5. Ronald A. Heifetz, *Leadership Without Easy Answers* (Cambridge, MA: Belknap Press, 1994), 73–76.
6. Roy F. Baumeister, Kathleen D. Vohs, and Dianne M. Tice, "The Strength Model of Self-Control," *Current Directions in Psychological Science*, vol. 16, no. 6 (December 2007), 352–353.
7. As quoted in Stephen E. Ambrose, *The Victors* (New York: Simon & Schuster, 1998), 41.
8. Anthony Sampson, *Mandela* (New York: Alfred A. Knopf, 1999), 10–12.
9. Jerome H. Parker IV, "Fox Conner and Dwight Eisenhower: Mentoring and Application," *Military Review*, vol. 85, no. 4 (July–August 2005), 92–95.
10. *Webster's New Collegiate Dictionary* (Springfield, MA: G. & C. Merriam, 1979), 985.
11. See Baumeister et al., "The Strength Model"; and John Tierney, "To Choose Is To Lose," *New York Times Magazine,* August 21, 2011, 32–37, 46.
12. As quoted in Tierney, "To Choose Is To Lose," 46; emphasis in the original.

BIBLIOGRAPHY

ANC. "Nelson Rolihlahla Mandela." *ANC Online*. http:/anc.org/za/people/Mandela.html.

Anderson, Jon Lee. "The Destroyer." *New Yorker*, October 27, 2008, 54–65.

Augustus. *Res Gestae Divi Augusti*, P. A. Brunt and J. M. Moore, eds. and trans. London: Oxford University Press, 1967.

Bachrach, Deborah. *The Importance of Margaret Sanger*. San Diego: Lucent Books, 1993.

Bak, Richard. *Henry and Edsel: The Creation of the Ford Empire*. Hoboken, NJ: John Wiley & Sons, 2003.

Baldwin, Neil. *Henry Ford and the Jews: The Mass Production of Hate*. New York: PublicAffairs, 2001.

Barry, Kathleen. *Susan B. Anthony: A Biography of a Singular Feminist*. New York: New York University Press, 1988.

Bass, Bernard M. *Bass & Stodgill's Handbook of Leadership: Theory, Research, and Managerial Applications*, 3rd ed. New York: Free Press, 1990.

Baumeister, Roy F., Kathleen D. Vohs, and Dianne M. Tice. "The Strength Model of Self-Control." *Current Directions in Psychological Science*, vol. 16, no. 6 (December 2007), 351–355.

Bennett, Harry, with Paul Marcus. *We Never Called Him Henry*. New York: Fawcett, 1951.

Bethe, Hans A. "Comments on the History of the H-Bomb." *Los Alamos Science*, vol. 3, no. 3 (Fall 1982), 42–53.

Bird, Kai, and Martin J. Sherwin. *American Prometheus: The Triumph and Tragedy of J. Robert Oppenheimer*. New York: Alfred A. Knopf, 2006.

Black, Jeremy. "Napoleon and Europe." *History Today*, vol. 48, no. 1 (January 1998), 10–12.

Blair, David. *Degrees in Violence: Robert Mugabe and the Struggle for Power in Zimbabwe*. New York: Continuum, 2002.

Blight, James G., and Janet M. Lang. *The Fog of War: Lessons from the Life of Robert S. McNamara*. Lanham, MD: Rowman & Littlefield, 2005.

Bliss, Michael. *William Osler: A Life in Medicine*. Oxford: Oxford University Press, 1999.

Blumberg, Stanley A., and Louis G. Panos. *Edward Teller: Giant of the Golden Age of Physics*. New York: Charles Scribner's Sons, 1990.

Brinkley, Douglas. *Wheels for the World: Henry Ford, His Company, and a Century of Progress, 1903–2003*. New York: Viking, 2003.

Brunt, P. A. *The Fall of the Roman Republic and Related Essays*. London: Oxford University Press, 1988.

Bryan, Charles S. *Osler: Inspirations from a Great Physician*. Oxford: Oxford University Press, 1997.

Burns, James MacGregor. *Leadership*. New York: Harper & Row, 1978.

———. *Transforming Leadership*. New York: Atlantic Monthly Press, 2003.

Campbell, J. B. *The Emperor and the Roman Army, 31 BC–AD 235*. New York: Oxford University Press, 1984.

Carden, Maren Lockwood. *Oneida: Utopian Community to Modern Corporation*. Baltimore: Johns Hopkins Press, 1969.

Chan, Stephen. *Robert Mugabe: A Life of Power and Violence*. Ann Arbor: University of Michigan Press, 2003.

Chesler, Ellen. *Woman of Valor*. New York: Simon and Schuster, 1992.

Clancy, Louise B., and Florence Davies. *The Believer: The Life Story of Mrs. Henry Ford.* New York: Coward-McCann, 1960.

Clark, Matthew D. H. *Augustus, First Roman Emperor: Power, Propaganda and the Politics of Survival.* Bristol: Phoenix Press, 2010.

Cohen, Eliot A. *Supreme Command: Soldiers, Statesmen, and Leadership in Wartime.* New York: Free Press, 2002.

Collier, Peter, and David Horowitz. *The Fords: An American Epic.* New York: Summit Books, 1987.

Compagnon, Daniel. *A Predictable Tragedy: Robert Mugabe and the Collapse of Zimbabwe.* Philadelphia: University of Pennsylvania Press, 2011.

Cushing, Harvey. *The Life of Sir William Osler,* 2 vols. New York: Oxford University Press, 1925.

Darwin, Charles. *The Descent of Man and Selection in Relation to Sex,* rev. ed. New York: D. Appleton, 1897.

———. *The Expression of the Emotions in Man and Animals.* New York: D. Appleton, 1873.

———. *On the Origin of Species.* New York: New York University Press, 1988.

De Blois, L. *The Roman Army and Politics in the First Century before Christ.* Amsterdam: J. C. Gieben, 1987.

De Duve, Christian. *Life Evolving: Molecules, Mind, and Meaning.* New York: Oxford University Press, 2002.

DeMaria, Richard. *Communal Love at Oneida: A Perfectionist Vision of Authority, Property, and Sexual Order.* New York: Edwin Mellen Press, 1978.

Divine, Robert A., ed. *Exploring the Johnson Years: Foreign Policy, the Great Society, and the White House.* Austin: University of Texas Press, 1987.

Douglas, Emily Taft. *Margaret Sanger: Pioneer of the Future.* Garrett Park, MD: Garrett Park Press, 1975.

Dwyer, Philip. *Napoleon: The Path to Power.* New Haven: Yale University Press, 2008.

Ellis, Geoffrey. *Napoleon.* London: Longman, 1997.

Englund, Steven. *Napoleon: A Political Life.* New York: Scribner, 2004.

Everitt, Anthony. *Augustus.* New York: Random House, 2006.

Farrell, Michael P. "Two Sticks of a Drum: Elizabeth Cady Stanton, Susan B. Anthony, and the Circle of Ultras." In Farrell, *Collaborative Circles: Friendship Dynamics and Creative Work.* Chicago: University of Chicago Press, 2001, 205–265.

Fogarty, Robert S. *Special Love/Special Sex: An Oneida Community Diary.* Syracuse, NY: Syracuse University Press, 1994.

Ford, Henry. *My Life and Work.* Garden City, NY: Doubleday, Page, 1922,

Fox, George. *Journal,* Norman Penney, ed. London: J. M. Dent & Sons, 1948.

Freud, Sigmund. *Civilization and Its Discontents,* James Strachey, ed. and trans. New York: W.W. Norton, 1961.

Frost, Brian. *Struggling to Forgive.* London: Harper Collins, 1998.

Fuller, Timothy, ed. *Leading and Leadership.* Notre Dame, IN: University of Notre Dame Press, 2000.

"Gardner Hews Out the Great Society." *Newsweek,* vol. 67, no. 9 (February 28, 1966), 22–30.

Gardner, Howard. *Leading Minds: An Anatomy of Leadership.* New York: BasicBooks, 1996.

Gardner, John W. *Excellence: Can We Be Equal and Excellent Too?* New York: Harper, 1961.

———. *Living, Leading, and the American Dream,* Francesca Gardner, ed. San Francisco: Jossey-Bass, 2003.

———. *On Leadership.* New York: Free Press, 1990.

Gergen, David. *Eyewitness to Power: The Essence of Leadership, Nixon to Clinton.* New York: Touchstone, 2000.

Goethals, George R., and Georgia J. Sorenson, eds. *Encyclopedia of Leadership,* 4 vols. Thousand Oaks, CA: Sage, 2004.

Golden, Richard L. "William Osler at 150: An Overview of a Life." *Journal of the American Medical Association,* vol. 282, no. 23 (December 1999), 2252–2258.

Goodchild, Peter. *Edward Teller: The Real Dr. Strangelove.* Cambridge: Harvard University Press, 2004.

Goodspeed, Thomas Wakefield. *A History of the University of Chicago: The First Quarter Century.* Chicago: University of Chicago Press, 1972.

————. *William Rainey Harper: First President of the University of Chicago.* Chicago: University of Chicago Press, 1928.

Gray, Madeline. *Margaret Sanger: A Biography of the Champion of Birth Control.* New York: Richard Marek, 1979.

Greenleaf, Robert K. *Servant Leadership.* New York: Paulist Press, 1977.

Greenstein, Fred I. *The Presidential Difference: Leadership Style from FDR to George W. Bush,* 2nd ed. Princeton: Princeton University Press, 2004.

Haidt, Jonathan. *The Righteous Mind: Why Good People are Divided by Politics and Religion.* New York: Pantheon Books, 2012.

Halberstam, David. *The Best and the Brightest.* New York: Random House, 1972.

Hall, G. Stanley. *Life and Confessions of a Psychologist.* New York: D. Appleton, 1923.

Hamm, Thomas D. *The Quakers in America.* New York: Columbia University Press, 2003.

Hammer, Joshua. "Big Man." *New Yorker,* June 26, 2006, 28–34.

————. "In the Pit of Africa." *New York Review of Books,* vol. 54, no. 20 (December 20, 2007), 30–36.

————. "The Reign of Thuggery." *New York Review of Books,* vol. 55, no. 11 (June 26, 2008), 26–29.

Haythornthwaite, Philip J., et al. *Napoleon: The Final Verdict.* New York: Arms and Armour Press, 1996.

Heifetz, Ronald A. *Leadership without Easy Answers.* Cambridge, MA: Belknap Press, 1994.

Helsing, Jeffrey W. *Johnson's War/Johnson's Great Society: The Guns and Butter Trap.* Westport, CT: Praeger, 2000.

Herken, Gregg. *Brotherhood of the Bomb: The Tangled Lives and Loyalties of Robert Oppenheimer, Ernest Lawrence, and Edward Teller.* New York: Henry Holt, 2002.

Herring, George C. "The Wrong Kind of Loyalty: McNamara's Apology for Vietnam (review of *In Retrospect*)." *Foreign Affairs,* vol. 74, no. 3 (May/June 1995), 154–158.

Hogan, Joyce, and Robert Hogan. "Evidence for the Big-Five Personality Dimensions." In Goethals and Sorenson, vol. 1, 95–98.

Horne, Alistair. *The Age of Napoleon.* New York: Modern Library, 2004.

Hughes, Thomas L. "Experiencing McNamara (review of *In Retrospect*)." *Foreign Policy,* no. 100 (Autumn 1995), 154–171.

Ingle, H. Larry. *First among Friends: George Fox and the Creation of Quakerism.* New York: Oxford University Press, 1994.

Janis, Irving. *Groupthink.* Boston: Houghton Mifflin, 1982.

"John Gardner: Uncommon American." Produced by Tom Simon and Rick Stamberger. Working Dog Productions, 2001. Documentary film.

Johns, Sheridan, and R. Hunt Davis, Jr., eds. *Mandela, Tambo, and the African National Congress: The Struggle against Apartheid, 1948–1990.* New York: Oxford University Press, 1991.

Jones, Rufus M. *The Faith and Practice of the Quakers.* Philadelphia: Book and Publications Committee of the Religious Society of Friends, 1958.

Juckes, Tim J. *Opposition in South Africa: The Leadership of Z. K. Matthews, Nelson Mandela, and Stephen Biko.* Westport, CT: Praeger, 1995.

Keegan, John. *The Mask of Command.* New York: Penguin, 1988.

Kellerman, Barbara. *Bad Leadership.* Boston: Harvard Business School Press, 2004.

Kelley, Harold H. "Attribution Theory in Social Psychology." In *Nebraska Symposium on Motivation,* 1967. Lincoln: University of Nebraska Press, 1967, 225–227.

Kennedy, David M. *Birth Control in America: The Career of Margaret Sanger.* New Haven: Yale University Press, 1970.

Kephart, William M., and William W. Zellner. *Extraordinary Groups: An Examination of Unconventional Life-Styles,* 4th ed. New York: St. Martin's Press, 1991.

King, Lester S. *Transformations in American Medicine: From Benjamin Rush to William Osler.* Baltimore: Johns Hopkins University Press, 1991, Chapter 9.

Klaw, Spencer. *Without Sin: The Life and Death of the Oneida Community.* New York: Penguin, 1993.

Koelsch, William A. *Clark University, 1887–1987: A Narrative History.* Worcester, MA: Clark University Press, 1987.

Kotkin, Joel. "Mr. Iacocca, Meet Mr. Honda." *Inc.*, vol. 8 (November 1986), 37+.

Kotter, John P. *A Force for Change: How Leadership Differs from Management.* New York: Free Press, 1990.

Lacey, Robert. *Ford: The Men and the Machine.* Boston: Little, Brown, 1986.

Lacey, W. K. *Augustus and the Principate. The Evolution of the System.* Leeds: Francis Cairns, 1996.

Lader, Lawrence. *The Margaret Sanger Story and the Fight for Birth Control.* Garden City, NY: Doubleday, 1955.

Landrum, Gene N. *Profiles of Genius: Thirteen Creative Men Who Changed the World.* Buffalo: Prometheus Books, 1993.

Langer, Phillip, and Robert Pois. *Command Failure in War: Psychology and Leadership.* Bloomington: Indiana University Press, 2004.

Lewis, David L. *The Public Image of Henry Ford: An American Folk Hero and His Company.* Detroit: Wayne State University Press, 1976.

Libby, Stephen B., and Morton S. Weiss. "Edward Teller's Scientific Life." *AAPPS Bulletin*, vol. 14, no. 6 (December 2004), 16–22.

Lodge, Tom. *Mandela: A Critical Life.* New York: Oxford University Press, 2006.

———. *Politics in South Africa: From Mandela to Mbeki.* Indianapolis: Indiana University Press, 2002.

Lord, Carnes. *The Modern Prince.* New Haven: Yale University Press, 2003.

Machiavelli, Niccolo. *The Prince*, Harvey C. Mansfield, trans. Chicago: University of Chicago Press, 1998.

Maister, David, Charles H. Green, and Robert M. Galford. *The Trusted Advisor.* New York: Touchstone, 2000.

Mamdani, Mahmood. "Lessons of Zimbabwe." *London Review of Books*, vol. 30, no. 23 (December 4, 2008), 17–21.

"The Man behind the Fist." *Economist*, vol. 382 (March 31, 2007), 27–30.

McMaster, H. R. *Dereliction of Duty: Lyndon Johnson, Robert McNamara, the Joint Chiefs of Staff, and the Lies that Led to Vietnam.* New York: Harper & Collins, 1997.

McMillan, Priscilla J. *The Ruin of J. Robert Oppenheimer and the Birth of the Modern Arms Race.* New York: Viking, 2005.

McNamara, Robert S. *In Retrospect.* New York: Times Books, 1995.

———. "A Life in Public Service," interview by Harry Kreisler, *Conversations with History*, Institute for International Studies, UC Berkeley, April 16, 1996; http://conversations.berkeley.edu /content/robert-s-mcnamara.

Meredith, Martin. *Mugabe: Power, Plunder and the Struggle for Zimbabwe.* New York: Public Affairs, 2007.

———. *Nelson Mandela.* New York: St. Martin's Press, 1997.

———. *Our Votes, Our Guns: Robert Mugabe and the Tragedy of Zimbabwe.* New York: Public Affairs, 2002.

Milkis, Sidney M., and Jerome M. Mileur, eds. *The Great Society and the High Tide of Liberalism.* Amherst: University of Massachusetts Press, 2005.

Millar, Fergus, and Erich Segal, eds. *Caesar Augustus: Seven Aspects.* Oxford: Clarendon Press, 1984.

Mintzberg, Henry. "Society Has Become Unmanageable as a Result of Management." In Mintzberg, *Mintzberg On Management: Inside Our Strange World Of Organizations.* New York: Free Press, 1989, 335–373.

Moore, Rosemary. *The Light in Their Consciences: Early Quakers in Britain, 1646–1666.* University Park: Pennsylvania State University Press, 2000.

Morris, Errol, director. "The Fog of War: Eleven Lessons from the Life of Robert S. McNamara." Columbia Tristar, 2003. Documentary film; http://www.errolmorris.com/film/fow_transcript .html.

Napoleon. *Napoleon on the Art of War*, Jay Luvaas, ed. and trans. New York: Free Press, 1999.

Nevins, Allan. *Ford*, vols. 1–3. New York: Scribner, 1954–1963.

Nies, Judith. *Seven Women: Portraits from the American Radical Tradition.* New York: Viking, 1977.

Nowak, Martin A. *SuperCooperators: Altruism, Evolution, and Why We Need Each Other to Succeed.* New York: Free Press, 2011.

Noyes, Pierrepont B. *My Father's House: An Oneida Boyhood.* Gloucester, MA: Peter Smith, 1966.

Oakley, Francis. *Kingship.* Malden, MA: Blackwell, 2006.

Olson, Sidney. *Young Henry Ford.* Detroit: Wayne State University Press, 1997.

Otsuki, Satoru, Tanaka Fumiya, Sakurai Yoko, Masaru Ibuka, and Nihon Hoso Kyokai. *Good Mileage: The High-Performance Business Philosophy of Soichiro Honda,* Yuki Tung, trans. New York: NHK Publishing, 1996.

Ottaway, David. *Chained Together: Mandela, De Klerk, and the Struggle to Remake South Africa.* New York: Random House, 1993.

Parker, Robert Allerton. *A Yankee Saint: John Humphrey Noyes and the Oneida Community.* Hamden, CT: Archon Books, 1973.

PBS. "The Long Walk of Nelson Mandela" and "Chronology." *PBS Online,* 1999. http://www.pbs .org/wgbh/pages/frontline/shows/mandela.

The Pentagon Papers. Gravel Edition, 4 vols. Boston: Beacon Press, 1971.

Peters, Thomas J., and Robert H. Waterman, Jr. *In Search of Excellence: Lessons from America's Best-Run Companies.* New York: Warner Books, 1982.

Peterson, Joyce Shaw. *American Automobile Workers, 1900–1933.* Albany: State University of New York Press, 1987.

Petty, Richard E., and John T. Cacioppo. "The Elaboration Likelihood Model of Persuasion." In Leonard Berkowitz, ed., *Advances in Experimental Social Psychology,* vol. 19. Orlando: Academic Press, 1986, 123–205.

Plato. *The Republic,* Desmond Lee, trans. New York: Penguin, 2003.

Plutarch. *Fall of the Roman Republic: Six Lives,* Rex Warner, trans. Harmondsworth, Middlesex: Penguin, 1959.

———. *The Rise and Fall of Athens: Nine Greek Lives,* Ian Scott-Kilvert, trans. Harmondsworth, Middlesex: Penguin, 1960.

Power, Samantha. "How to Kill a Country." *Atlantic Monthly,* vol. 292, no. 5 (December 2003), 86–100.

Pruette, Lorine. *G. Stanley Hall: A Biography of a Mind.* New York: D. Appleton, 1926.

Raaflaub, Kurt A., and Mark Toher, eds. *Between Republic and Empire: Interpretations of Augustus and His Principate.* Berkeley: University of California Press, 1990.

Rapport, Michael. "Napoleon's Rise to Power." *History Today,* vol. 48, no. 1 (January 1998), 12–19.

Reid, Edith Gittings. *The Great Physician: A Short Life of Sir William Osler.* London: Oxford University Press, 1931.

"Robert S. McNamara." *SecDef Histories.* Department of Defense. http://www.defense.gov/specials /secdef_histories/bios/mcnamara.htm.

Ross, Dorothy. *G. Stanley Hall: The Psychologist as Prophet.* Chicago: University of Chicago Press, 1972.

Rost, Joseph C. *Leadership for the Twenty-First Century.* Westport, CT: Praeger, 1991.

Rubenzer, Steven J., and Thomas R. Faschingbauer. *Personality, Character, and Leadership in the White House: Psychologists Assess the Presidents.* Washington, D.C.: Potomac Books, 2004.

Rudolph, Frederick. *The American College and University: A History.* Atlanta: University of Georgia Press, 1990.

———. *Mark Hopkins on a Log: Williams College, 1836–1872.* New Haven: Yale University Press, 1956.

Rush, N. Orwin, ed. *Letters of G. Stanley Hall to Jonas Gilman Clark.* Worcester, MA: Clark University Library, 1948.

Sakiya, Tetsuo. *Honda Motor: The Men, the Management, the Machines.* Tokyo: Kodansha International, 1982.

Sampson, Anthony. *Mandela.* New York: Alfred A. Knopf, 1999.

Sanders, Sol. *Honda: The Man and His Machines.* Boston: Little, Brown, 1975.

Sanger, Alexander. *Beyond Choice: Reproductive Freedom in the 21st Century.* New York: Public Affairs, 2004.

Sato, Masaaki. *The Honda Myth: The Genius and His Wake,* Hiroko Yoda and Matt Alt, trans. New York: Vertical, 2006.

"A Sense of What Should Be." *Time*, vol. 89, no. 3 (January 20, 1967), 16–21.

Shapley, Deborah. *Promise and Power: The Life and Times of Robert McNamara*. Boston: Little, Brown, 1993.

Shotter, David. *Augustus Caesar*, 2nd ed. London: Routledge, 2005.

Smith, David James. *Young Mandela*. New York: Little, Brown, 2010.

Southern, Pat. *Augustus*. London: Routledge, 1998.

Sparks, Allister. *Beyond the Miracle: Inside the New South Africa*. Chicago: University of Chicago Press, 2003.

Stanton, Elizabeth Cady, Susan B. Anthony, and Matilda J. Gage, eds. *History of Woman Suffrage*, 3 vols. Rochester, NY: Susan B. Anthony, 1887.

Stengel, Richard. "The Making of a Leader." *Time*, vol. 143, no. 19 (May 9, 1994), 36–38.

Storr, Richard J. *Harper's University: The Beginnings*. Chicago: University of Chicago Press, 1966.

Suetonius. *The Twelve Caesars*, Robert Graves and Michael Grant, trans. London: Penguin, 1979.

Teller, Edward. *Memoirs: A Twentieth-Century Journey in Science and Politics*. Cambridge, MA: Perseus, 2001.

Thomas, Robert David. *The Man Who Would Be Perfect: John Humphrey Noyes and the Utopian Impulse*. Philadelphia: University of Pennsylvania Press, 1977.

Thucydides. *History of the Peloponnesian War*, Rex Warner, trans. New York: Penguin, 1972.

Topalian, Elyse. *Margaret Sanger*. New York: Franklin Watts, 1984.

Van Patten, James J. *Watersheds in Higher Education*. New York: Edwin Mellen Press, 1997.

Veysey, Laurence R. *The Emergence of the American University*. Chicago: University of Chicago Press, 1965.

Waggenspack, Beth Marie. *Elizabeth Cady Stanton's Reform Rhetoric, 1848–1854: A Perelman Analysis of Practical Reasoning*. Columbus: Ohio State University, 1982.

Waley, Arthur. *Three Ways of Thought in Ancient China*. Stanford, CA: Stanford University Press, 1982.

Wallach, Michael A., and Lise Wallach. *Psychology's Sanction for Selfishness: The Error of Egoism in Theory and Therapy*. San Francisco: W. H. Freeman, 1983.

Ward, Geoffrey C. *Not for Ourselves Alone: The Story of Elizabeth Cady Stanton and Susan B. Anthony*. New York: Alfred A. Knopf, 1999.

Watts, Steven. *The People's Tycoon: Henry Ford and the American Century*. New York: Alfred A. Knopf, 2005.

Weber, Max. *From Max Weber: Essays in Sociology*, H. H. Gerth and C. Wright Mills, eds. and trans. New York: Oxford University Press, 1946.

Wellman, Judith. *The Road to Seneca Falls: Elizabeth Cady Stanton and the First Women's Rights Convention*. Urbana: University of Illinois Press, 2004.

Wildes, Harry Emerson. *Voice of the Lord: A Biography of George Fox*. Philadelphia: University of Pennsylvania Press, 1965.

Wills, Garry. *Certain Trumpets: The Nature of Leadership*. New York: Simon & Schuster, 1994.

Wilson, Edward O. *The Social Conquest of Earth*. New York: Liveright, 2012.

———. *Sociobiology: The New Synthesis*. Cambridge, MA: Belknap Press, 1975.

Wilson, Louis N. *G. Stanley Hall: A Sketch*. New York: G.E. Stechert, 1914.

Wind, James P. *The Bible and the University: The Messianic Vision of William Rainey Harper*. Atlanta: Scholars Press, 1987.

Wren, J. Thomas, ed. *The Leader's Companion: Insights on Leadership through the Ages*. New York: Free Press, 1995.

York, Herbert F. *The Advisors: Oppenheimer, Teller, and the Superbomb*. San Francisco: W.H. Freeman, 1976.

Zanker, Paul. *The Power of Images in the Age of Augustus*, Alan Shapiro, trans. Ann Arbor: University of Michigan Press, 1988.

INDEX

CPSIA information can be obtained
at www.ICGtesting.com
Printed in the USA
LVHW021728101121
702938LV00013B/876